For Michigan Fans Only!

by
Rich Wolfe

Published by Lone Wolfe Press, a division of Richcraft. Distribution, marketing, publicity, interviews, and book signings handled by Wolfegang Marketing Systems, Ltd.—But Not Very.

Photo Credits:

First Color Insert: University of Michigan Athletic Department, Bentley Historical Library, Tom Ufer, Glenn Schembechler, Barbara Cossman at University of Michigan Athletics for design of Bo Schembechler's Memorial Service, *Life Magazine, Oakland Tribune* photographer Carl Bigelow, Schembechler Enterprises, Inc.
Second Color Insert: *Sports Illustrated, Look Magazine*

Chapter 1, 2, 3, and 6 Photos: Tom Ufer, University of Michigan Athletics, Bentley Historical Library

Chapter 4 and 5 Photos: unknown

p. 80 Ira Jaffe; p 206 Theresa Wangler; Mike Wallace, New York, NY, Wallace House, Ann Arbor, MI, Bentley Historical Library, Ann Arbor, MI

Dustjacket: University of Michigan Athletic Department, Bentley Historical Library, *Sports Illustrated*

Chief Researcher: Janet Myllymaki
Layout: The Printed Page, Phoenix, AZ
Author's agent: T. Roy Gaul

Rich Wolfe can be reached at 602-738-5889

ISBN: 978-0-9846278-1-3

***<u>PAGE TWO.</u> In 1941, the news director at a small radio station in Kalamazoo, Michigan hired Harry Caray who had been employed at a station in Joliet, Illinois. The news director's name was Paul Harvey. Yes, that PAUL HARVEY! "And now, you have the rest of the story....**

DEDICATION

Bill Cormack of San Francisco, California &
Dave Cooper of Bloomfield Hills, Michigan,
long time Michigan fans and friends

ACKNOWLEDGMENTS

Wonderful people helped me make this book a reality, starting with Beth Ball of Maryland Heights, Missouri, and Lisa Liddy at The Printed Page in Phoenix, Arizona—wonder women who seem to use magic and are indispensable.

Special thanks to Bruce Madej, Tara Preston, and Dave Ablauf from the University of Michigan Athletic Department; and Mary Passink from the University of Michigan Football office. My appreciation to Mark Bast, Grand Rapids, MI; Pauline Dora, CT; Birgit Rieck, Wallace House, Ann Arbor, MI; Theresa Wangler, Bingham Farms, MI; Ira Jaffe, Farmington Hills, MI; Steve Parker, Richmond, VA; Bill Cormack, San Francisco, CA; Curtis Wright, Los Gatos, CA; Dave Cooper, Bloomfield Hills, MI; Elaine McCarthy, Storrs, CT; Harvey Sackett, CA; Ira Weintraub, Ann Arbor, MI; John Hrycko, Dowagiac, MI; Malcolm Moran, PA; Neil Roseman, Ellicott City, MD; Nick Maczkov, Larkspur, CA; Ruth McCutcheon, Menlo Park, CA; Scott Elrod, Belvedere, CA; Mike Ambroziak, Phoenix, AZ; Chris Carson, San Francisco, CA; Glenn Schembechler, OH; and particularly to Tom Ufer, Ann Arbor, MI. Not to be forgotten are Jon Gustin, Mark Morosky, Sondra Taylor, Bella Koleva—all working in Pontiac, MI.

A tip of my hat to all of the wonderful fan stories that did not get into the book...we ran out of space for over a dozen or more people with wonderful stories. However, you can look for their stories in *For Michigan Fans Only: Volume II.*

It really was a pleasure talking and meeting with so many wonderful Michigan fans, past players and coaches...all are so gracious and helpful. Michigan, you are a "class act".

CHAT ROOMS

PREFACE

I grew up in Iowa and graduated from Notre Dame. The Michigan Wolverines have ruined more of my Saturdays than all the weddings of my 25 nieces and nephews combined!

Growing up I was an avid Iowa Hawkeye fan. Let the record show that Ron Kramer ruined nine days of my youth. After every Iowa game, I would listen to a scoreboard show on radio station WMT in Cedar Rapids. They had a magnificent post-game show that included all the Big 10 fight songs, as well as the fight songs for Notre Dame, Alabama, Southern Cal, and other major football powers. They also would give the Slippery Rock score every Saturday much like they do to this day at the Big House. I shouldn't even like Michigan. I subsequently found out there's not a lot to dislike about Michigan.

Even though Michigan was a big rival of Iowa, I grew to really like their fight song. Whenever one first hears "The Victors", it's difficult not to get caught up in the rhythm and the words. My dislike for Michigan was also tempered by the fact that when I was eleven years old, my oldest brother married a beautiful gal from Dearborn. Two days after the wedding, I went to my first big league baseball game, a **DOUBLEHEADER*** at Briggs Stadium with the Tigers and the White Sox. As a result, at a young and impressionable age, I became a huge Tigers fan. I remember shooting baskets in the granary on the farm listening to WJR in Detroit with Van Patrick extolling the virtues of the Tigers and Goebel beer.

On the way home from my brother's wedding, we stopped in Ann Arbor to see the stadium which in those days held 101,001 fans. Each member of my family posed individually in front of the scoreboard with the camera being positioned at mid-field.

***In 1943 the Chicago White Sox played forty-four DOUBLEHEADERS. Last year they played one.**

I'm sure we were the only people to think of taking a picture where we were "the one" in the 101,001 scenario.

When I was at Notre Dame, the world was different (for one thing, it was flat). We didn't play Michigan in football, but we did play them in baseball. Freshmen were not eligible for the varsity in those days, but the first varsity game I saw when I was a freshman was against Michigan. The Michigan catcher was Bill Freehan; he looked like a giant! He certainly did not look like a college baseball player, but like he belonged in the big leagues; a man amongst boys. So, I am thinking...Ron Kramer was huge, Bill Freehan was huge; does everyone who plays sports at the University of Michigan have to be a giant?

I was delighted when Notre Dame started to play Michigan in football because of the reputation of the two schools, which includes, but is not limited to, academics. Even when the Elvis Grbac to Desmond Howard pass on fourth down beat Notre Dame in 1991, one just had to shake their head and say: "Wow, that was a gutsy call and an incredible effort and a heck of a play and as much as I hate losing I can accept it." Maybe it was just God's way of getting even for making the wind stop before Harry Oliver's field goal a few years previously.

Growing up in Iowa at that time, I had no love lost for either Woody Hayes or Bo Schembechler. The general perception was that they were evil people doing evil things. My perception changed when, years later, I got to know Jack Harbaugh very well. Harbaugh was an assistant to Bo for many years and later the head coach at Western Michigan University. Jack is just a super guy even if he is from Ohio (as was Bo). He told me so many Bo Schembechler stories about what a wonderful guy he was, that I went from really disliking Bo to admiring him (with one exception, his firing of **ERNIE HARWELL***). As an aside, every

***When ERNIE HARWELL was a young man in Georgia, he was Margaret Mitchell's paper boy. Mitchell wrote *Gone With the Wind*....Harwell was baptized in the Jordan River.**

Iowa and Notre Dame fan hopes that Jim Harbaugh stays at Stanford forever.

But my real admiration for the University of Michigan took a quantum leap when I wrote a book on Tom Brady in 2002 and interviewed many Michigan people. We'll expound about Brady in much greater detail later in this book.

Upon becoming my own publisher ten years ago, this fans' book concept seemed like a good idea to test. The first scheduled fans book was to be about Notre Dame fans but it was shelved when "Win One for the Gipper" was replaced by "Just Win One." The actual first "Fans" book, *For Yankee Fans Only,* sold out. The second, *For Red Sox Fans Only,* sold out immediately. Twenty thousand more were reprinted. The book, *For Cub Fans Only,* not only became the best-selling book in the history of the Cubs, it sold over three times the previous record.

Publishing can be a vicious business with phony reviews and spurious stories constantly planted on the Internet by publishers trying to protect their investments and new releases. The trade-off is that "the more you get ripped, the better you're doin." Their shenanigans do not bother me since I cannot type, have never turned on a computer and have never seen the Internet. Perhaps I am a Luddite at heart, but one thing is certain: the only critics who count are the readers like you.

Since the age of ten, I've been a serious collector of sports books. During that time—my favorite book style is the eavesdropping type where the subject talks in his or her own words—without the "then he said" or "the air was so thick you could cut it with a butter knife:" waste of verbiage. Books such as Lawrence Ritter's *Glory of Their Times* and Donald Honig's *Baseball When the Grass Was Real.* Thus, I adopted that style when I started compiling oral histories of the Mike Ditkas and Harry Carays of the world. I'm a sports fan first and foremost—I do not even pretend to be an author. This book is designed solely for other sports fans. I really do not care what the publisher, editors or critics think. I'm only interested in Michigan fans having an enjoyable read and getting their money's worth. Sometimes, a person being interviewed will drift off the subject, but if the feeling is that Wolverine fans would enjoy the digression, it stays in the book.

In an effort to get more material into the book, the editor decided to merge some paragraphs and omit some of the commas, which will allow for the reader to receive an additional 20,000 words, the equivalent of 50 pages. More bang for your buck...more fodder for English teachers...fewer dead trees.

I've been blessed to be able to do more than three dozen sports books, and I can honestly say that this is one book that I hated to see come to an end. It was so enjoyable to work on a project where great—but often forgotten—American values like sportsmanship, integrity, loyalty and enthusiasm are so evident.

The best thing about the University of Michigan is: "it's a classy place". It has first-class academics, first-class athletics, in a first class city, and first-class fans; wonderful fans who are knowledgeable, passionate and civil. It has been a pleasure working on this book.

Chapter 1

SWEET HOME BIG HOUSE

The Land of Ahs

IF A FOOTBALL COULD TALK, IT WOULD SOUND LIKE BOB UFER

TOM UFER

After graduating from Bowdoin College in Maine, Tom Ufer went home to Michigan and worked for Ufer Insurance with his brother David and his father Bob...and has been there ever since. From 1976 to 1981 however, Ufer was also able to work as a "spotter" in the broadcast booth with his father.

Dad was very close to Bo Schembechler and his wife, Millie. Dad actually had the same birthday as Millie, April 1st. The birthday parties with the coaching staff would either be at our house or at Bo's house, which were about three blocks apart. Millie Schembechler wrote a wonderful poem I show off on my office wall that talks about the No. 1 Michigan fan in the land, my dad. It's about 10 sentences and was written in 1976.

My grandfather graduated from the University of Michigan in 1915 and my grandmother in 1917. My grandfather was an All-American track runner. In Dad's senior year in high school, he led the state of Pennsylvania in scoring in football. He was very fast. When Dad came to Ann Arbor in 1940, following his mother and father, he played football and track. Dad broke every record from the 100-yard dash to the half mile. He gave up football in honor of track and went on to run in the L.A. Coliseum. He ran in **BOSTON GARDEN*** and Madison Square Garden

***The actual name of BOSTON GARDEN was "Boston Madison Square Garden."**

as well. He held a world record for four years and a Michigan record for 37 years in the indoor quarter. He graduated from Michigan in 1944 and started broadcasting in 1945. He broadcast 363 games over five decades from 1945 until October 16, 1981. He passed away 10 days after doing that last game.

The thing that was unique with Dad was his love for Michigan. He would say, "I don't care who wins as long as it's Michigan." He had an opportunity in 1955, and not a lot of people realize this, to do national broadcasting. ABC and **NBC*** offered him auditions to come up to New York and give it a shot. At that time he was in the hospital with internal bleeding of an ulcerated colitis. The doctor said, "If you go national and do this 12 months a year, you'll kill yourself with all the pressure and all your preparation."

> The thing that was unique with Dad was his love for Michigan.

He basically locked in the 10 weeks a year with Michigan football, and it was a total labor of love doing those five decades of Michigan football. Having been an athlete here and with his parents having gone to Michigan, he truly did love the school. He owned the insurance business for many decades as a means to an end. That allowed him to have the free time in the fall to focus on the football team.

He and Bo were very dear friends. Dad was very instrumental in 1968, along with his good friend Don Canham, in mentioning Bo as a coaching possibility for the following year. As Bo became more famous and did quite well at Michigan, Dad's fame grew, and he became an unbelievable spokesman for the University

***NBC** Sports President, Dick Ebersol, recently paid $50,000 at a charity auction to have Carly Simon tell him the name of the subject person in her song, "You're So Vain." Only Simon, Ebersol and that person know the identity, rumored to be Warren Beatty, James Taylor or Mick Jagger.**

of Michigan. Bo used Dad for recruiting. The second weekend of February, Bo would bring in his top recruits to Michigan. That Saturday night was when Dad usually spoke. He would tell these kids, "You're not a Michigan Man for four years; you're a Michigan Man for life." It was all from his heart, having been an alum and having played football here. Bo said, "Thank God for Ufer, all the kids he helped to come to Ann Arbor."

> ...17,000 Michigan fans turned around as one and started chanting Dad's name. "Ufer! Ufer! Ufer!"

Dad would emcee or be the speaker at the pep rally and events before the Ohio State game. When Woody Hayes, the infamous Ohio State coach, came to town for the games, Dad was the only one that Woody allowed to interview him. Woody knew Ufer had made fun with him over the years, but he also knew that Ufer did his homework and really prepared for his broadcasts. Dad respected Woody as one of the great coaches in college football.

Dad was really well respected by all the Big 10 coaches because he was so professional with his broadcasting. The preparation he did was interesting. A sportswriter came to the booth about three years before Dad passed away and said, "Ufer! Oh my gosh! Look at all these...cards. Look at all of your preparation! You could paint that window black and do three games off your...cards with all the stuff you prepared!" Meaning he only used 15-20 percent of what he prepared for the games. Dad was heard throughout the Midwest on WJR, a 50,000 watt station, for the last five years of his career. That was very instrumental in getting Michigan back on the map as one of the great college football programs after taking a little time off in the early '60s. Bo put us back on the map where we have been for the last four decades, and Dad was very instrumental in getting Michigan the players and spreading the Michigan word.

When he was preparing as we were driving to different insurance meetings, Dad had...cards and he'd memorize the names and numbers of the kids. For example, I'd give Dad the number of a kid from **NORTHWESTERN***, a second—or third-string tailback, and he would give me his name. I'd ask, "Dad, what do you care about the third-string tailback from Northwestern? The kid's probably not going to get in the game and what's it matter about his stats, his height, weight, and average carry per game?" He said, "Tom, you know, there is a mom and dad up there in Chicago that may be listening, and if that kid gets in, I'm going to make darn sure that I know his name." He'd have that type of preparation. It was really amazing.

Early on, Bo had lost a couple of bowl games, in particular, the Rose Bowls. A fun memory for me at the Rose Bowl was in 1981. Dad gave a speech at the junior college on December 31, the day before the Rose Bowl. He gave a half-hour speech in front of 10,000 people to get these kids ready for the game. He was telling them they could give something to Bo that no other Michigan team had given him and that was his first Rose Bowl victory. They had 60 minutes of football and a lifetime to remember. Each one of the kids came up and honked the Schembechler blowing horn that Dad used in his broadcast. Twenty-two kids got up to briefly speak and honk the horn. The next day, Bo went on to beat Washington 23-6. As the game ended, we were up in the press box, and about 17,000 Michigan fans turned around as one and started chanting Dad's name. "Ufer! Ufer! Ufer!" As a 26-year-old kid standing next to his father, I was unbelievably proud.

Another broadcasting moment that encompassed the fan and cheerleader he was came on October 16th, 10 days before he passed away from prostate cancer. They had the banner out that said, "Bob Ufer—The M Club Supports You." The team came out and touched it and then the band came out and

***The late Randy Walker, head coach at NORTHWESTERN from 1999-2005, is the only coach to beat every Big 10 team. When he was head coach at Miami (Ohio), his team beat Northwestern.**

spelled our name. Dad gets on the **P.A. SYSTEM***, he was doing his final game and knew it, and there were 101,000 people with their heads turned up toward the press box. Dad said, "I want to ask you all two simple questions. Who is the finest coach in America today? (Bo) Who? (Bo) And who's the finest team in America today? (Meechigan) Who? (Meechigan) Let's all join together and sing the finest college fight song ever written—Meechigan Victors!" He had 101,000 people ready to go to war. We were playing Iowa. He passed away 10 days later.

About 1976, General Patton's nephew, who lived in the Chicago area and listened to Dad's broadcast on WJR, calls and asks, "Mr. Ufer, would you like to have my uncle's horn from his WWII jeep?" My dad said, "Oh my gosh! Is the sky blue? Is the grass green? I'd love the thing! I'll get it involved in my broadcast!" What Dad did then was beautiful; he'd have a separate microphone hooked up to this horn. Then if Michigan scored a touchdown, there were three honks. There were two for a field goal and one for an extra point. They would get going at big games and Dad would just sit on it—Honk! Honk! Honk! Honk!

They still talk about the game in 1979. It was the 100th year of Michigan football. Michigan is playing Indiana and the score is tied 21–21. There are five seconds left in the game when Johnny Wangler rolls back from the 45-yard line and throws a completion to Anthony Carter at the 22-yard line. He breaks one tackle and then breaks another at the 4. He goes into the end zone and Michigan wins in the final second of the game. Michigan goes absolutely out of their minds. When you listen to the replay, Dad goes absolutely crazy and all you can hear is the honking of the horn. It was a classic: "King Carter! King Carter! The finest play in 100 years of Michigan football! That

***The PUBLIC ADDRESS announcer for the Houston Astros (Colt '45s) in 1962 was Dan Rather. John Forsythe, the actor, was the P.A. announcer for the Brooklyn Dodgers in 1937 and 1938.**

will go down for the next 100 years as the finest!" It was one of those moments in time.

Anthony was a two-year All-American, a little kid about 5'10". He used to wear three pairs of tube socks because his legs were so skinny; he wanted to make his lower legs a little bigger. What an unbelievably skilled athlete. Bo gets him from Florida and AC had a great four years here. Dad just had a ball with ol' Anthony Carter, ol' AC, No. 1! He also gave all the kids nicknames: Anthony "Carter the Darter," "Dynamic Donnie" Dufek, "Galloping Gil" Chapman, Butch "Don't Call Me Harold" Wolfolk. Dad was doing this back in the '70s—he had all these nicknames for these kids. Bo was General George Bo Patton Schembechler! He used to call Woody Hayes "Dr. Strange Hayes." Earl Booth was "Darth Vader" Booth!

Dad loved the Michigan-Michigan State games and really loved the Michigan-Ohio State rivalry. Bo and Woody played each other for 10 years. Bo won five, Woody won four, and they tied once. In seven or eight out of the 10 years, that final game in November decided the winner of the Big 10 championship. Dad had an absolute field day. The 6:00 and 10:00 shows on WJR were all Michigan-Ohio State. Back then they were selling Woody toilet paper with a picture of Woody's head on every square. It was just crazy. They had pep rallies on Friday nights and Dad would lead 3,000-4,000 kids on campus, getting them all pumped up for the Meechigan-Ohio State game. Those were the special ones. He was so proud that Bo put Michigan back on the map where they stayed for many years. Michigan and Ohio State were the two giants of the Big 10, and really of college football, and Dad was able to bring that to fans all across the Midwest.

WJR got all this fan mail for Dad. For years in the '60s and '70s, they were always the Michigan State station. Then station management came to Dad in 1976. Remember now that Bo has been going for six years and has really taken over the state of Michigan and the Midwest with the premier football program.

The station wanted to move from Michigan State to Michigan. A lot of people said, "You can't bring Ufer in—he's crazy!" The ratings for the six years that Dad did it went absolutely off the wall, Detroit, Michigan, the Midwest, they absolutely loved Dad as the voice of Michigan football. He would get letters from these people who called themselves football widows: "Mr. Ufer, you saved our marriage. We didn't like football, but now we love to sit down and watch Michigan on TV, turn the sound down, and turn you up. You bring so much enjoyment not only to my husband but also to me and my kids. I don't really understand football, but you bring us joy for three-and-a-half hours every Saturday in the fall." You realize then how big college football is. Dad used to say football was a religion and Saturday was a holy day of obligation.

The man involved in building Michigan Stadium in 1918 and 1920, the great coach Fielding Yost, had the foresight to build a 75,000 seat arena with the footings for another 50,000. He would tell everybody back in 1920 when it opened, "Someday it will grow to this!" In the early '40s, when Dad ran track over at Yost Fieldhouse, Yost would sit on the end on his stool with a big cigar and fedora. He talked at great length with his West Virginia drawl about the stories of the past and future of Meechigan. Dad decided, as Bo started winning and he was having more fun with his horn and other things he had incorporated into his broadcast, that he was going to start using "Meechigan"!

Dad used to say football was a religion and Saturday was a holy day of obligation.

Dad was "on" 24/7. He loved life and people. He thoroughly loved doing Michigan football. He coached my brother's and my Little League team for years. He started both the booster clubs in 1969. He was very involved with the community. He was just an "on" guy and loved life!

About 10 years ago, I put out a couple of CDs. We sold tens of thousands of them to raise $1.3 million for scholarships in Dad's name to over 120 local high school kids going to Michigan as student athletes. We gave Lloyd Carr a check for $250,000 and $100,000 to the student academic side, all from sales of those CDs. Again, Dad's been dead 29 years and we still sell a couple thousand a year. People in their 50s and 60s now have their kids here and reminisce about the '60s and '70s with Bo and Dad. He was the spokesman for the University of Meechigan. It was a labor of love. We're very proud to keep his legacy alive. You listen to these CDs and if you're not smiling in a few seconds, you're not breathing. Kids are buying the CDs still because they *want* to touch yesteryear. They want to touch positive times.

In 1976, Ron Nessen, press secretary for President Gerald Ford, calls our house a couple times and Dad hangs up on him twice, thinking it was a prank call. The third time he answers it, he hears, "Ron Nessen, calling from the White House. We, like you, are going to kick off in November. We're going to kick off President Ford's re-election campaign for 1976 and want you to be in Crisler Arena in front of 15,000 people and lead the way as the emcee." To listen to the 15-minute introduction that Dad did for President Ford is a treat. I have it on CD too.

Dad does this and I'm at Bowdoin College at the time as a junior. Lo and behold, the 30-second clip of Ford for his election in the fall had about eight seconds of Dad as emcee.. Dad is arm and arm with Ford and the...picture of them is on the front page of the *Boston Globe*, the *New York Times*, all these papers. We have a couple of papers from overseas too. The headline read, "President Ford kicking off his re-election campaign with Michigan Sports Announcer Bob Ufer at Crisler Sports Arena."

Dad was the cheerleader, the consummate fan, the All-American with a world record in track, the football player. He knew what it meant to be a Michigan athlete. He came up in 1940 and never left. It came through loud and clear in the broadcast.

It's amazing, even now, how you walk through the tailgates and you can hear Dad's CDs rockin' and rollin'! Everybody is smiling and reminiscing. Dad used to say, "You come into life naked and you leave naked, but try to touch all the bases while you're here." He really did that in life. He loved life and loved Michigan.

It's amazing, even now, how you walk through the tailgates and you can hear Dad's CDs rockin' and rollin'!

Most of the football players attempt to use the collegiate game as a stepping stone to go pro. Dad stayed because of his health, and the rest, as they say, is history. As one of his kids, I am unbelievably proud. Dad passed away six weeks after I was married in 1981 so he didn't get to know my daughters. People talk about "Bompa" Grandpa Ufer even now in their classes! And the professor has a smile on his or her face.

My youngest daughter, Kendall, goes to the University of Michigan. She was thrilled the other day and texted me, "Dad, you won't believe it! We're using the Michigan Hero cards and there is a picture of Bompa on one of the cards." That's her grandfather and my father. The legacy and memories live on, from one generation to the next. I miss him.

(For CDs, go to www.ufer.org. All proceeds go to the Bob Ufer Foundation Scholarship Fund.)

THE BEST DAMN BAND IN THE LAND... AND WE'D DOT THE i TWICE IF WE WANTED TO

CAROL (MAU) FLINT

Carol Flint's daughter describes her as a "band geek." But that served Flint just fine when she was a student at the University of Michigan. A member of four different bands while in college, Flint says, "I would join any band so I could get into the sporting events." That included football, hockey, and men's and women's basketball. Working as a senior program manager at Xilinx, near San Jose, CA, has not lessened Flint's love for music. She plays in two hand bell groups, sings in her church choir, directs her son's Boy Scouts troop band, and even taught middle school marching band for seven years.

When I was selecting colleges, I only applied to one place. I knew I wanted to go to Michigan. My dad had gone to Michigan and some of his family had too. It seemed like a natural choice.

While I was at Michigan I was in the marching band for five years. We went to two Rose Bowls, a Sugar Bowl, a Bluebonnet Bowl in Houston, a Holiday Bowl, Super Bowl, and a **WORLD SERIES***. Being in the band and doing those things are probably my fondest memories from Michigan.

***The last WORLD SERIES day game was in 1987.**

One particular Rose Bowl game, my freshman year, was the first bowl game that Bo won. Everybody was just so excited after that game. On that trip the band played at a pep rally with Bob Ufer—that was really exciting! He was quite an inspirational guy. Shortly after that, he died. It was one of his last big pep rallies. Because it was a bowl game, the band performed for the football team. It was interesting that the team had never seen the band perform—they were always in the locker room when we were playing.

We did our pregame show, the football team was introduced, and then Bob Ufer gave his pep talk to the players. He said, "You always remember the highs and the lows. If you go out there and goof up or have a bad game, that's the thing you'll always remember; you'll always remember that bad game. If you go out there and win and win Bo's first bowl game, that's what you'll always remember. You won't remember the mediocre parts; you'll remember the highs and the lows."

Michigan played Washington that year. Our Michigan band shared dorm space with the Washington band. Every single meal—breakfast, lunch, and dinner—someone would stand up and say a knock-knock joke and then sing their fight song. Finally, after we won the game, we went back for dinner thinking the Washington band wouldn't sing their fight song that night—but they still did. We were ready for it! That year we had performed an Elton John song, "Funeral for a Friend," so we stood up and sang that song for them. They were amazed and gave us a standing ovation.

We would typically go out a whole week before a bowl game. We played at the pep rallies, alumni events, even at a New Year's Eve party for the students. One alumni event was a formal dance. After we performed, a jazz band played and we listened to the band and danced. All the alumni wanted to dance with the band members. That was a lot of fun—we were the celebrities!

One year we went out to the Rose Bowl and played UCLA. Again, we shared dorm space with their band. Their band also had an intramural football team and Michigan had both a men's and women's intramural team. We talked our directors into letting us have a football game, band against band. It wasn't too hard since our director, Eric Becker, was the coach for the women's team. Our songwriter was the coach for the men's team.

> ...the sound was amazing inside the stadium.

So the band vs. band football game began. At one point we looked around and noticed all the local television station cameras. They usually came out to the field to film our practices for the hype before the Rose Bowl. This time they found the two schools' bands on the field having a football game. Word quickly spread and soon there was a whole row of cameras filming our football game. At one point, when we were way ahead like 45–0, we put our women's team in against their men's team! Later that evening, my aunt and uncle in L.A. saw the game highlights on the news showing a play where our women scored a touchdown against their men's team!

I remember all the times in the tunnel before pregame, when the Michigan team came off the field from their warm-ups, and all the band members were yelling and cheering and giving high fives—although some players were too tall to reach. The drum cadence was getting them all excited. When the other team came in from their warm-ups, we would stand perfectly still at attention, looking straight ahead and trying to psych them out.

My very first football game as a freshman, we came running out of the tunnel for pregame, and the sound was amazing inside the stadium. It was something else. I'll never forget that first time running out of the tunnel. The crowd was so loud you could hardly hear the drumbeat, and you're standing right next to the drummers. You just had to watch everyone's feet! It was such a shot of adrenaline; everyone's feet were coming up higher than in practice. The sound was just overwhelming, and I remember concentrating so hard on the band show so as not to make any mistakes. It was amazing!

School would usually start on a Thursday so the band would arrive on Saturday and have "Band Week." It was all day Saturday through Wednesday. School started on Thursday, as did regular practices. Our rehearsals for Band Week started at 8:00 a.m. and went until 11:30 or 12:00. Then we had our lunch break and continued on from about 1:00 until 6:00 p.m. We had a dinner break and were back at it until 8:00 p.m. or dark.

> "You'll want to come in good physical shape."

Then there were sectionals or extra-rank practices. After a couple of days we had tryouts to see who made it into the band. They were open to anyone who came to Band Week, but then there were tryouts to see who would actually march. My freshman year, I made it! There were two more spots in the pregame show than there were at halftime because of the diagonals on the *M*s. I got one of those spots, so I was first alternate and marched every game for five years!

The first few days of camp we spent a lot of time on Elbel Field. In that first week, we had a playing test to put us in "chair order" that determined what part you would play. The week's music was handed out. Then we spent most of the time outside learning the unique style of marching. The band practice field was an asphalt field painted to look like a football field and had identical markings to the field at the stadium. A lot of our formations involved cueing up the yard lines and where you were on the *M* in the middle of the field.

Before my first camp, I received a letter at home saying "You'll want to come in good physical shape." Well, I thought I was but found out I wasn't. It does take a lot of time and energy to do the entry cadence, the double-time high step—we practiced that over and over again. Your legs would feel like lead. We did marches back and forth and up and down the field time after time that first week to learn that style. That was the first full two days: learning how to march. You have to all learn to look identical. After tryouts, we started learning the shows. First we practiced without music, just marching to a drum beat, and then we had to start to learn to march and play at the same time. We had tryouts every week. A rank was a unit of 12 and every unit had a rank leader. That rank leader picked the weaker players or the ones who didn't try as hard that week, and they were challenged for their spot.

You could get challenged if you missed a rehearsal, if you weren't there when they took roll. It didn't matter if you showed up two minutes after that. If you weren't there when they took attendance, you were absent. Rehearsal started at 4:45 p.m. and attendance was taken at 4:40 p.m. because the one taking attendance was in the band, so she had to be ready too. We had this saying, "To be early is to be on time. To be on time is to be late. And to be late is unforgivable." So you got there and were ready to go or you would end up being challenged.

The last game of the season the seniors did a little postgame show of their own. We picked out some favorites from the years we were in the band and made our own formations. My last game happened to be a year Michigan played Ohio State in Ann Arbor. We played "The Yellow and the Blue" at the end. It brought tears.

The band members spent so much time out on the field together and practicing—we got pretty close. About five or six years ago now we had a band reunion. At Homecoming, you're so busy with Alumni Band that you don't have much time to visit, so the band had a reunion in the summer for three or four days. We took turns visiting different people's houses and had fun catching up.

A HARD WAY TO MAKE AN EASY LIVING

NEIL ROSEMAN

Roseman graduated from the University of Michigan with a bachelor's degree in both political science and economics. He currently lives in Ellicott City, Maryland, and owns two businesses. He's living one of his dreams of having Michigan season tickets and flying to every game.

One day, I was reading the *Michigan Daily* and noticed a classified ad for a job as the manager for the Michigan football team. **I actually thought it was a joke. To me, that was a godlike job.** Why would they ever put something like that in the newspaper's classifieds? I called up and found out it was legit, so I went to meet the head manager and was hired. If you want to call it hired; it's not like we got paid.

At the time, there were about eight managers and a head manager, a senior who had done it for three years. Specifically, we each were assigned to a coach. I was assigned to Coach Jerry Meter and the defensive line. The manager's job was to set up and take down practice, taking down all of the tackling dummies and sleds.

On game day, we went around with juice and donuts to wake up players at 5:00, 6:00, or 7:00 a.m. Sometimes we had to do the bed checks at night. We got to the stadium early to make sure everything was set up. During the practices before games we would also retrieve the balls and throw them back as part of their pregame warm-ups. Then we held the earphone cords on the sidelines, which was a big deal.

Five of us would hold the earphone cords; they weren't **WIRELESS*** at the time, so you had to follow your coach around with 50 feet of wire in your hand. As the coaches went up and down the field, you could reel in the wire and let it out. All of the wires would get tangled up and crossed. The big ABC trucks would run over them. And when the coaches went on the field, especially when they're really upset and yelling at a referee, we had to reel them back in. We controlled how far they went out with how much wire we gave them.

It was amazing. It was the best year of my life. But I only did it for one year. I had started another business my second year and being a manager was *so* time consuming. We were there before the players got there, we were there after they left, and we traveled with the team as well. That was almost 25 years ago.

I'm a little guy (5'6½") who never played football. I remember being at practice the first couple of days when the freshmen were there; they came in early at that time. The upperclassmen weren't there yet. When the upperclassmen finally came in, I thought to myself that the hits weren't too big of a deal. I'm not saying that I could play, of course; I had never played football before. Then later on at practice, we actually went to the Big House and had a scrimmage with referees and everything. What I didn't realize was that at practice they weren't hitting at 100 percent; they were maybe only hitting at about 20-25 percent. Once I realized that, I thought, "Oh my God...I would die...I would die quickly!"

Another new experience was my first team meeting. I had no idea how everything worked and I was told to go to the meeting.

***In 1974 Billy Martin was managing the Texas Rangers and Frank Lucchesi was his third base coach. Martin tried using a TRANSISTOR hook-up to his coaches to relay signals. One game the system was broken, but Martin kept yelling instructions for a suicide squeeze into the microphone. Red Sox pitcher Luis Tiant finally stepped off the mound and yelled: "Frank, Billy said he wanted the suicide squeeze."**

The whole team was sitting at desks, those little school desks. Bo started to talk about the upcoming season. He had one of those overhead projectors where you write with grease pencils. He was going through the schedule, and he says, "First off, Notre Dame comes to town. And we're going to kick their...!" You have to hear the tone in his voice and see the veins popping out of his neck. It was really intense. We had come off a 6–6 season, which was the worst season in Bo's history at Michigan, and weren't ranked. South Carolina was ranked No. 1 at the time and Maryland was No. 2. Bo continues, "And then we're going to South Carolina—we'll take that Rebel flag and...! And then Maryland's going to come to town—what the f--- is a Terp?" Now remember, this was back in the days when there was no Internet and nobody had ever heard of the Terrapins. I didn't know what a Terp was at the time. He went through the whole schedule like that. I knew then that I was in for something different.

When traveling with the team I was told to wear khaki pants and a blue blazer. We won our first five games. We were 5–0 and ranked No. 2 in the country, right behind Iowa. Most people think the big speech before a game is done in the locker room, right before you go out on the field. At Michigan, the big speech was done at the hotel before you went to the game.

"Do you know why we must win?"... "Because we are Michigan!

After you ate breakfast or lunch, everyone went into the meeting rooms where the players met with the offensive or defensive coaches. Then everyone came together for Bo's speech. During his talk, which was about the Iowa game, one-third of the team would be so jazzed that they'd start bouncing their legs up and down; their feet were in place but their knees were moving. I can't recall the first part of this speech, but in the last part, he said, "Do you know *why* we must win? Because they're No. 1 and we're No. 2! Do you know *why* we must win? Because this game is on national television!" Back then, that was a big deal because most games weren't on national television. And he continued, "Do you know *why* we must win? Because they shut us out last year 26–0! Do you know *why* we must win? Do you know *why* we must win?" Everyone kind of mumbled why. "Because we *are* Michigan!" He's screaming and his veins are popping and he looks up and says, "Let's go!" And then he walks out first and everybody else falls in behind him. When we all walk out the door, they're playing "Hail to the Victors" in the hallways of the hotel with hundreds of fans singing! They're patting us all on the back saying, "Go Blue, Go Blue!" They thought I was a player because I'm dressed like one.

That was another highlight of my life, being patted on the back and cheered like I was part of the team. That speech from Bo was incredible. However, we lost that game on the last play of the game. That was when Chuck Long was at Iowa and they had a really good team.

We won the next game fairly easily. Then we had to go to Illinois. Jack Trudeau was at Illinois and they were a really great team. Bo pitches the same speech and the ending phrase was, "We cannot and will not be denied again!" You just don't see that nowadays; it was like General Patton rallying the troops. That's what sticks out for me.

One time I was setting up for practice at the stadium—it wasn't called the Big House back then—I was in the tunnel walking down from the locker room and Bo was sitting at the end of the tunnel gazing out at the stadium. There were only 10 people in the stadium at the time. We were just setting up for the practice. I walk up and paused right next to him and he started talking out loud to me and himself. This was a big deal! Bo usually does not talk to managers. Well, he had these blue prints in his hand and he's talking to me, but he's really not. He said, "You know what they want me to do? They want me to approve all these luxury boxes and suites here at Michigan Stadium." I told him, "No way. Too much corporate money in college football." And that was the end of the conversation. He was just looking at the stadium, thinking about how it would look, with the plans in his hand. That talk was back in 1985 and he had not approved anything.

They brought in referees for our scrimmages. There was a freshman sensation who was the top recruit that year. I'm holding one of the down markers on the sideline. That freshman comes across the middle and jumps high for the ball, which was actually coming toward me on the sideline. He jumps high to catch the ball and is helicoptered by a defensive back—he comes in and just nails him. He did a 360 in the air and then falls on his back with the ball in his stomach. I was wondering if he was okay because if it were me, I'd be dead. The referee went and leaned over him. He took the ball out of his hand and told him, "Welcome to the Big Time, son!"

I'm a happy-go-lucky guy who can handle adversity pretty easily. The most painful thing I went through as a manager is when the team lost. You were not allowed to talk on the way home. I'd be on the bus going to the airport, getting on the plane, going back to the Detroit airport, and on the bus back to Ann Arbor, all with no talking. You had to contemplate where you had screwed up, where you had missed a block or other assignments. They made that entire six-hour time frame, or however long it was, talk free after a loss. You didn't know where the rule was coming from, you just knew that everyone was doing it, so you followed along. Nobody stands up and says, "Don't talk." It's just that nobody's talking and you're just a manager, so you're not about to talk.

If a play didn't run right in practice, Bo would say, "Run it again!" So the offense would run off tackle and gain maybe one yard. Bo would be a little upset and say, "Run it again!" Of course, the defense knew what the offense was going to run because Bo just said to run it again. Bo had this philosophy that it didn't matter if the other team knew your play. All of the trickery and secrecy didn't matter; you should be able to tell the opposing team what you are going to do and then run it down their throats for another four yards.

Another thing that really stuck with me was when I was a freshman. I was 18 years old and had no money. My parents lived in Illinois and I was at school in Michigan and it was all new to me. I had no idea about what was happening the next day. At the end of the year, we were going to the Fiesta Bowl to play Nebraska. So we were practicing and practicing and the dorms were going to close in two days for Christmas. But we're still practicing for four more days, followed by three days off, and then a flight to Tempe to play in the Fiesta Bowl. Well, all of a sudden, I had no place to stay because the dorms were all closing. So I went up to Coach Meter, the coach that I was assigned to, and said, "Coach, I don't know what to do here. I want to practice with the team, but I don't have any place to stay as of tomorrow." So he said, "Let's go in and see Bo." So we walked in and Bo was getting ready for practice. He proceeds to tell Bo the situation, and Bo said, "Well, put him up in a hotel." It didn't seem logical to me at the time that they were going to spend $70 a night to put me in a hotel for three days. To me, it felt like I was part of the family, and they weren't going to let me not have someplace to sleep.

One unbelievable experience I had during a game was when I was holding the earphone cords for Coach "Mo" (Moeller). He was the defensive coordinator at the time and was just irate at an official for a call and was storming the field. Of course, if you do that, you can get a 15-yard penalty. So all of the other coaches were saying, "Do not let him do that. Pull him in. Do not let him go out that far." So I'm caught between him yanking me and them telling me not to let him out. So I start reeling him in. I'm pulling him back and he can feel it tugging at his waist. He turns around and said, "Let me f------ do whatever I want to f------ do!" I was mortified because that just probably happened on national television. I've got the coaches telling me to pull him in and he's screaming at me. We're in the middle of a game and it's critically important. I finally just pulled him in because that's what everybody was yelling at me to do. He came back about 10 minutes later and apologized to me. So that was cool.

One of my pet peeves as a fan of Michigan football is that the banner and several other things are the wrong color. The banner should be Maize and Blue. If you look at it, it's more of a Spanish yellow, not a Maize, and the color of the banner doesn't match the color of the players' uniforms as they go out underneath. I started getting into Michigan football, got my season tickets, made a donation, and started to get to know people in the Athletic Department. I shared my thought that the banner isn't right, and after a year or two nothing ever happened. People agree with me, but nothing ever happened.

Finally, I said that it's time for me to stop complaining and just take the bull by the horn. I made a few calls. This banner is on national television every game so it's not just 110,000 people watching it; millions of people are seeing these colors that are just off. I called up Mary Walker in the Athletic Department and said I was prepared to pay for the new banner. So after multiple phone calls, getting to the right people, and getting the M Club, I paid for a new banner.

It just seemed important to me. I'm so proud of the Maize and Blue; it seems like everything should be the right colors. David Brandon, the athletic director, seems even more committed that the colors are right. There are several things that are the wrong color. When you come down the tunnel, it says "Go Blue," but once again, it was that Spanish yellow, not Maize. Now that has been changed to Maize. David Brandon was really committed that we do the Michigan brand correctly. Several things in the stadium were the wrong color and are now being corrected. Obviously, I can't afford to donate an elevator shaft, a concession stand, a family planning center, or all these different things that people donate millions of dollars for, but this was great for me. It's a passion.

MAMA WANGS' WINGS

THERESA WANGLER

Theresa Wangler's son John played quarterback for Michigan in the late 1970s. Former players and friends visit her tailgate every home game, complete with homemade food known as "Mrs. Wangler's Tailgate Café." John Wangler, the former quarterback, is the founder of Top Cat Sales, a wholesale distributor of licensed apparel and footwear.

We started tailgating before and after the games after Johnny graduated in 1981. As most things do, it started out small with some of Johnny's classmates and a few of our friends, but it would grow and grow and grow. We make a different menu every time and serve whatever the boys are in the mood for along with a variety of main dishes, including hors d'oeuvres, desserts, a big basket of fruit, and an assortment of beverages. I always have a large basket of candy because a lot of little children come to the tailgate and they love grabbing the **CANDY***.

We tailgate in The Victors parking lot, which has become home base for a lot of former players. When they come back to the games they always stop by and remind us what they would like for me to bring to the next tailgate.

***P. K. Wrigley and Milton HERSHEY were bitter business rivals. When Wrigley bought the Chicago Cubs, Hershey tried to buy the Philadelphia Phillies...and sell chocolate gum. Hershey failed in both efforts.**

While John was playing, he was a drop-back passer; his classmates referred to him as "Winging Wangs," whatever that means. So I became Mama Wangs, and still they come back to see Mama Wangs. Anthony Carter was a few years behind John, but he was John's main receiver. He's from Florida, and when we were going to all of the games Anthony became quite close to us. He would call me his "Michigan Ma."

The big play that everyone constantly talks about is the last-second pass that Johnny threw to Anthony Carter. Michigan was on the 47-yard line and had to win the game to stay in the race. So Johnny threw a pass and Anthony caught it and ran down the field on October 27, 1979. Michigan won the game by six points. That just happened to be the day before my birthday and about three days before his dad's birthday, so he said that was our birthday present. We have the football that was used at that game in our den.

The menu at the tailgate varies every week, but the last game of every season we play Ohio State, and whether it's home or away, I make chili. It's usually cold outside. A friend from Hawaii told me that you have to serve chili over rice, so I have been serving the chili over rice with onions and cheese on top. I make about 40-45 pounds of chili meat to have enough. Now every year I don't bring even one bean home, every single drop of that chili goes. Everybody waits for the chili—now it's a trademark of the last game.

Each weekend we serve between 45 and 150 people. If we happen to be playing Michigan State or Notre Dame, there's always 140-150 people, but most of the time it's between 40 and 75. Although it started out small in the early days, it has mushroomed into this big party for every Saturday home game.

We're in the parking lot early to set up and visit. We close up to go into the game and reopen afterward. After every game it takes about an hour to an hour and a half to clean up.

The marching band stops right in front of us, 250 strong. The little ones run out to have their pictures taken with the drum major

Johnny is currently a manufacturers' representative for **adidas***and Reebok. He invites many of his customers. We have this nice big canopy set up. Our tailgate neighbor had a sign made up for the canopy that reads "Mrs. Wangler's Tailgate Café." People come by and think this is really a café and someplace they can buy food. They ask to buy a beer, and I say, "Are you trying to get me in trouble? I don't have a liquor license. Just take it." Some fans of the opposing team come by as well. We have become a landmark there.

Some of the past players come by regularly. We've had Butch Woolfolk and Fred Brockington. Jim Breaugh, the former quarterback, comes a lot. Rick Leach comes occasionally; Anthony Carter comes up from Florida once or twice a year. BJ Dickey, another former quarterback, sometimes shows up. Stanley Edwards stops by. We see quite a few of the boys that played around the same time as Johnny, and a lot of the players after Johnny come too. Every week it changes.

I enjoy it. A lot of Johnny's customers come too, but even if they don't, I love seeing all of the former players. It can be a lot of work, but I enjoy every minute of it, so I don't look at it as work. There are 365 days in the year and of those I spend seven Fridays and seven Saturdays tailgating, so 14 days is not a lot of work. Now I have favorite bakeries and meat markets to order from. And I make everything homemade. The tailgating has been a wonderful tradition for our family. Johnny has six children and it's a big deal for them too. It's a way of creating some memories for the grandchildren as well. I enjoy every minute of it!

***"adidas" is named after its founder, Adi Dassler. "adidas" is never capitalized.**

TAILGREAT

IRA JOEL JAFFE

Ira Jaffe is a partner with Jaffe, Raitt, Heuer, and Weiss Law Firm in Southfield, Michigan. Jaffe was raised in Detroit and graduated from Massachusetts Institute of Technology (MIT) and the University of Michigan Law School. Jaffe has an enormous UM memorabilia collection and is known for his tailgating extraordinaire with partner Dr. Mel Lester, feeding up to 1,500 football fans every home game.

Going to all the games throughout the years, clearly, anybody who knew me thought I was a little crazy. We got to the point where our children were starting to grow and we wanted to have our house be the place that they brought their friends, rather than us not knowing their friends.

So we decided to finish the basement. It's a very small basement, but we decided to finish it nonetheless. A friend of ours was just going to draw up some plans and he asked what colors we wanted. I thought, well, you don't make a basement elegant, so let's do it in Maize and Blue. So we did, and the minute we were making it Maize and Blue, the imagination started going wild as to how to make it a Michigan basement. So that's what we did.

Over the years, I naturally had a certain amount of paraphernalia, but then, having created a Michigan basement, friends or anyone I had taken to a game as a guest would go into a store and see something Maize and Blue and say, "Oh my goodness! I know some idiot who would like that!" People started buying things for me, as well as me seeing things and knowing I had a place to put them. So I started collecting. Now the basement has things like a 1940 *Life* magazine with Tom Harmon on the cover. A friend sent it to Tom with a letter describing his friend as a big fan, and **TOM HARMON*** sent it back autographed with a nice letter. That's very special.

My wife saw that Michigan won the national basketball championship some years ago and was at an auction. She was able to bid on the shoes that basketball star Rumeal Robinson was wearing when he made the free throw that won the National Championship. I have thousands of things...who knows how much?...a lot! Some are real special and some are just things anyone could get.

A friend of ours has a son who played on the Michigan football team, and he had some players over for a barbecue during the summer. We have pictures with the star players in our swimming pool and playing on the tennis court next door. Some of these guys star in the NFL, so those are fun. Over the years, people that were deemed to be supporters of an athletic program in college could do different things to interface with players. These things were legal but aren't anymore. My tailgating stories, once again, go back to my father. In going to a game, my father would go to a deli, buy some sandwiches, and we would go to a little park by the stadium to tailgate.

My father had four tickets and my sister wasn't interested in going, so I could always bring a friend. Those were great memories. Dad died when I was 19. So the minute I had a son I could take to the games, I brought him and we'd bring some sandwiches, and candy when he was young.

It's just part of my personality to be open to people. I joined something called the Victors Club. Every college has one; if you contribute a certain amount of money to an athletic department you get to buy better football seats and get a parking

***Ricky Nelson and John DeLorean married daughters of *TOMMY HARMON.**

pass. Thirty-five years ago, maybe longer, I invited a friend of mine and his two sons to the game and it was supposed to rain. I had a friend who had just purchased a motor home so I called him and said, "Listen, I have a deal for you. I have a parking pass; we'll use your motor home. I'll bring the food and booze and then we'll be dry and it will be fun." Now all of a sudden, we had a motor home with parking right near the stadium. We started doing that every week.

Being gregarious, I would say to people, "Come on over and have a drink or a sandwich before or after the game." And people did. We were in the best location, and Michigan was getting more popular as Bo Schembechler came and started making them win all the time. What was five people turned into 10, into 30, and then into 100! It just kept getting bigger! I could have stopped it by not having the food and not inviting people, but I loved it.

In 1980, I bought a Dodge Maxivan. It was all white—a big ole ugly thing! I took it to a converter and had the top cut off—put a three-foot riser on it—and painted it Maize and Blue with a matching interior. We went to the games in that. We then brought up a friend's truck. I would get an extra parking pass and we started serving a couple hundred people.

We were bothering folks in the parking lot because so many people were coming. They asked us to move out of that good location. Right adjacent to the stadium there was a little terraced hill. I asked if we could go up on that hill and they said sure! It was literally 10 yards from the stadium entrance. We started doing the tailgate parties there. We would carpet the hill and put up five or six pop-up tents. We'd bring a Ryder truck and generators.

... we were serving 1,500 people every week!

We stopped doing it when they expanded the stadium four years ago. At that time, I think we were serving 1,500 people every week! I'd bring 50 dozen bagels, 25 dozen donuts, and 25-30 lbs. of corned beef, roast beef, and turkey. We had a full bar. No one else brought food.

The kids I knew from the fraternities , or my kids knew, would come with 20-30 kids because they could get a good meal. My wife would ask me, "Do you know these people?" I didn't care. It was fun—my labor of love! I had a party store that delivered a lot of things and I went to the supermarket for the fill-ins.

I had to take all day Friday off to help prepare. I'd have four or five fellas who worked for a friend of mine's apartment complex come and help load. We would have 30-40 coolers filled with different things. Then I had a crew of three or four different secretaries or bookkeepers who worked in my office. They and some of their children would come early Saturday morning, and we would go up in a caravan and a rent-a-truck. They helped set it up.

You can't just leave the food out with that many people. You need a person who refreshes it, cleans it, and puts it back out. After the game, we had to bring that all home, wash it, and re-sort things—then do it again for the next home game! I had a crew of about 10 helping me!

Thank goodness I have a wonderful wife because I don't know how I'd ever have done it without her. She never even liked it. It consumes me. At least she knew what my little quirky thing was!

Some of the better stories are from when we went to the bowl games, especially the Rose Bowl. We would rent several buses in L.A. and have everyone meet outside the Century Plaza Hotel and serve donuts, coffee, and bagels. Then the buses of people would go to the stadium and have a party. In '97 Michigan was playing for the National Championship and everybody was calling asking about the tailgate and wondering if I could get tickets. It was also an El Nino year where there was supposed to be a lot of rain. We tried to get into the corporate tent area.

At first, they wanted Michigan's endorsement. Then they wanted insurance. Then they wanted financial information. We finally selected a menu and had everything arranged and told people about it. They told us that we couldn't have a spot because everybody that had a corporate tent the year before had reupped, so we were out.

He responded, "Oh, I'm the president-elect of the Tournament of Roses."

I was in a really bad mood and this guy started calling me saying, "Hi Ira!" with a big *up* voice, "Are you coming to the Rose Bowl?"

I wasn't very nice to him, unfortunately. I just unleashed on this guy about the story I just referred to. He asked who I was dealing with and I told him, "Rose." He said, "Oh! I know Rose! Let me see what I can do!"

He called me back a few days later all cheery and said, "I talked to Rose and you're right, you can't get in." He said, "I can probably help you out!" I said, "Oh yeah? How? Who are you?" He responded, "Oh, I'm the president-elect of the Tournament of Roses."

He became my best friend! He got us the right to use what they call the Rose Bowl Aquatic Center right on the grounds of the Rose Bowl. We had five buses of people. We had so many people we surpassed the limit on how many people were allowed at the aquatic center. So we had tailgating *outside* the Aquatic Center. That's when we won the championship!

TAILGREATER

DR. MEL LESTER

Dr. Mel Lester has traveled and lived in other places around the world, but has always returned to Detroit. For 31 years during football season, there was no place else he would rather be than the parking lot at the University of Michigan, with his friend Ira Jaffe, hosting the country's best tailgate.

My connection to Ira had nothing to do with football in the beginning. I was chairman of the board and CEO of a very large medical laboratory company in Detroit. We decided to change counsel, and one of the board members suggested Ira Jaffe. So the three of us had lunch, talked a little while, and I hired him! I said, "You're my new attorney!" That was the beginning of a professional relationship.

When fall came, I had a small tailgate at the game; I mean, the way normal people do it! I realized that right across from me in the parking lot Ira Jaffe was doing the same thing. We had been tailgating right across from each other for several years and never knew one another. We saw each other, started to talk, and wondered why we were tailgating across from each other. Invariably, some of the people who stopped at his tailgate stopped at mine! They were just coming across! So we said, "Why don't we do it together?" and set up side by side.

We put up one tent after another in the parking lot, and one day the associate athletic director, Fritz Seyferth, who is close friend of Ira's and mine, came and said, "You guys can't take up that much space here! You're getting in the way and people are complaining!" "Well, Fritz," we said, "we've got permits." He said, "I know that, but I can't explain that to everybody.

Why don't you move over here? You'll be as close as you are and be out of the way." We reluctantly moved and, again, we were growing with more tents and he was unhappy again. There was a grassy hill adjacent to us that nobody tailgated on, and Seyferth said, "Why don't you just take the hill and get off the blacktop?"

We decided to do it, but we had to put carpeting down because when it was raining or snowing it got wet and slippery. We went out and bought outdoor carpeting and before the game we went out there to nail this carpeting down on the grass. Then we were setting up more and more tents! Every year it got bigger and bigger and bigger. We did that for 31 years. We entertained anywhere from 500 to 1,000 people as it grew and grew at every tailgate. We had people coming from all over the country and people knew who we were.

One day I got a telephone call in the late summer from a woman who said, "I'm embarrassed to make this phone call because you don't know me. My name is such and such and I live in Los Angeles. Our daughter is coming to Michigan as a freshman. A close friend of mine in L.A. says he's a close friend of yours." He was an old Detroiter and I knew him very well. All of his family was still in Detroit and still good friends of mine. "He told us that you and Ira Jaffe put on the biggest tailgate in America. And I must go to your tailgate when I go visit my daughter. Actually, the first football game, UCLA is playing Michigan in Ann Arbor and we're coming!" I said, "That's wonderful! First of all, you are absolutely invited to the tailgate. Second, your daughter is invited to the tailgate, but there is a caveat: she's got to bring two of her friends because a lot of what we do is about kids. We want to get to know the kids who are here in Ann Arbor. So if that's agreeable, you are most welcome and I will send you directions as to how to get to the tailgate." That was just wonderful with her! I got all the information about where she was from in L.A. and where she was staying in Ann Arbor and I faxed her some information. I said, "When you get to the tailgate, please get here early enough to have fun and be sure your daughter comes with two friends."

I called the hotel and had some roses in the room for her when she and her husband arrived. The tailgate started, and I had totally forgotten about them because there were so many things to do. Suddenly, one of the gals who worked for us says that there was some lady here from L.A. looking for me. So I went over and met her and her husband. They were the most delightful people! The daughter did come and brought two friends, so my wife and I got to meet them. I was talking to the daughter and said, "Look, your mom and dad are 2,500 miles away. Gerry and I are 25 minutes. We are your parents away from home. If you need anything, here is our phone number. You call us and we'll take care of it for you." We had the most delightful time with them. About two weeks after the game, a package arrived and it was this beautiful piece of crystal sent from California.

They said that they were going to do a program on the best tailgates in America.

Their daughter came to every single football game for four years, and after she graduated, she became a financial consultant on the East Coast, got married, had two children, and kept coming back to football games—like family. That's what the tailgate was all about!

A number of years ago, the Food Network was based in North Carolina, and I got a call in the spring. They said that they were going to do a program on the best tailgates in America. They had done some investigating and said they understood that we were one of the best. They wanted to come up in the fall and do a whole shoot on our tailgate. I said, "I'll have to check with my partner, Ira, but I'm sure he'll say it's okay!" Again, I forgot about it, and I got a call before the first football game from the Food Network. They said they were coming up for the first game and asked how to find us and what time to be there.

Well, it doesn't matter what time the game starts, whether it's an early game or a late game, we're always up there at 7:00 or 7:30 in the morning.

We went up there with our trucks. Everything is perfectly lined up so it comes off the truck in the order it has to go out to the tailgate site. It starts with the carpeting. They were there already with cameras! They photographed the whole thing! We set it up so that Ira supervised everything coming out of the truck and I supervised everything being laid down. The first piece of carpeting is pulled out, and I mark the spot where the first corner goes on the grass. When I'm satisfied, I drive a spike into it. From there, we lay everything else. Food Network filmed the whole thing.

I prepare all the specialty items myself. For instance, back in the days when we were cooking for 500 to 1,000, if I was making ribs, I would make between 25 and 30 slabs! If I was making soups or chili, I'd make 46 gallons. I'd make pastas and salads. If I made a Caesar salad, I would make it with 20 heads of romaine lettuce. It was all on us for 31 years! I would start cooking on Tuesday of that week. I've got a professional kitchen and have storage space for professional cutlery and pots and pans. I made pasta primavera, linguini with clams, spaghetti, chili dishes—that's what we did! Ira took care of the basics—bagels, lox, cream cheese, corned beef, turkey, tuna fish—whatever! For dessert, we had ice cream. We'd hire a cappuccino man on the cold football days. We had bars like you couldn't believe with specialty drinks. We just had to be sure we didn't have underage drinkers. We did our best.

> It was a labor of love—we wouldn't have missed it!

The Food Network covered six tailgates in the country, the six best! They went to the University of Washington because the fans come up in boats from Lake Washington. They thought that was cool, as do I. They did one of the southern schools and

I can't remember the other schools. But, for the last one they put on, they said, "The Granddaddy of them all, the biggest, best tailgate in America is the Jaffe/Lester tailgate at the University of Michigan!" We did a lot of kidding around with them during the whole filming. I remember once they were looking at a lot of the chafing dishes and all the food that I had made. I made a remark, "Well, if you don't treat them well, the customers will never come back!" Ira said, "Customers? Have you been charging all these years?" They saw the setup too, how the whole thing was organized. They couldn't believe it! Once the carpet was down and the tents were all set up, God help anyone who put a table in the wrong place because Ira would kill them! Every table had its own spot, a tablecloth, And its own products and food. We had a popcorn machine going. It was a carnival, yet we never missed a football play! We had a staff of gals who helped us set up and didn't go to the game. They'd stay there while we were in the game. Some of us would come out at halftime to see what the plan was for after the game. The tailgating started before the game and ended an hour or hour and a half after the game. We kept partying afterward. So the ladies were out there watching to make sure no one was fooling around in the area. They cleaned up too. They were experts! We could break down the whole tailgate in 30 minutes; it took us 45 minutes to put up. Then we went to the houses and put it away for next week!

It was a labor of love—we wouldn't have missed it! When we were up there at 7:00 a.m. getting set up and it was cold or rainy or whatever, we'd look at each other and say, "Where else would we rather be than here?" We loved it and had so much fun.

YESTERDAYS TOMORROW

PATRICK VAN HULL

Patrick Van Hull grew up in Plymouth, Michigan and always had a passion for baseball...going to University of Michigan summer baseball camps and rooting for the Tigers, **CUBS*** *and Braves. Van Hull graduated from Michigan in 2002 with a BS in Industrial and Operational Engineering. He works for Rio Tinto Mineral as a supply chain planner with the U.S. Borax Mine.*

I went to my first game when I was three years old. My dad had season tickets the entire time I was growing up; section 4, row 27, seats 18-21. We sat next to the same people for years and years! You saw kids grow up and was almost a family-like atmosphere especially from the stand point you just know you would see these people every fall. When I graduated from high school, I only completed an application to one school. I applied early and got in early.

On September 22, 2001, Michigan was playing Western Michigan. That was the first game after 9/11. That was my senior year and I was living in an apartment with other guys. There were five guys...all good friends. From a generational standpoint, everybody knows where they were on Sept 11. Everyone can remember what they were doing and who they were with. These were they guys I was there with, sitting in front of my TV

***More NFL games have been played in the Meadowlands than any other stadium. Until 2003, WRIGLEY FIELD held the record even though Wrigley had not hosted an NFL game since 1971.**

mesmerized. The days progressed and we realized the events had been canceled... no Michigan football. We even resorted to watching the computer play video games against each other on Play Station 2 because we were so hard up for college football.

Eventually, that first week moved on. They reshuffled the schedule and the Western Michigan game was moved to the 22nd. We went to that game, and as part of being a senior, we had great seats. Everyone was prepared to wait in line a little bit longer for security. It was that sense of normalcy—once we go back and see Michigan football again, everything is going to be right.

I can still remember the feeling of walking into the stadium—especially the ring around the top where they traditionally have pennants from the different schools. All of those had been replaced with American flags. You saw increased police presence. You saw military. It was just a very surreal kind of setting but it was just the thing to do. Everybody was so looking forward to being at Michigan Stadium.

We got in our seats. I still get chills thinking about watching that team coming out of the tunnel and onto the field. They had a moment of silence and there were 110,000 people just dead silent...not a word...you could hear people breathe. They had a fly-over and a giant flag covering the entire field. They started the National Anthem and you could just feel the chills go through the stadium. The electricity—how the world had changed in the last two weeks. The band never sounded so clear, so strong. To be there with your best friends in the world, the family, the people that were all there because it was the biggest and best thing they could do on that given Saturday was go see Michigan play football. As the National Anthem was played, that feeling continued and when they finished I remember looking over at my friend, Mark Outslay, and his hat and sunglasses couldn't cover the fact that most people there—senior, college guys—tears flowing down their faces.

Still, to this day, it solidifies how much Michigan football is to life. That's what it took us to get back to life. That was normal. To see that team come out of the tunnel and to see those helmets...it sits as a very strong memory and speaks to how much of an influence a game played by 18-20-year-old boys, more or less, drives everybody's lives. That really shows the importance of Michigan football and what it means to watch that team and say that you're a fan and to be an alumnus. Michigan football is the one constant that has been there forever.

Yesterday was the start of the season and I woke up at 5:00 a.m. like it was Christmas morning, waiting for the kickoff! Still seeing the team come out of the tunnel yesterday...still feeling those chills... still screaming with all I can every time they score...being in Lodo's Bar in downtown Denver...screaming the fight song, "The Victors," with hundreds of Michigan fans... there is nothing like it. I could go on and on just talking about what it means. My life would be so significantly different if it weren't for University of Michigan and growing up around that football team. Lodo's Bar is the Alumni Association's game watching bar so every Saturday the bar is overrun with Maize and Blue.

Chapter 2

FANDEMONIUM

Open The Gates and Open Them Wide, Wolverine Fans Are Coming Inside

MICHIGAN MEMORIES ARE FREE AND WORTH EVERY PENNY

HARVEY P. SACKETT

Harvey Sackett grew up in Sunnyside, Queens, New York. He received his undergraduate degree from Ohio State University, yet he knew the words to Michigan's "The Victors" before he knew the words to the National Anthem. He lives in California with his wife Patti and regularly visits their son Kevin, a senior at Michigan. His father was a graduate of the Michigan Dental School.

I was the sports editor of my high school newspaper. While there, I had the good fortune to interview Cazzie Russell when he was playing for the New York Knicks. We were able to arrange that because I was a Michigan fan and he was a Michigan All-American. I had actually seen him in one of the most epic college basketball games every played. Michigan played against Princeton's Bill Bradley in what used to be the Holiday Festival. It was during a time when Michigan had been, quite frankly, horrible in basketball for literally decades. Then suddenly they had this terrific team and Cazzie Russell was the star. It was basically David against Goliath, Bill Bradley against the number one team in the country.

Bradley fouled out with a few minutes to go in the game. Michigan was down and Cazzie Russell had a last-minute game-winning shot to win the game.

As we were walking down the stairs of the old Madison Square Garden—I was only 13 or 14 at the time—all of these Michigan fans were singing "The Victors." I couldn't understand why they were singing because the game had already ended. So as I was walking down the stairwell and said, “Dad, why are they singing that song?” He said, “It’s because they are Michigan Men!” It was school spirit! My exposure to Michigan cam early.

When I was in high school, even though I was a pretty good student, my dad was quite concerned that I was too immature. I was young for my age going to college and not focused enough to really deal with what he saw as the academic demands of being an undergraduate at Michigan. Basically, I wasn’t even allowed to apply to Michigan—and I would have been accepted too!

> He said, “It’s because they are Michigan Men!”

My idea of college was a Big 10 school. That’s all I had ever seen, going back to my first visit to Ann Arbor when I was just 13 or 14. I had no concept of college being a small liberal arts school or anything like that. So I...well...I guess you could say...I settled on going to Ohio State. I had a wonderful experience, but once I graduated from Ohio State, my love for Michigan just came to the forefront again.

To this day, to the chagrin of my Ohio State friends, lifelong friends, I root for Michigan when the two schools play. I never root against Ohio State because they’re my alma mater, but I made it known about five years ago that “my heart’s with Michigan.” And my son is a senior at Michigan now.

My sister was a student at Michigan State when I was a kid. We went to visit her on a spring weekend. We were driving back from East Lansing and my dad wanted to stop in Ann Arbor. I had never been there. We got to Ann Arbor, and it was just my dad, my mom, and me. We got into Michigan Stadium and it was completely empty, other than the three of us sitting there. I was overwhelmed by sitting there, even before it was called “The Big House.” Just knowing this was such a special place and seeing the look on my dad’s face. Before the scoreboards were electronic, they had the upcoming season's schedule painted on the back of the scoreboard outside of the stadium. So you could just get excited about the upcoming season, because you could see the schedule.

Just sitting there, it seemed surreal because we seemed small, and yet you knew you were seeing such a large stadium, just the three of us in complete silence.

I remember once coming out of the stadium—when I was at Ohio State—and hearing the replay of Bob Ufer. I had never heard Ufer call anything, so just hearing him call this play, I truly got chills up and down my spine because I had never heard emotion from a play-by-play announcer. His love for Michigan transcended radio. That was something that really resonated with me.

The first time I took my son to the Big House, it was deja'vu of when my dad took my mom and me to the stadium while empty. My wife, my son, and I went out for our first Michigan game. They were going to play Michigan State the next day. It was a Friday afternoon and we walked into the stadium and basically sat pretty much, or as close as I could remember, in the exact same seats where my dad, my mom, and I had sat when I was just about my son's age maybe 38 years earlier. That was a very special experience. We have a picture that my wife took of my son and I arm-in-arm after the game with big smiles on our faces and the scoreboard in the background after Michigan beat Michigan State.

In September 1996, my wife Patti, my son Kevin, and I are going to our first Michigan game together as a family. We were going to Boulder, Colorado, to see Michigan play Colorado. Patti was a little bit leery about us taking this trip because Kevin was in third grade and she was worried about him missing two days of school. She's focused on him getting his homework done even though we were going away for the weekend to watch Michigan play football. We were staying at the Boulderado Hotel, which is an old hotel right near the campus and the football stadium. Kevin doesn't know too much about college football at this point. He was wearing Maize and Blue from top to bottom. But above and beyond that, though he's for Michigan, he really doesn't know too much about its history.

While we were sitting in the lobby, there was a guy sitting across from me. He and I struck up a conversation and it's very clear, because he's wearing Maize and Blue from top to bottom, that he's a very serious Michigan fan. He happens to say to me in passing that Bo Shembechler is staying at the hotel. Well I, being like another little kid, get real excited and say, "Bo's staying here?" Well, Kevin picks up on this and says, "Dad, who is Bo?"

So I go on to explain to him that Bo Shembechler is one of the *great* coaches in Michigan football history, if not *all* of college football history. Kevin looks at me and says, "I want to meet Bo." So I said, "Well, it may not be that easy to accomplish, but let's see what you and I can do. And you still have to do your homework."

So, we sit in the lobby all afternoon until about a half hour before dinner comes around. We go upstairs, go to dinner, and at the end of dinner he says, "I want to go back in the lobby and meet Bo." We go back into the lobby and sit there for a couple more hours and no Bo.

We go to sleep that night and get up Saturday morning and have breakfast in the hotel. Right after breakfast he says predictably, "I wanna go back in the lobby to meet Bo." I said, "Okay, but you haven't done your homework yet and we have to go to the game."

So we sit in the lobby until about 11:30 a.m. and the lobby starts to empty out because people are going to the game. Kevin's homework is still not done. We were literally getting up from the loveseats to go to the elevator when I see this man walk through at the far end and he looks like Bo. We stop for a second and sure enough, it is! I said, "Kevin...there's Bo!" and he looks at me as if I'm kidding and I say, "No! It's him…there he is…go on up to him."

So he goes up to Bo and says, "Excuse me Coach, could you please sign my hat?" Bo smiles and says, "Sure!" Then he puts his hand on Kevin's shoulder, takes his hat, and signs it for him. Now I'm watching this and I don't know whether to laugh or cry. I'm just so excited and so overwhelmed about my son meeting Bo Schembechler. Bo waves to me and I say, "Hi Coach," and with that, Kevin and I walk toward the elevator. Kevin doesn't say a word. He's just looking at the bill of his cap with Bo's signature…and he doesn't take his eyes off that cap. We go up the elevator and still not a word out of Kevin. We walk into the room, he sits on the bed, and for five minutes he's just looking at that cap. He finally looks up at me and says, "That really wasn't Bo, was it?" And I say, "Yes…it was."

The fact that we had waited and waited and at the very last minute saw him was just very special.

And then hearing my son—well, it's hard for me to talk about this now—when we dropped him off as a freshman a few years ago, we asked him that night what his first game was like. He said that when the band came out and started playing the "The Victors"—well, he just completely lost it.

So I skipped a generation, but you could call it two-and-a-half generations. This is something that my dad passed off to me and I passed off to Kevin. It's very special.

I try to go to at least two games a year. It's not just simply, "Oh, I'm going back to Ann Arbor for a game." If somebody said to me,"What's the perfect day?" I'd describe it this way. The "perfect day" for me would be, because I love food, going to Zingerman's in the morning to pick up my order, tailgating at the same spot at Arch and State, watching all the students get excited and ready for the game, walking down River Street, seeing the stadium and walking in, and then having the band come out to play. For me, that's it—that's the perfect day.

TIME WELL WASTED

DAVE GREENFIELD

Dave Greenfield, 28, is a second-generation Michigan grad. He is a financial software engineer living in San Francisco, CA.

My senior year at Michigan I moved in with seven new roommates, all guys and all seniors at Michigan. When the first football game came around, we were discussing tailgate plans for the game, and one of my roommates mentioned he had a older friend—Bill Glawe or just Glawe, as he was known—from back home in Midland who was a huge Michigan football fan and drove down for most of the home games.

We didn't get too much background on Glawe at the time, but we knew that he had a van big enough to drive us over to the golf course with supplies. The first game of the season Glawe pulled up his van to our house with his mom around 10:00 a.m. Most of us were still shaking off our Friday night cobwebs, but Glawe had spent the whole day before shopping for supplies, making sandwiches, and prepping a feast for a BBQ. He even brought two coolers, one full of beer and one full of soda.

I remember meeting Glawe. He is the kind of person you can't miss, even if you were in a room with 40 other people. He's a tall guy, with giant 70s-style glasses and a volume setting that someone turned up to MAX a long time ago and then threw away the remote. He was probably in his late 40s at the time and from a much-different-than-UM-student working-class

Midland culture, so he stuck out a bit in our group. But he brought the beer, the bratwurst, and the van, so we were willing to give him a shot.

About 10 hours later, Glawe was a legend in our house. He provided us with a full day of great food, drinks, high-decibel Michigan football stories, overanimated Euchre reactions, and random fan interactions. Probably the part of the day that best sums up Glawe was how he brought two oversized bags of Blow Pops with him to give away to Michigan fans in and on the way to the game, and he definitely didn't go home with any.

Over the course of the year (and the next year when some of us lived nearby) Glawe became the centerpiece of our Michigan football tailgates. Each game I learned a little more about Glawe. He had met my roommate in Midland when both of them were working at a Domino's Pizza. The two had bonded since Glawe was a huge Michigan fan and my roommate was on the path to enrolling at Michigan at the time. I found out the reason he brought two coolers (we were fine with just beer). He had overcome his own demons with drugs/alcohol in the past and didn't drink anymore. The more I learned, the more it struck me that on most days I didn't have much, if anything, in common with Glawe. But come game day, we could hang out for 10 hours and be best friends.

Knowing more about Glawe's background, we all grew to appreciate how much Glawe did to set up our tailgate experience. The fact that he brought a cooler of beer, despite not even drinking beer, said a lot. He even started buying beef hot dogs for one roommate who didn't eat pork for religious reasons. Around when we were set to graduate from UM, they started selling the commemorative bricks outside Michigan Stadium. We all knew that as big a part of our Michigan football experience as

... we told him the brick was on its way; he had a smile from ear to ear and had to hide a little bit of a tear...

Glawe was, we needed to make him a part of the Big House. I remember when we told him the brick was on its way; he had a smile from ear to ear and had to hide a little bit of a tear welling up in his eyes.

Last year I made it out to my first football game since moving to California five years ago. One of my other roommates made the trip out from Florida. We knew that for the experience to be complete, we had to invite Glawe up for a tailgate. Sure enough, five years later, he was ready to go with only 24 hours notice, up bright and early in his van headed to Ann Arbor to meet us. Just like old times, he made it up while we were still recovering from Friday night.

Being out in the working world now, we were more than happy to sponsor his ticket this time. A small repayment for the food, beer, and entertainment he provided during our college days. I don't make it out to games too often now, living in California, but I do know that anytime I go for a game, I will be happy to sponsor a ticket for Bill Glawe.

Looking back on the memory, I'm glad we made it official with the brick. To our group of friends, even though he may not have the Michigan degree that we all ended up with, Glawe was just as much a great part of the Michigan football tradition as the stadium full of 100,000 fans, the championship teams, and the winged helmet. Great to be a Michigan Wolverine!

THE WRITE GUY

JOHN BORTON

John Borton has been the Editor of The Wolverine *since 1991. and loves it. A graduate of Sienna Heights University, Borton writes internet newsletters twice a week. He maintains a daily website—www.thewolverine.com—and is editor of a monthly magazine. Borton and his wife, Darlene, have been married for 23 years and live in Somerset, Michigan with their two children.*

In the fall of 1991, my very first year at the magazine, things were a little looser in terms of media and access. I had an interview lined up after practice with Desmond Howard. I went to the newly built Schembechler Hall and met with Desmond. At the time he had a decent year at Michigan, but nothing that had put him into the extreme limelight that he was about to enjoy. Desmond came out of practice and we just sat down on the floor because he was tired from practice and he said, "Nobody really knows who I am now, but I am hoping they do by the end of this year." Well, that happened to be the year that he won the Heisman Trophy and Michigan won the Big 10 and went to the Rose Bowl. After that, Desmond Howard certainly became a household name. At the time he was only the second Heisman Trophy winner in the history of the University of Michigan... before Charles Woodson. Gary Moeller, who was the Head Coach at that time, was coming down the stairs at Schembechler Hall and here we are sitting on the floor in this little office. He peeked over and said, "Are you okay, Desmond?" and Desmond replied that he was doing well. He was just hoping to be recognized a little bit in that season. By the end of that season, you couldn't come anywhere near him in a one-on-one interview situation. It was all teleconferences with people in media outlets across the country.

In a similar vein, Tom Brady was fighting for his life to earn the starting job as Michigan's starting quarterback. He had lost out on that job and a chance to win a National Championship in '97 because Brian Griese, who had been at one time a preferred walk-on, had beat him out and was Michigan's quarterback through that undefeated season. I love Tom Brady to this day, because he was always one of the friendliest, most down-to-earth, nice guys when he talked with you. He was struggling and wanting to play, but he was always just a great, friendly guy. Things really unfolded for him: three-time Super Bowl winner and twice the MVP award in that game... it is amazing!

That the 1997 season was just an unprecedented ride....because Michigan's last National Championship was in 1948. Michigan had four straight four-loss seasons; three of those records were 9-4. The fans were getting more than a little bit on edge. There was a national magazine that had written an article called, *"M is Mediocre."* People were wondering. Lloyd Carr had been on the job for two years—was he going to be able to do the job? Then all of a sudden, the team starts reeling off win after win. They had a huge victory over Notre Dame at home early in the season. They fell behind by two touchdowns to Iowa at home, but they rallied to win that game.

I can still remember Michigan going off to Penn State that year and it was billed by ESPN as Judgment Day. Michigan was ranked #4 at the time and Penn State was #1. Michigan leap-frogged them that day with the most incredible performance. It was 34-8 at Penn State and Michigan just dominated the game. We were sitting, waiting for the coaches and players to come in for interviews after that game and...literally...the walls of that media room just shook. You could hear the players chanting, "It's great to be a Michigan Wolverine." That season turned from, "Okay, Michigan, is this going to be a 'run-of-the-mill' season" to something incredibly special with Charles

Woodson winning the Heisman Trophy that year. The defense on that team—it was just the best defense that I've ever seen out of a Michigan team. They went to the Rose Bowl and hung on to win the National Championship in a game over **WASHINGTON STATE***. I was on the field, seeing the players just running around and hugging Lloyd Carr on the podium. It was amazing. It was a climb to the top of the mountain for Michigan. Most fans had not seen this in their lifetime.

I remember going to the Big House in the '80s when Bob Ufer was the legendary Michigan broadcaster. He was so special because he was a complete Michigan "homer" fan and broadcast with unabashed love for Michigan for more than 40 years. In the last days of his career and really of his life, he was in the booth for what turned out to be his last game. I was in the stands that day. The band had spelled out his name on the field. He waved and took to the mike in front of the 100,000 crowd in Michigan Stadium. That's my biggest memory of just being in the stands and watching something that was very special. They had spelled out "U-F-E-R" on the field. There was no doubt that the entire crowd was cheering for him. It was absolutely deafening in there. He had the enthusiasm and love for Michigan football that they all shared. It's that sort of deal where you're almost part of the family. He brought to them the sport that they love. It was an amazing and wonderful goodbye. That was his last broadcast.

Lloyd Carr was the coach for 13 years, but I remember when he was just an assistant coach in the early 1990's. We had interviews at Schembechler Hall when I was just a new guy. I was walking down the hallway and Lloyd Carr, who at the time was

***Pullman, home of WASHINGTON STATE University, has a population of twenty-five thousand. Martin Stadium, the home stadium for the Washington State Cougars holds thirty-eight thousand... In the late 1950s, the Cougars had a home game during a blizzard. The paid attendance was 1. The Athletic Department gave that paying fan a lifetime pass to Washington State football games.**

an assistant coach, got to talking to me about *The Wolverine,* about what it involved. He looked at me and said, "Do you do this full time?" He was just incredulous that you can have a full-time job devoted to covering a college football team. You think about it now, with the internet and the blogs and the media that is so in depth. In the last year or so when Lloyd was head coach, he made a reference to, "Those of you who cover our program minute by minute." I'll never forget him asking, "Do you do this full-time?" And my answer was "Yes." It's been 20 years of very full-time. We cover exclusively Michigan. It's a school-specific publication and website.

The rivalries are all a little bit different. Notre Dame—not being a Big 10 school but certainly that game on a national basis—has all of the pageantry and history. To go into that stadium is an amazing feeling because you have a team that feels like it's "them against the world." A Michigan win against Notre Dame is amazing. For years and years the Wolverines had struggled and were almost snake-bitten through a time of losing to the "luck of the Irish". When Remy Hamilton kicked that field goal back in '94 in the last minute... there's a euphoria there that just seems to propel a season. There's such incredible pride on both sides and it's a rivalry marked by mutual respect, by great efforts and by the great personalities of the players and coaches on both sides.

In Michigan State there is a proximity that almost breeds a little contempt...you're so close and Michigan has had an edge in that series since the 1960s. Michigan has really dominated in large part. Mike Hart summed it up the best a couple of years ago when he said, "They say we're like big brothers, maybe we are." MSU would be the little brother and that thought just grinds on Michigan State. There is certainly a real edge to that series. When Michigan State won the last two games, there were postings online. Now there are posting of how many days since Michigan has beat Michigan State in either basketball or football. I remember John Wangler, the Michigan quarterback, saying at one point that Michigan State gets more mileage out of one win over Michigan that Michigan gets out over 10 wins over the Spartans.

Michigan vs Ohio State is called "The Game" ... there is no doubt it is. Michigan won most of the '90s and Ohio State has really held the upper hand the last couple years. That grinds either side. It is special. Going into Ohio Stadium—The Snake Pit—as Bob Ufer referred to it ... with Maize and Blue clothing, you are taking your safety in your own hands. That is a passionate fan base to say the least. In all of college football, it is certainly one of the most hostile places to play if you have winged helmet and Michigan on your uniform.

When I think back when I was just a kid—the feeling of waking up on an Ohio State day—it's very similar to what a kid experiences waking up on Christmas morning with anticipation of what presents you were going to open.

Football has changed in lots of ways. Bo Schembechler used to pound the ball and love the running game—he was all about the option football game for a long time. He moderated somewhat and would throw the ball. With Gary Moeller and Lloyd Carr, the offenses became more open and they had the great pro-passers from Elvis Grbac to Brian Griese, Tom Brady, Drew Henson, Chad Henne. They had some amazing passing attacks. Rich Rodriguez ... it's almost back to the future...loves to run the ball. Having read option quarterbacks and keeping it on the ground—you go through all sorts of style changes-but the essence of Michigan football remains the same. It's unbelievable pride in that winged helmet and the anticipation of 113,000—a record for any game college or pro—and as the game approaches and the players gather in the tunnel. When they burst out and run across the field and leap and touch the banner, that place explodes. It's unbelievable. It's that feeling that it's the same. It's seven times a year for home games, eight if the Michigan fans are lucky that they will gather on a Saturday

Bob Ufer

MICHIGAN
M
MICHIGAN

Those Who Stay Will Be Champions

The Team, The Team, The Team

To the Glory of God
and in Celebration of the Life of

Glenn E. "Bo" Schembechler

April 1, 1929 - November 17, 2006

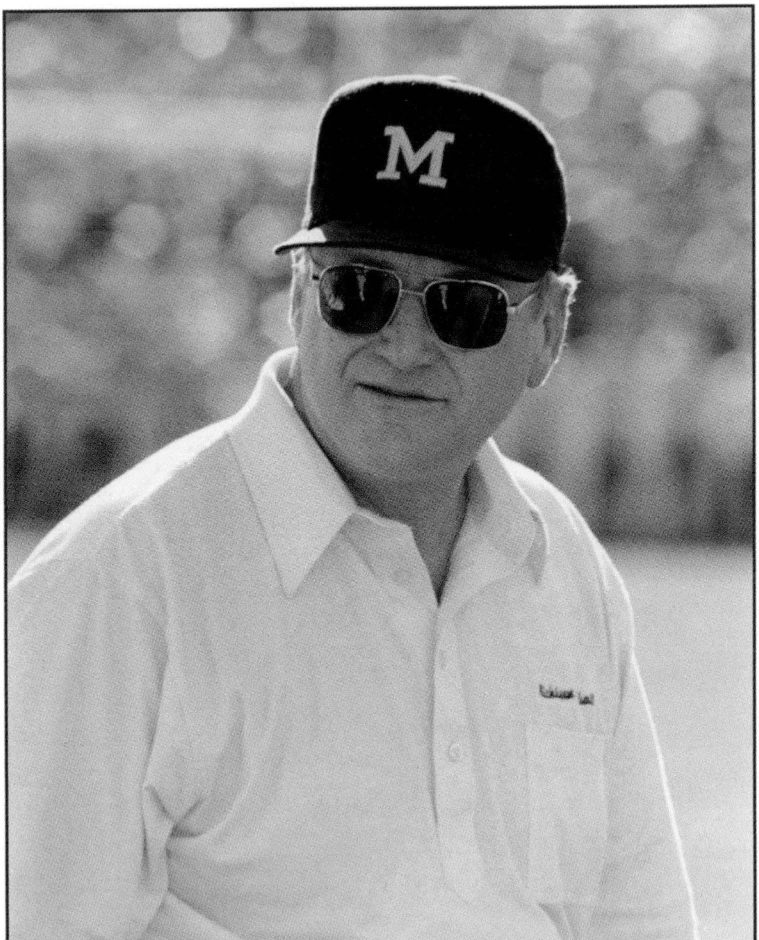

Monday, November 20, 2006
St. Andrew's Episcopal Church
306 North Division Street,
Ann Arbor, Michigan 48104

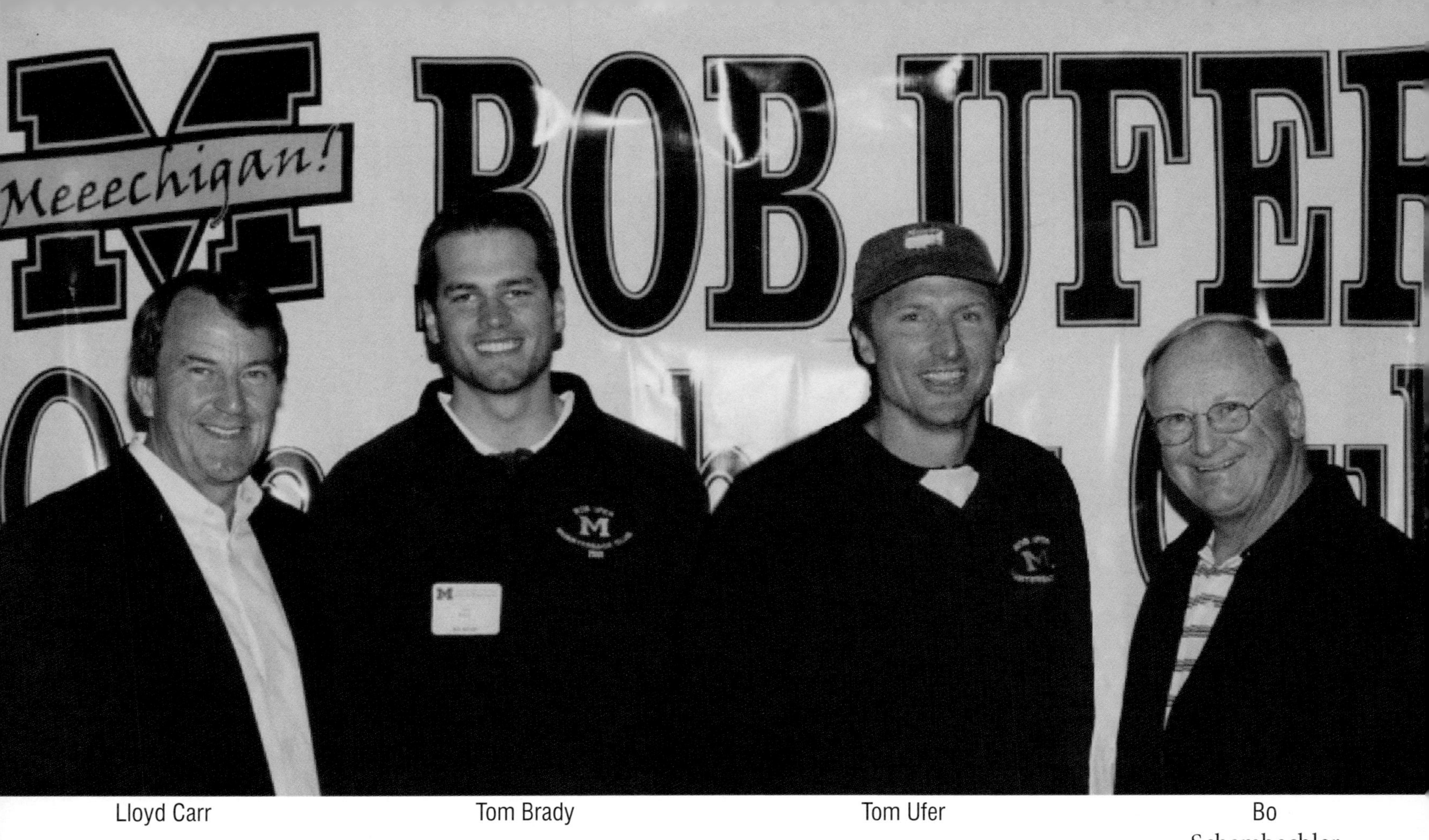

Lloyd Carr Tom Brady Tom Ufer Bo Schembechler

Last minutes of Tom Brady's great career at Michigan

LIFE

MICHIGAN'S GREAT HARMON

NOVEMBER 11, 1940

10 CENTS

YEARLY SUBSCRIPTION $4.50

afternoon and see what they have seen with their fathers and their grandfathers. It's amazing pageantry.

One of the most amazing things I've ever seen was at the University of Connecticut game with the story of Brock Mealer. Elliot Mealer, now a third year player on the Michigan football team, had committed to come to Michigan. Their family experienced an unbelievable tragedy. The family was traveling to a Christmas Eve service in their home state of Ohio. There was an elderly man that ran a stop sign and hit the family vehicle. The father was killed and the girlfriend of Elliot was also killed. Elliot's brother, Brock, was paralyzed and Elliot hurt his shoulder in that accident. Brock was not a football player, but being Elliot's brother, he was really adopted by the Michigan football team and fans.

He went through as much rehabilitation that he could but the doctors told him there was a "1 percent chance" that he would ever walk again. He was challenged by Michigan's strength and conditioning staff, including Parker Whiteman and the head strength and conditioning man, Mike Barwis. "You come here and work out with us." For months and months, they pushed him. They worked him out and treated him like they would treat a player. On opening day, Rich Rodriguez, the head coach, had said, "We want Brock to lead us out onto the field." And that's exactly what happened. He had the arm brace crutches with him, but he *got up* out of that wheelchair and *walked* from the tunnel of Michigan Stadium to the midfield where the banner is. They lowered the banner so he could reach up and touch it.

I've never seen a greater moment in all my life in that stadium. That place exploded! You saw a lot of coaches lowering their sunglasses because they were tearing up. I get emotional thinking about it now. It goes beyond football games. When you see something like that and you see the impact that can be made on people's lives...the inspiration. Brock wore a t-shirt that read, "1%" and "Glory to God". That was an amazing moment and one I'll never forget.

IT'S HARD TO CHEER WITH A BROKEN HEART

JACK HOWARD HUMPHREY

For Jack Humphrey, Michigan football is a family tradition. He graduated in 1971 with an Electrical Engineering degree and earned his masters from Purdue.. In high school Humphrey played guitar in a rock band around Detroit. He worked for Texas Instruments as a consultant in marketing, sales, and engineering management. Now retired, he lives in Colorado, which he calls, "paradise."

What color are tears? When you're crying, you can't really tell because everything blurs, but I know what the answer is.

This goes back to the '70s when I was living and working in Detroit as a sales manager for Texas Instruments. My father lived in Southfield. He developed brain cancer. He was an avid Michigan football fan and a member of the Victors Club.

After eight hours of open brain surgery, the prognosis was neutral. The doctors said, "We don't know if we got it all. It was very extensive but we did the best we could." My father returned home and he no longer had a will to live. He didn't want to get out of bed.

At that time, Schembechler was the Michigan coach, and he had reoccurring coronary problems. On Bo's first trip to the Rose Bowl he had a heart attack and his team and the people in the stands could not figure out why their coach wasn't there New Years Day. He was in the hospital instead. Bo had also been operated on for a heart related problem during the off season and that had made the news.

I was over visiting my dad as he was languishing in bed. My stepmother was sorting the mail and spotted a letter from the University of Michigan Athletic Department. "Take this up to your father." she said. I took it up to my dad and he opened it. It was from Bo Schembechler! It said, "Dear Charlie, I understand you have been under the weather..." It went on for a couple of paragraphs being positive and upbeat about the team for the coming year and how we needed to get out and support these kids. Dad read the letter, set it down, muttered something under his breath, threw off the covers, said, "Tell Florence I'm coming down for lunch" and he got out of bed. It was like a light came on! He had the will to get out and exercise and he mostly recovered. He even drove his automobile.

Throughout that summer, life was very good. The Victors Club has a season kick-off meeting held in Crisler Arena. They catered a lunch in a private room. Bo Schembechler was there to give a thumbnail of who was on the roster and what was new with the team this year. He had a guest speaker at the lunch. Then everybody would walk over to Michigan Stadium, where they would hold a private team practice of the team. That was just one of the great fringe benefits of being a member of the Victors Club—other benefits included special allotments of games and Rose Bowl tickets.

Anyway, that year Ara Parseghian was Bo's guest speaker. I went over and said to Bo, "Coach!" He turned and looked at me and I said, "You wrote my father a letter and he's here and I really want to thank you." He stopped the interview, came over and shook my father's hand. He congratulated him on his recovery but you could see in his eyes that Bo was looking into a death pallor and it bothered him. The season progressed and, as was typical in those days, we got to the last weekend in November when Michigan squared off with Ohio State in the game that determined who won the Big 10 Championship and went to the Rose Bowl. My father's health had been slowly deteriorating as the tumor returned and as we approached that weekend in November, he could no longer walk without assistance.

> ...I know that tears are blue. How do you put a price on that?

I talked to my brother who lived in Houston at the time and we decided that we needed to do something special for my Dad. I rented a recreational vehicle and my brother flew in from Houston. My father's two closest friends from D.C. I don't like calling in favors, but this time I pulled some strings. Don Canham Jr. was one of my fraternity brothers at Michigan. His father was the Athletic Director at Michigan. I explained to Don that we wanted to take my dad to the Ohio State game. We had a way to get him down there, but there was no way he could go in and out of the stadium because he just *couldn't* walk. Don talked to his father and they managed to get me a parking spot for the RV that was on the apron of the Ohio State University stadium. Through the side window of the RV, we could look through the entrance way and see a portion of the field. Everybody got together and we drove down to Columbus. We parked the RV during the game. The four male folks that could walk, my brother, Dad's two friends and I went into the stadium and watched the game. My father and stepmother stayed in the RV. They had the windows open and they could hear the cheering. They had a nice TV, that I had provided, tuned to the game and they could see some of the action through the RV's window.

Michigan won and there was a great celebration. My father said he wanted to go out afterwards and celebrate and we had to figure out how to do that. We drove to one of the better restaurants in Columbus. My brother and I walked in and explained the situation—we had a member of our party suffering from brain cancer and couldn't walk—the owner said to pull the RV around to the back door and he sent out a group to set up a table in the RV, bring out the menus and served us anything we wanted in the RV. We had a great victory celebration.

The next morning, when the sun rose, Dad looked at us and said, "I'm going to die. I can feel it. Take me to the hospital." We drove from Columbus to Henry Ford Hospital in Detroit and he was admitted. He proceeded to get worse and about the second week in December, he passed away. As I cleaned out his possessions from the hospital room, there was a letter from the Victors Club with six tickets to the Rose Bowl, and several round trip plane tickets from Detroit to Los Angeles—first class. He had bought those tickets as a positive affirmation because he wanted to live to support the team at the Rose Bowl, and not give up on life.

During the funeral and burial, I was very stoic and kept my composure. My dad had died, but I took the airplane tickets and my fiancé and I flew to LA and on New Year's Day, 1977. The two of us sat in six seats at the Rose Bowl and watched Michigan play. I don't remember much of anything because I was crying.

That's how I know that tears are blue. How do you put a price on that?

THERE WOULD BE NO NATIONAL DEBT IF DON CANHAM WAS RUNNIN' THE COUNTRY

BILL BOOTH

Bill Booth is a partner Ward, Plunkett and Cooney which has represented the University of Michigan Athletic Department since the mid-1960's. Booth grew up in Saginaw, Michigan, graduated from the University of Michigan in 1953, and attended University of Detroit Law School. Booth and his wife, Ann, live in Bloomfield Hills.

When I was 10-years old Mr. Hawkins invited me and his son, Hawk Hawkins, to go to a football game in Ann Arbor. We took the train from Michigan Central Terminal in Saginaw and we pulled right up next to the University of Michigan Stadium. We were playing one of the service academies. Through the eyes of a 10-year-old it was an exciting experience! The train was filled with people "Rah Rahing" and there might have been a drink or two. Everyone dressed "to the nines" for the game and that impressed me. They had on their suits, hats and topcoats. The train made one stop on the way down and then pulled right up to the stadium. There was also food—we had a dining car experience of tailgating—I guess you would call it. We walked from the train across the field to the stadium. That field became paved later on for parking. It was a great game and the weather was nice. Michigan didn't win. The service academies were dominant football teams at the time. I slept all the way home of course...it was a long day. Young Hank Hawkins and I were only 10-year-olds. That started it!

My dad then bought four season tickets. He was not a Michigan Man, as you say, but we went to ball games all through what would now be middle school through high school. I graduated from Arthur Hill and did quite well there -if I do say so—and was accepted at University of Michigan. As students, we'd never miss a game. We'd go from the fraternity house to the stadium and a lot of hoopla went on!

Years later I received a call from Mr. Crisler's secretary, "Bill, Mr. Crisler and Benny would like you to come to Ann Arbor to have lunch with them. Are you available Wednesday?" Of course, I was always available for them. I drove to Ann Arbor from Detroit, met them, had a couple of drinks and, as men do, we shared our stories to one another. Benny Oosterbaan played football with Mr. Hawkins, so that was an entrée.Our firm represented the Athletic Department in a case brought against them and we won. Our firm never sent them a bill. Mr. Cooney instructed me that it was our contribution to the University's Athletic Department.

Then Mr. Crisler said, "Well, Bill, we appreciate what you did but you never sent us a bill." I gave him the Mr. Cooney story and he said, "I know you have four football tickets but you're always sniffing around for extra tickets. How would you like six more tickets?" I had 10 tickets together and they were very good seats. Only about 65,000 fans were coming to the games then. Bump Elliott was the coach, a wonderful guy and coach. The real coup was that I was given a parking pass for a motor home. This was all gratis for a long while. Then one day my friend Don Canham called me and asked me if I still wanted the tickets and the pass. I started paying for them from then on. That was okay too!

Michigan beat USC 49-0 in the '48 Rose Bowl. USC was lucky to score 0!

Chapter 3

PUT ME IN COACH

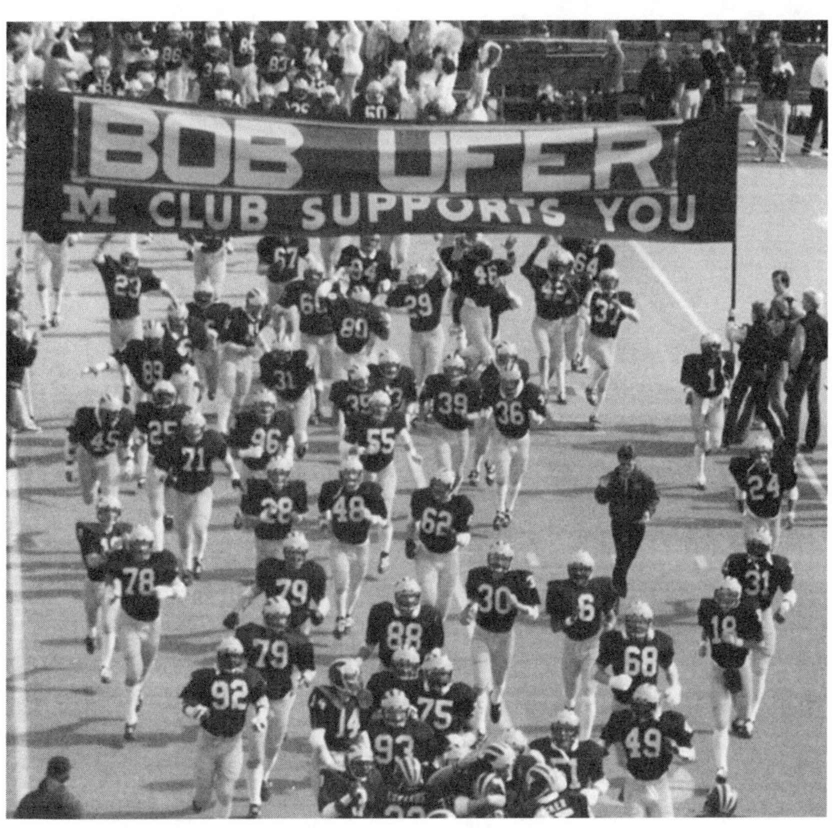

It Was A Ball

WHY CAN'T SUGAR BE AS SWEET AS BO SCHEMBECHLER?

FRITZ SEYFERTH

Fritz Seyferth played for Bump Elliot and Bo Schembechler graduating in 1972 with an Industrial and Operational Engineering Degree. When he retired from pro football, Seyferth entered business with B.F. Goodrich in Akron, Ohio, and Arthur Young & Company in New York City. In 1979, Seyferth started working with Bo Schembechler as his administrative assistant and recruiting coordinator. Nine years later, Bo became athletic director and he again recruited Seyferth to be associate athletic director. They started the fundraising office for the University of Michigan Athletic Department and their first project was The Center of Champions, which became Schembechler Hall.

My first day working for Bo, February 1, 1979, I was coming from New York City and a large corporation where when mistakes are made you learn to put your head down. The bullets may fly for a little while, but they would eventually stop. If you could keep your head down, you could avoid getting confronted with a lot of issues and problems. So it's my first day at the office, and we have a large boardroom table with perhaps 12 coaches sitting around it. Bo gets a phone call at 8:00 in the morning and leaves. He comes back about five minutes later and slams the door about off its hinges! Bo was really upset and starts screaming at the staff, "I want to know which one of you promised this young man he was going to start at quarterback for us next season?" I thought, "Boy…like anyone is going to volunteer an answer." So I just waited for it all to calm down and two coaches immediately raised their hands. I thought, "Wow! That's pretty dumb... they're going to get killed!" To their credit, each of them got up and said, "Coach, he may have thought that by the way I talked to him, but I told him with his athletic ability that he had the opportunity to compete, he could compete to start. I did not promise him that he was going to start." The other coach said the same thing. With that, Bo continued his rage to make a point, "Don't let that ever happen again! There is only one way you play at Michigan—you earn it! That was a wake-up call for me about what kind of program I was part of, and it was very different from where I came from in New York City...

Cam Cameron was a first-year assistant coach for Bo Schembechler. I was the recruiting coordinator. At about 8:15 one night, we get a phone call from Cam that he's got J.J. Flannigan, the top running back recruit in the state of California, coming to Michigan. I get Bo on the phone with the recruit and Bo says, "J.J., I understand you want to come to Michigan." He says, "Yes I do, Coach." Bo says, "Well, I understand that in talking with Coach Bill McCartney at **COLORADO*** today you committed to go to Colorado." J.J. says, "No, Coach, they've hired my high school football coach to be the running backs coach there thinking I would go to Colorado, but I want to go to Michigan." Bo says, "J.J., I'll tell you what we're going to do. I want you to think this over. We're going to talk in 24 hours, and if you've committed to go to Colorado, you're going to Colorado. If you haven't, we'd be delighted to have you at Michigan." So Cam Cameron gets on the phone and wants to know what happened and we explained it to him. Twenty-four hours later, Cam called back with J.J. Flannigan, who said, "Coach, I'm going to Colorado." Bo said, "Congratulations, J.J., you've made the right decision. Good luck!" Cam got on the phone and said, "Coach, I'm confused. What do you want me to do?" Coach said, "Cam, just recruit kids that tell the truth."

***At Coors Field in DENVER, in the upper deck, there is one row of purple seats that encircle the stadium designating the "mile high" level.**

Michigan had never gotten a top running back out of California before. It is very natural for a young assistant coach to be on fire and try to win the day. When it comes right down to it, the program stands for something, and we need all who are going to be a part of it to honor the culture they represent. It all starts with the head coach...

It snowed the Tuesday of the 1969 Ohio State game. We had about eight inches of snow and there was no indoor practice facility. The team was assembled in Yost Fieldhouse and Bo told us, "Men, you all stay here, while all the coaches and managers go out and shovel the field." After about 45 minutes, they came back all tired and drenched in sweat and Bo says "OK... let's practice!" That shows the commitment of the coaches and staff. They didn't ask us to do it, because they wanted us to be ready for practice. They did it. Then we went on to the Sheraton and had the encounter.

In 1969, we were staying at the Sheraton Hotel in downtown Ann Arbor before playing the biggest game of our lives against the undefeated and No. 1 Ohio State University. We all had seen our movie the night before, were delivered our hot cocoa, and Bo's been around to say goodnight to everybody, only for us to be woken up at 4:00 in the morning with fire alarms going off and smoke in the hallway! It was clear there was a fire of some kind. The players grabbed blankets and anything they could and got outside and literally stood in the street—many in their boxer shorts with a blanket around them, and we are thinking this is not the way to get ready for the biggest game of our lives. We eventually did get back to bed that morning and found it didn't deter us at all as we went on to beat Ohio State 24–12 in what really set the rivalry in place between Bo and Woody and Michigan and Ohio State. While we may have had to overcome some adversities, Michigan was a team that was ready to play that game and didn't let standing in the snow or rain get in our way...

In 1988, Bo became the Athletic Director. He wanted to start a fundraising office to build a new football facility, renovate the **GOLF COURSE***, add new tennis facilities, etc. We needed to know what we were doing, so he asked me to lead it, and I knew nothing about fundraising. After gathering the do's and don'ts of fundraising, I came back and told Bo that one philosophy is to assess people who have a great interest in your school and have the capability of making a gift. If you overestimate what they can give, it's okay. Bo says, "I'll tell you what. I have a different idea. How about we ask people what they would like to do and then provide them the greatest experience of their lives so that they want to do that every year after that?" They might even increase their gift after that. That became the philosophy of fundraising at the University of Michigan Athletic Department. We invited people to become part of the family, treated them like family, and encouraged them to do all they possibly could to make them feel good to be part of the program. I've taken that philosophy over to the University of Michigan's Cardiovascular Center where they have had probably the most successful fundraising project in the history of the University of Michigan, starting with a goal of $40 million dollars and raising over $105 million by the time I left!

In 1981, Michigan played UCLA in the Bluebonnet Bowl at the **ASTRODOME*** in Houston, Texas. The traffic in Houston is really congested so we had a police motorcycle escort take the team to practice and the game. We were returning from the game with the motorcycle policemen in front of us, and a car was not pulling over in the tremendous traffic jam. The sirens are going

***While playing GOLF in 1567, Mary Queen of Scots was informed that her husband, Lord Darnley, had been murdered. She finished the round.**

***On June 15, 1976, the Pirates were "rained in" at the Houston Astrodome. Ten inches of rain flooded the ASTRODOME parking lots and access roads. The teams made it to the park but the umpires, fans, and stadium personnel did not.**

and the lights are flashing and the busses are trying to go down the highway, but this car would not pull over. The police officer pulls next to the car and with his boot, kicks the door in and the car moves over. All of us look at each other, "Can you believe what you just saw?" We proceed up a couple of miles and there is another car not pulling over and the policeman takes his baton out of his holster and knocks the rearview mirror right off the car. The car pulls over. We all look at each other, "Football is clearly a lot more important in Texas than it is in Michigan..."

When the President got up there to speak, he gave one of the most eloquent and wonderful speeches...

Gerald Ford was our honorary chair of the Center of Champions Campaign that became Schembechler Hall. In preparation for the kickoff dinner for the donors who were hopefully going to support this project, I had sent President Ford an outline of suggested topics he might consider intertwining in his talk. The Secret Service took me to the airport to pick up President Ford so we'd have a chance to talk before the dinner. On the ride to his hotel, I asked him if he received my note and he said he had not. At that, I was stunned and was wondering how this evening would come together if the President didn't understand the purpose of this mission and outline of what we were trying to accomplish. I gave him some topics to consider and left it at that.

When the President got up there to speak, he gave one of the most eloquent and wonderful speeches intertwining almost everything suggested to him and more. He did it in such a way that was very natural and very Gerald Ford and was so meaningful to the audience. It gave me a perspective that these gentleman that become President must be exceptionally bright people, and we got a chance to witness one such person that day.

Lloyd Carr had the largest dictionary you've ever seen in your life on a podium outside his office. He always had an open door for any of his athletes, but his condition was that they would come in and have to look up a word and explain to him what that word meant before they began their discussion. That was pointing out the importance of academics and their continual growth and that every day you get better or you get worse. That dictionary was a reminder to everybody who walked by that they were here, number one, for academics and the growth of the individual.

I was meeting with Lloyd during the summer before the 1997 season. Michigan had the most difficult schedule for the '97 season. We were talking about how to get a team prepared for such a demanding schedule. We talked about the concept of visualization and how what you have in your mind is what you make possible. Lloyd subsequently read the book by Jon Krakauer, *Into Thin Air,* and had found that one of those people on the expedition, Lou Kasischke, was in the area, and he invited him to come in and talk to the team. Lloyd's theme was that if we can take one team at a time, we can win this year. Lou came in and said, "Men, as you climb higher and higher into the thinner air, you have less oxygen and you can't think as clearly. So one of the things you have to have is a discipline that every step you put down is rock solid. Once that foot is planted firmly on the ground, you have the opportunity to take the next step. But you cannot move onto the next step until the first one is firmly planted because if you fall, you fall to your death." Lloyd took that analogy and had ice picks made for every player on the team. They all signed the ice picks and hung them in the football building as a reminder that we are going to take one step at a time. We have to win the next game. It doesn't matter what game we are playing in two or three weeks. We're going to focus on one game at a time. That analogy led the team to win the National Championship that year while facing one of the most difficult schedules in the nation. That's an attribute to the quality of Lloyd Carr's thinking—how he is committed to helping the athletes become all they can be. It's about the individual mental and physical growth of every individual on the team...

1969
IT WAS ABOUT PRIDE, IT WAS ABOUT WINS, IT WAS ABOUT TIME

GARY MOELLER

Gary Moeller was a three-year letter winner at Ohio State University. Starting his Michigan career as an assistant coach with Bo Schembechler, Moeller had the rare distinction of serving as both offensive and defensive coordinator during his time at Michigan. He was head coach from 1990–1994. In 1995 Moeller was hired by the Cincinnati Bengals as a tight ends coach. In 1997, he joined the Detroit Lions as assistant head coach and linebackers coach and in 2000 he became the Detroit Lions' head coach. In 2001, Moeller joined the Jacksonville Jaguars.

January 10, 1969, was my first introduction to the University of Michigan. That day, six young assistant coaches and Bo Schembechler drove to Ann Arbor, Michigan, from Oxford, Ohio. We were all very enthusiastic and really looking forward to becoming a part of Michigan. I had the opportunity...I don't know if it was an opportunity or a job...to drive Bo. He and I were in the lead car. It was really funny because Bo supposedly knew the directions and obviously knew how to get to Ann Arbor. But once we got into Ann Arbor, we got lost. It was dark that night, and when Bo had been there before interviewing with Don Canham, the interviews were outside the city. He didn't really visit the campus. So we didn't know where on campus we were going. We got lost that night, but it was a beautiful night...the snow was coming down...and we were so fired up and excited to get this chance to coach in the Big 10.

Everybody wanted to know who this Bo character was coming into Ann Arbor as their football coach from Miami of Ohio. Was that a big enough school? They couldn't pronounce his last name...even the people on TV would get it incorrect. We were very excited about working with the players, but we worked very hard. A number of those players left that year and dropped out of the program because it was too tough, yet we liked that in a lot of ways because we wanted the players that wanted to be there to stay.

We looked at this later; I think that Michigan had as many good football players at that time as any time that I was here in Ann Arbor. That was a very talented team that Bump Elliott had left us, so we had a leg up, which a lot of people didn't really understand. We obviously didn't know what would happen, but we were looking down the road at eleven months from the date that we came into town: November 22, 1969. We would be involved with one of the greatest games in college football history. Ohio State was being compared strictly to the Minnesota Vikings in the National Football League and was probably the team of the century. They had won the national title in 1968 and had beaten Michigan 50–14 in Ohio Stadium. We didn't know how great this game was ever going to be until we got into the game that week. We did have the players to compete with anybody.

We had lost to Missouri 40–17 and we lost to Michigan State, another archrival, 23–12, so we were 3–2 going into Minnesota. One of our star tailbacks was left behind because he didn't practice. He turned out to be a really good football player for us later on. Being 3–2, a lot of people were writing us off, but realize too that in 1968 Bump Elliott's team was 8–2. They lost their opener to California and lost to Ohio State 50–14. Something that really added fuel to the fire in that 50–14 loss was that after Woody had scored the 48 points, he went for two after the last touchdown instead of the extra point, so he could get to 50. That really fired our players up and played on their minds throughout that entire next year. Woody going for two really helped us.

Our players were getting better all the time and were getting more familiar with our system. The game before Ohio State that year we beat Iowa 51–6. We had tremendous yardage. The excitement in the locker room after the game, I never saw anything like it. Those kids stood there and chanted, "Bring on the Buckeyes! Bring on the Buckeyes!" for a full ten minutes, and I'm not exaggerating. They were very excited and wanted to play Ohio State. We didn't know how much our kids knew about Ohio State. Sunday was a day we would meet the team to look at the film of the previous game, and they didn't really want to look at the **IOWA*** film. They did look at it, but they wanted to get on with the Ohio State film. So much excitement, and again they kept talking about the Buckeyes and the 50–14 score from last season. This team wanted to get back at them. They had played much better than the score had shown and they knew they could compete against this team.

I was a young coach at the time...realize that Bo Schembechler was 40 years old, there were a few other guys about his age, but everybody else was under that. I said to Bo, "Don't you think these guys will get too high too soon?" He looked at me and said, "You know what we have to do...we have to just let them go...see if they'll go higher and higher...that's the way we'll win it, if they continue to do that." Every day they carried that same enthusiasm and same excitement. Everything went wrong that week in preparation before that game. For starters, we had ice, sleet, and snow on the practice field on

***In 1939, the Heisman Trophy winner was Nile Kinnick of IOWA. He is the only Heisman Trophy winner to have his university's football stadium named for him. In 1934, Nile Kinnick was Bob Feller's catcher on an American Legion baseball team.**

Monday and Tuesday. We could hardly get out to practice, so the coaches and the freshmen players who weren't eligible to play and managers went out and shoveled the field so we could have a small area to work out. Something would happen to mess up our practices, but the players still carried their enthusiasm. On the Friday night before the game, we stayed at a hotel in Ann Arbor and the electricity went out. We were going to check players, so we went around to each guy's room with flashlights. The heat went out also because the electricity was out, so we were scrambling to get extra blankets to give to the players. When things like this happen and everything is just not in our control, as a coach you get uptight because you think that it's going to disrupt their thinking and keep us from having a good game. But these guys knew they were going to win! The players that were in Columbus the prior year felt and knew they were going to beat Ohio State. They convinced the team and coaching staff, who weren't living as close to that loss in Columbus the year before.

We go to the stadium the next day, and the enthusiasm and talk was still there. We started on the field and Bo's got the team in the tunnel. The coaches were all in position, so when the players come out of the tunnel, they go to their position coach to get warmed up for the game. This day when they come down the tunnel all the players are saying "Bo, Bo, Bo, they're on our field, they're on our field." There is Woody on the field with his players warming up on our end. Well, Bo knows that Woody knows—he's been in Ann Arbor many times—that you don't warm up on that end. So Bo sends someone out, and Woody turns to look at Bo, who motioned that you belong down on the other end. Woody half snickered and took his team to the other end. That fired up the players again because Bo got fired up again.

When the game started, they went down and scored, and we'd come right back to score. At halftime Michigan lead 24–12, and that was the final score as well. We were playing supposedly the greatest team in college football. Our guys knew that they could play against them because they had the year before. Now realize, we have players like Dan Dierdorf, Jim Mandich, Tom Darden, Tom Curtis, and the sophomore class was very talented. Because of all of the preparation and the enthusiasm the kids put into it, we just had a great feeling that we were going to win. It made it a special, special game. And it gave us the opportunity to go to the Rose Bowl. This helped everybody, including the media and the players, to accept the program that we put in. Bo was accepted in a better light now. He was a coach that knew how to win, and all of his discipline and toughness that he demanded from his players was now accepted. This helped the belief in our players, in our recruiting, and with the fans. It started off Bo's 21 years in football and brought Michigan back to its heights and glory. He won many championships the next 20 years.

Leadership at Michigan was *special.*

Bo and all of the coaches always felt that everyone on that football team was going to be a leader one day. Anybody could be a senior on our football team; even if you walked on and never got on the field, you were involved in the Michigan program. As long as you did what everyone else did and were supportive of our team, and you helped tell the other players what it is to be a Michigan football player, you could be on that team and be a leader. Leadership at Michigan was *special.* As seniors, you sat in the front row, followed by the juniors, then the sophomores, and all of the freshmen clear in the back. We didn't care how good a recruit you were, you needed to work your way up. We demanded that the seniors knew how to act so the rookies would know how to be a Michigan football player. They had no idea. When you go into college or pro ball, you don't know what it's like, so you look to the older players. The seniors would show the rookies how to practice at Michigan. We felt that the leadership at Michigan gave the guys a head start.

Three years after I graduated in 1967, I was hired to go to Oxford and coach at the University of Miami as the freshman coach. Then in 1969 I came to Michigan and was excited as anybody could be to coach there. People knew I was from Ohio State, and before the Ohio State game in 1969, one of the groundskeepers asked me, "Hey, are they going to let you go to the game? Can we trust you in that game?" I told him that of course I could be trusted. Obviously, it was a great honor for me to take over when Bo retired from football in 1990. I truly respected him and knew him as an assistant coach and head coach. He was a mentor to me and a close friend.

I want people to know that Bo went after his heart disease like anything else he did. He was a very determined individual...he worked out every single day. He wrote a book, *The Heart of a Champion: My 37-Year War Against Heart Disease.*

Bo and Woody were big competitors; they went back a long way together and competed against each other. They didn't talk much during that time, other than when they got out on the field. Bo may have talked with Woody's wife Anne because they were good friends...they used to take care of Bo when he was a graduate assistant at Ohio State. They were true competitors, but there was a true love between those two guys.

Two days prior to Woody's death, Bo had an invitation to speak in Dayton, Ohio. Woody was asked to introduce him and Woody agreed. Bo was furious because he knew that Woody had been sick. Anne Hayes tried to convince Woody not to go, but he wanted to do it. He did an excellent job of introducing Bo, and I know Bo appreciated it in many ways, but Woody needed assistance to get to the podium. Two days later Woody Hayes passed away. Woody and Bo had a lot of respect for one another.

Desmond Howard won the Heisman Trophy, which was a big thrill for us. In 1991 we were playing Notre Dame. It's fourth-and-1 around the 30–35 yard-line, and we lined up in a running formation and put Desmond Howard all by himself.

If they single-cover him, all we do is throw him a quick pass. If they double-cover him, then we run off tackle. So the quarterback was Elvis Grbac...who was a very accurate thrower...and Desmond Howard was the receiver. Notre Dame covered Desmond one-on-one, so Elvis checks to the run. All of a sudden, Notre Dame bails out, and they're playing two-deep coverage. When they put two guys out there, then Desmond has to take off down the sideline to try to beat them both. Desmond jumps the outside and beats them. Elvis looked like he was going to throw the quick pass, he pumped up like he was going to throw it. He sees Desmond take off, so he pulls the ball back down and lays the ball up high and Desmond makes a one-handed catch. Desmond is lying prone in a parallel position, stretched out as far as he can, and makes this fingertip catch. Obviously we scored a touchdown, helping us beat Notre Dame that year, 24–14. It was one of the *real great* catches. I called the play, but it was the great execution of it that made the difference.

This really started Desmond on his run for the Heisman Trophy...and became the Heisman winner. In an Ohio State game that same year, Desmond had a 93 yard kickoff return that set a record. The play is shown on TV a lot, with Desmond doing the Heisman pose. That was something we didn't like to see an individual at Michigan do...signaling himself out...causing attention to himself. We always believe it's the team, the team, the team—a lot of people had to block for Howard to run that kick back. He did a lot of work on his own and had some spectacular plays. He was a very talented young player and is still showing us his talents today on TV. He was very special.

Desmond Howard and Elvis Grbac played high school football in Cleveland at St Joseph's High School. In their career, between the two, they had thrown one pass to one another. Grbac never really started until his senior year of high school at St Joe's. We were reluctant to recruit him. He was a very good basketball player—being 6'6". We knew he could do a lot of great things.

NOTRE DAME NEEDS A QUARTERBACK, A HALFBACK AND ARA BACK!

JERRY HANLON

Jerry Hanlon played football under Coach Ara Parseghian at Miami of Ohio. Upon graduation, Hanlon coached at various high schools in Ohio, moving on to become assistant coach at the University of Dayton. His big move was with Bo Schembechler to Miami and then to Michigan. Hanlon coached with Bo and with Gary Moeller. Hanlon was Michigan's offensive line coach for 17 years and the quarterbacks coach for six years. He is credited with developing 19 All-American linemen at Michigan.

Everyone knows about Bo and my first year here at the University of Michigan in 1969. You've heard so many stories about how hard we worked—and we did! We worked everyone very hard, including ourselves and the other coaches. The people thought we were all a little bit crazy with the way that we approached things. However, I am grateful to that group of young men who were here at Michigan, who were not recruited by us but had to suffer through what we wanted to put them through for this program. They accepted our beliefs and what we were trying to do. I particularly will be ever grateful to how they endured and gave us a chance to prove that what we thought we were doing was right. A few of them left, but for the most part they stayed. Winning on the field created a feeling of success, and it certainly transported us into the modern era of Michigan football, which is known as the Schembechler era. That was one of the truly satisfying things that we shared here.

That first group of kids were good players and were used to winning, but we wanted to change things and make it tougher—and they accepted that. And when they started to feel that they could walk out on a field and beat anybody that they had to play, that, of course, made them a much better football team—and that's what we were trying to instill.

I remember that we were going into the second-to-last game of the season and had lost one game, to Michigan State. Ohio State was undefeated. We had a chance to win the Big 10 championship as we went to play Iowa. We were in a snowstorm going into Iowa. The next day, helicopters blew the snow off the field. Then the sun came out and it was a beautiful day. We absolutely waxed Iowa, and they were a pretty good football team. When we came off the field after that game, I had never seen any more excitement in any locker room in the history of football. They were ready to play Ohio State that day and were hollering, "Bring on State! Let's go get 'em! Let's beat Ohio State!" The coaches kept saying, "We've got to calm them down...calm them down. We don't want them to get too high." That was one thing about Bo Schembechler. He said, "When you play Ohio State, you can't get too high."

We had great practices all that week. When we went on the field that Saturday, it was against a team that was supposed to be the greatest team in the history of college football. Our kids went there knowing they could beat them. To see it happen and to be a part of that was really one of the great joys a person can have in the coaching profession.

That game, in and of itself, has been talked about numerous, numerous times. Everything started back when we put those kids through all of that hard work. We saw them continuing to grow, culminating after the Iowa game. Then it just grew into something that nobody was going to stop, even when we walked onto the field at Ohio State. That was a tremendous victory, and it propelled us into the limelight and into the Rose Bowl that year.

Bo Schembechler had a heart attack while we were at the Rose Bowl. While that didn't lose the game for us, I think it had an effect on the team, and we didn't play quite as well as we should have. We were staying at a monastery outside of Pasadena. Bo and I had been down having a talk with the priests who were there at the monastery. As we walked back up the hill, Bo stopped halfway up, and I said, "What's the matter?" He said, "I just got a little touch of indigestion or something; I'm hurtin' a little bit." So I walked on up with him and he went into the room. We always sat down and talked about the game the night before, just trying to cover the last-minute things. When he went on to his room, he said, "I'm not going to do this tonight Jerry. I don't feel good." So we didn't do our talk.

I had felt that something was wrong when I woke up the next morning. Bo had already talked to the doctors and had been taken to the hospital. It was a tough thing to have to endure, even if it had happened sooner, but it happened right on the morning of the game. Nobody knew exactly what was happening, except that Bo had some sort of reaction in the heart and they were taking him to the hospital. It worked as a detriment to us. It had affected not only the team but us as coaches. Although Jim Young took over and did an excellent job, we just didn't have enough to win the game that day.

Rick Leach was inducted into the State of Michigan Hall of Fame for baseball. Rick was not only a fine football player here for us, but he was a baseball player who went on to play professionally. I remember when he came to Michigan. He was a true freshman, and we started him at quarterback, which was almost unheard of! Freshmen hadn't been eligible for very long, but there he was...starting as a freshman. I remember Bo coming to me and saying, "Hanlon, I'll tell you one thing. I don't want him touched! You keep those linemen off of him!" What we were doing at the time was running an option attempt where we'd go down and pitch the ball while he's getting hit. So I said, "How am I going to keep him from being hit when we're running option football?" Rick still talks about that. We did try to protect him as best we could. He was one of those really great athletes, and over a period of four years here, he went to the Rose Bowl three times and Orange Bowl once. So that will tell you what type of leader he was and the type of program we had here at the time, where you could take a freshman and plug him in, and there were enough other good players that would help him out and make sure he got the job done. That was part of Michigan football.

"What's so important about working for Bo Schembechler?" ... "To get hired one more time than you get fired."

It was almost a brotherly relationship that Bo and I had. We respected one another, but we didn't always agree. People will tell you that, and I used it when they'd ask me, "What's so important about working for Bo Schembechler?" My stock answer has always been, "To get hired one more time than you get fired." On many occasions I was fired. I would disagree with him, and it sometimes got heated, where he said, "Get out of here, you're gone!"and then I would leave. It seemed like I would always get called back. The first couple of times it scared me. It was that type of relationship where we would disagree—both of us having strong wills. Finally, he would just give up on me, get me away, and then we would get back together. When we settled on what we were going to do, we knew it was the right thing to do. And I would like to say that I was always right when I argued with him, but there were many times when he had some valid points that I probably should have acquiesced to.

Jimmy Harbaugh was the most competitive football player that I had ever coached and it was somewhat of a detriment to him. If the ball was thrown 10 yards over his head, he would run and dive—even though he knew he couldn't catch it—just to prove that he wanted to do it so badly. And he would get a little bit perturbed at his receivers when they wouldn't do the same thing. So I had to sit him down a little bit to make sure he knew to let me coach the players so that he didn't get his receivers upset by saying, "You're not trying hard enough." Jimmy and I had a little bit of a confrontation going and we didn't speak very much, except about football, in his senior year—until late in the season. He came in, sat down, and said, "Coach, I know what you mean now; I think I'm starting to grow up." And since that day when he came to talk to me, we've been very close.

Even today, now that he's the head coach at Stanford, we talk every once in a while, and he's been very, very interested in what I have to say about football. He is going to be a very fine young coach. We had to learn what one another really meant, and when we did, we became very close.

Those are the type of kids that get started at Michigan, and there have been so many others. Mark Donohue was a kid who came out of Chicago. He was just an average-sized guard, but I never had a player who loved football more than he did. He was such a joy to coach because he would practice harder than anybody else. He may not have had as much talent, but he would get the job done, no matter what you would ask him to do.

Paul Seymour was one of my favorite players because Paul thought about the team as much as he did anybody else and much more than he did about himself. He came here as a wide receiver. He was 6'5" and 220–225 lbs., a pretty good size in those days. Then they usually would bulk up and get a lot bigger. But Paul was so big, and we needed a tight end after Jim Mandich graduated. We asked Paul to move from wide receiver to tight end. He balked a little bit, but then he said okay.

Of course, he was not only a great receiver, but a great blocker. Paul Seymour and Dan Dierdorf would double team and put you into the nickel seats someplace. Paul did a great job and wound up being an All-American tight end here at Michigan. The following year, we had two tight ends, Paul Seymour and a new kid named Paul Seal, who ended up playing professional football, but we didn't have a tackle. "Paul, remember when we moved you in one spot? Let's see if we can move you in one more." So we moved him from tight end to tackle. That was traumatizing for him because he considered himself a skilled athlete, and now he was going to become an old-fashioned, hard-nosed offensive tackle. Well, he didn't want to do it. But we said, "Well, you make up your mind, but it will be the best for the team."

When I came out of the building, there he was sitting on the hood of my car waiting for me. He said, "Well, what do you think, should I really do it?" And I said, "It's the best thing for the team." So he said, "Okay Coach, I'll do it." And from that day on, he never looked over where the tight ends were catching balls or running patterns. He became an offensive lineman and an offensive tackle—and a great one!

He ended up being an All-American here at tackle as well as tight end. And I told him that the pros had talked about if they drafted him, they would probably draft him not as a tight end but as an offensive lineman and offensive tackle. And the Buffalo Bills did draft him, as a tight end.

He thought that I had hoodwinked him a little bit. I said, "You're going to go to Buffalo and you are going to block for O.J. Simpson—all you are going to be is a glorified tackle." You're going to line up at tight end, but you still are going to be a glorified tackle. He laughed, but that really proved true. He was a great blocker in that offense. He and Reggie McKenzie, another offensive lineman that I had here that was so good, they were the leaders of all of that yardage that O.J. Simpson had with the Buffalo Bills.

I've stayed close with Paul and he's been one of my favorites, simply because he sacrificed what he wanted to do for what was good for the team and what I thought was good for him. I'll always be appreciative for what he did.

Dan Dierdorf was the epitome of what you want in an offensive run blocker. He could come off the ball and create a hole at the line of scrimmage better than anyone I have ever coached. He had that ability to stay low, move his feet, be aggressive, and all of those qualities it takes. So he became my cornerstone. If you're going to play football here at Michigan, you have got to play like Dan Dierdorf. You have got to come off the ball and learn how to pass, block, and do those other things. But the most important thing is that we want to control the line of scrimmage, and that's what Dan Dierdorf allowed us to do.

I was recruiting Dan for Miami University when he was a senior at Canton Glenwood High School. I had gone to the school and knew the head coach very well. I went to see Dan and he was in wrestling practice. So I spent time with the head coach and we watched him wrestle a bit. Then we went to the coach's office to wait for Dan to come and talk with me. Well, Dan had already made up his mind that he was going to Michigan, therefore, he didn't want to spend time talking to someone from Miami University. He sneaked out the back door and didn't come and visit me. There we were down at Miami University and he goes off to Michigan.

Two years later, Bo Schembechler and I were walking down the hall at Michigan and well, Dierdorf came down the hallway whistling and said to Bo, "Bo, I'm so glad you're here. It's nice to see you." Bo looked at him and said, "You're fat, you're out of shape, and you belong to me!" Dierdorf had shafted both of us when he went to Michigan. Dan said that from that day on, he regretted ever walking out that back door. And whenever he tells the story he adds that "Whatever you do, be careful, because whatever goes around comes around, and you had better not burn any bridges." He, too, became one of Bo's favorites, because when we needed to try to get the team to do something and to stay focused, Bo always hollered at Dierdorf. He knew that Dierdorf was the best player and if he hollered at him, every other kid on the team would know how serious he was about it. So Dan had to suffer, but he was, of course, one of the best linemen we've had here, and he set the model for what we wanted out of our players.

After we both retired, Bo had a small office at the football building. When I had some free time or was wandering around, I would stop in and we would discuss what was happening in today's modern football. And of course we always talked about how we would change things if we were running the show. They were interesting conversations, and he was always fun to be around and talk old times.

One of the first things we agreed on is that college football today is more a "college-pro" game, and it's changed quite a bit. We always felt that you played football to test yourself against good opponents and get ready to win your conference championship. That was what we based everything on—winning the Big 10 and giving our kids the chance to compete against good competition. You don't find that today. Very seldom do you find that in any place in college football. Today it's who can you get on your schedule to beat up so that you don't lose your BCS or national ranking. It's about having a chance to play in a BCS bowl game.

That, to me, is one of the big drawbacks. The kids should have an opportunity to travel around the country and play a good opponent and learn, not just from the football game but from being in a different area. It just doesn't seem to happen like it used to, and I'm sure Bo would agree with me.

The National Championship is all right, if it's voted on at the end of the season by somebody who knows a little something about football. If you don't happen to get it, then you have something to cry about all year long, until you start up again. Everything today is about the almighty dollar. I know that it's important for schools to make money and to promote all of their other sports, but we're putting too much emphasis on the sport of football to do that. The Big 10 used to be an organization that was there to help the universities if they had some problems and to tie them together and make sure things were going right among the schools. Now, they have become the dictatorial body that tells you what day you're going to play, what time you're going to play, and who you're going to play. I don't think that's what the original Big 10 Conference was supposed to be. When you see these things, to me, it takes away from what I was always taught. Maybe I'm a little bit altruistic thinking that football is for the players, for the students, and for the fans. That doesn't seem to be the basis anymore. It's more for the television networks and the money makers. Your fans don't even know what time to come to the game. They can't even make plans to come because we don't know what time the football games are going to start until sometimes a week before the game. To me, it's gone a little bit too far away from what college football was supposed to be.

Maybe I'm a little bit altruistic thinking that football is for the players, for the students, and for the fans.

The very last time that Bo talked to the team, we were sitting there in the office talking, and he said, "I've got to go talk to the football team." That was the night before the Ohio State game. He said, "I'm having a hard time walking." I said, "Do you want me to help you over there?" He said, "No! Get away from me, I'll do it myself!" But he was having a hard time walking. He of course had neuropathy along with a heart condition. So his legs did bother him. He said again, "I've got to go talk to the team." I said, "Hey, I'll be up there in the back. I want to hear what you've got to stay, to see if you still have it." So he went in and struggled getting over to talk to the group. Then he stood up in front of that group, just like there was nothing wrong with him, and gave a very passionate speech about how important the Ohio State game was and what it would mean to these kids. It was an excellent talk.

So when he walked out of there, I was coming back the other way and we passed in the hallway as he went back to his office. As I was leaving, I said, "Hey Coach! You still got it! So just hang in there!" Well, little did I know, the next day he went to Detroit to do some interview work and the next thing you know, he had a problem. He was rushed to the hospital. I didn't get a chance to see him anymore after that, but I was with him the night before. If Bo had to spend his last evening here, I think there wouldn't have been a better thing to do than to talk to a group of young men who could learn something from him and could see how passionate he was about the sport of football. I'm sure he influenced them for the good. And that was what his whole life was about, trying to influence young men for the better. He did a pretty good job of it.

When I retired from coaching, they had asked me if I would like to go into the booth and be the color man for the University of Michigan. Of course, I really loved that because it made me stay close to the game. I had studied tapes and film to try to keep up with what was going on in football. I always remembered Bob Ufer. Ufer was a very colorful man, but he also was a really, truly good person. When Bob came into your office, he was always so cheerful and upbeat that when he left you felt good about yourself! He had that kind of attitude. But things did not come easy to Bob. I found out from him that if you're going to work in radio, you better be prepared.

I remember him coming to my office to get the film so he could study the opponent that we were going to play the next week. He would actually look at that film and broadcast what was happening on there, so that he could get used to the names of the people and the opponents. He knew Michigan by heart, but he would study the other team so he knew who was carrying the ball and what they could do. He worked extremely hard at it.

When I went into this business, I remembered Bob and the fact that you had better be prepared. He always told me one thing:

"Jerry, don't try to say everything in the first five minutes." So I used that for a long time. I enjoyed my time with WJR. Frank Beckman is really one of the fine broadcasters and announcers. It was a pleasure to get to work with him. We not only got to cover the season but went to several bowl games. It was a nice experience. It was a little disappointing when they sold the company. One of my former players took over my job and he's very good at it. Jimmy Branstetter played tackle for me here. And he now is the color man for the University of Michigan. I may have lost a job, but I gained another one of my kids doing something really great.

I was inducted into the Cradle of Coaches, which is an Honorary Coaches Hall of Fame at Miami University. **MIAMI*** has turned out many, many great coaches—names like Paul Brown, Weeb Ewbank, Walter Alston, Ara Parseghian, Paul Dietzel, Earl Blaik, Dick Crum, Bill Mallory, Bo Schembechler, the list goes on and on. It honors men who have graduated from Miami University or have coached there and then went on to bigger jobs and have become icons in the coaching profession. I was never a head coach in college and I was probably the first assistant coach in college football to become a member of the Cradle of Coaches Hall of Fame. It was a great honor and I wear that distinction proudly.

Sometimes you wonder whether or not you had chosen the right profession. Maybe you should have worked a little bit harder or tried to be a little bit better, but when you play golf with these guys and have the feeling that they still like to have you around; I think that maybe I had made the right decision and stayed in the right position. As you get older, it's those things that come more to the forefront.

***Do you confuse MIAMI of Ohio and Miami of Florida? Miami of Ohio was a school before Florida was a state.**

RUNNING WILD, LOOKIN' PRETTY AND DANCIN' WITH LADY LUCK IN PASADENA

JIM CONLEY

Raised in Springdale, Pennsylvania, Jim Conley played football, basketball, and **SOCCER*** *in high school. He chose Michigan largely because of Bump Elliott and his dad's love of Michigan. He was captain of Michigan's 1964 Rose Bowl team. Conley worked for General Motors until 2002, then started his own manufacturer's representative company.*

My class was the first class—my senior year—to go back to two platoon football. Freshmen were not eligible to play. Then in my sophomore year, which was in 1962, you had to play both ways...both offense and defense. In my junior year, they changed it to where they had limited substitutions. The used to substitute two players on the third down, two players on the fourth down, and two players on first down. Then in my senior year it became the 2 platoon system that you see now. Shortly after that, they made freshmen eligible again when they cut the scholarships back to 85.

We had approximately 65 eligible players on our team so it was unique in a way. We had a lot of players that would have played and could have been...for an example...a great linebacker. But if you couldn't play an offensive position well enough to earn the right to play the defensive position...then you were lost in

***More U.S. kids today play SOCCER than any other organized sport, including youth football. Perhaps, the reason so many kids play soccer is so they don't have to watch it.**

the shuffle. There were many good players that could play one way—but not the other way—so they lost out. It was a unique time in football for everybody.

My senior year, we were fortunate to have a very, very wonderful sophomore class. Even though we had a lot of significant injuries, we went on to the Rose Bowl and beat Oregon State 34–7. We had beaten them so bad that they've never been back.

One of my teammates, Bill Yearby, was an All-American for two years. He played left tackle right beside me...or rather—I played beside him. He was just absolutely a spectacular football player. Before the Rose Bowl game, Coach Elliott came to me and said, "You better keep your eye on Yearby, he seems to be really, really fired up."

We were just getting lined up after the kick-off. Bill and I were on defense and on the left side of the line. Before Bill even got ready, the offensive tackle shot offside and just hammered him. Bill, of course was blowing smoke by then. He was anxious to get back at the guy and I was trying to keep him under control. We go back and line up again—the guy jumps offside and nails Yearby again! By then, Yearby is absolutely filled with smoke because he's been hammered *illegally* twice! I had calmed him down and I said to him, "As soon as that fat guy puts his hand down...we're goin!" So they came back to line up again and this time Bill and I fired offside and knocked their tackle head over heels.

A flag goes up because we were offside and the referee called me and the other captain in and said, "I don't know what's going on here, but I want it to end!" I said, "They started it!" And the Oregon State guy said, "What? No! They started it!" and then the referee looked at me and said, "I feel like I'm dealing with my kids, not college football players!"

Bill was probably the best defensive player that I had ever played with. He was just a great All-American and a great guy...

Players would step up when there was an injury. I remember when Frank Nunley came on the field to replace Barry Dehlin. Frank stepped up as a sophomore and he said, "What do I do? What do I do?" and I said to him, "Yearby and I are going to knock these people down in front of you and you're going to make the tackle." That was his first play in college football. He went on to play 10 years for the 49ers. It wasn't like we were putting in someone that didn't know what to do...he was just a little nervous.

Back in the early 60's, when they had only one captain...they would put his picture on every ticket. So when I was captain—I had my face on every ticket and Bump Elliott said to me that was probably the reason why we didn't sell out.

Even a greater fact is that we graduated 92% of our players. The name "student-athlete" is really applicable to our team and our players. It was a thing that Bump Elliott really, really stressed on us. There is an interesting story about Bump. It was when Bo Shembechler beat Ohio State in 1969 to set the world straight that Michigan football was back. He gave the game ball to Bump because he felt that Bump had left him a lot of great players on that squad. Bo felt that Bump deserved the game ball more than anybody else. All of Bump's staff went on to coach somewhere.

The best thing that I can say about my time in Ann Arbor was the fact that we really believed in the "team". We were close together on and off the field, we had absolutely no dissension on our team...we had the leadership of a great senior class. To me, that was just the formula that works.

In looking back through all of my years, thinking of everything that I could possibly say about Michigan...I would say it was when Bo came back and said, "The team, the team, the team".

That was really true for our group of guys.

THE REASON MANY PEOPLE ARE CUB FANS: THEY CAN'T AFFORD WORLD SERIES TICKETS

FRANK MALONEY

Frank Maloney grew up in Chicago, played football at Mount Carmel High School, and was recruited by the University of Michigan. "Best decision I ever made in my life," Maloney says. He loved coaching and at the age of 21, became head coach at Mount Carmel High School. He migrated back to the University of Michigan as assistant coach to Bump Elliott for six years, then moved on to **SYRACUSE*** *University as head coach for seven years. His final stop was the Chicago Cubs, where he is currently Director of Ticket Operations.*

I decided to go to Michigan late in the summer. Of course they didn't have as many dorms then, but the South Quad is where most of the players went. Since I was late, the dorms were all filled. Don Dufek got me a room in a house on Packard Street.

The main mode of transportation between Ann Arbor and Chicago in those days was the train. I can remember so many times taking that train from Chicago back to school after vacations, pulling into the old station downtown. I would carry my suitcase all the way up State Street and down to Packard in snow and cold. Those were great memories. It certainly toughens people up

***In the 1999 Orange Bowl, Florida beat SYRACUSE 31-10. Florida coach Steve Spurrier awarded the game ball to himself.**

In those days, athletes were more students than they are now. We really had to toe the line as students, but we had fun too. I remember our favorite places—the popular place was the Pretzel Bell. When you turned 21 years old, you went down and drank a pitcher of beer at the Pretzel Bell and they rang the gong 21 times. That was a great tradition. I was really sorry to see a few years later that the Pretzel Bell went on its way. It used to be on Liberty Street in Ann Arbor. I also have great memories of Schwaben's. It was near the downtown area and was a very popular bar for students. We used to love to go on Wednesday nights.

In one of my history classes, Professor Reichenbach came storming out on the stage in a Prussian military outfit. He used to come to Schwaben's and sit down for a couple of hours and talk history with the students. Of course, he never bought a beer. We would have to buy the professors the beer. It was a great experience because we really loved listening to him. He was well into his years and just a remarkable character.

I had an astronomy teacher named Hazel Losh. She was a legend up there. I took astronomy because we had a science requirement. She was probably 70 years old when I took the course. She was amazing and loved football players. Every time the snow started in December, everybody raced over to her house to shovel her sidewalks. Every Saturday at the football games when the Michigan banner was out on the field...Hazel Losh was escorted by some of the lettermen out there. She was a marvelous teacher—a tremendous personality. Michigan had a lot of those—that's what really impressed me.

I have a lot of great memories as a coach. I went back to Michigan in 1968 and was hired by Bump Elliott as an assistant line coach. After one year, Bump retired and became the assistant AD and Bo Schembechler came on the scene.

I've narrowed my great memories down to two. One was of course the infamous 1969 game with Ohio State. As everybody knows, we were a 20-point underdog going into that game. That year was the 100th anniversary of the founding of college football. It was quite a ceremonial year. The game was probably the most famous upset in Michigan history when we beat Ohio State 24–12. That's a memory I will never forget. I was the defensive line coach on that team.

In 1972 we played Stanford in the Rose Bowl. In those days the Big 10 teams went to California around a week before Christmas. You were scheduled to do that for many reasons...a trip to Disneyland, a trip to Universal... all of the pageantry.

That year we faced some unusual California weather. It rained for days. The problems it created for us! We had no place to practice (Bo was a great believer in practice) and were going to have to find a gymnasium. The West Coast didn't have artificial surfaces because they normally didn't have this rainy weather. So we had no artificial place to go—no field to practice on. We practiced one day in a gymnasium, but that was ridiculous. Coupled with all of this, the forecast was for rain and more rain.

Bo, being a very proactive guy, commandeered buses to take the team over the Sierra Nevada mountains to the desert. We all boarded the buses, left our families, and took the trip through the mountains. We went somewhere near Bakersfield. Sure enough, it was bone dry and desolate. We found a high school to practice. After practicing for a couple of days, everyone was getting pretty bored.

One night Bo thought, "Well, we have to entertain the boys." He got a couple of buses and took us into town for a movie at one of those little old theaters; it was *Dirty Harry* with Clint Eastwood.

Jim Brandstatter—now the color announcer at Michigan—could imitate John Wayne, Clint Eastwood...he was a dead ringer for them all. I can remember him on that bus going on and on. That got our morale back up.

After three or four days in the desert, it was getting close to game time and we really should have been at the Rose Bowl Luncheon. So we boarded the buses to go back. All that rain in the mountains had turned to snow and we couldn't get through! So we chartered a United jet that came in over the mountains to fly us back. The flight didn't take more than 10 or 15 minutes! We had a terrific game but lost to Stanford in the last minute of play.

> Michigan is a marvelous school.…It's the exceptional Big 10 school.

Without sounding negative, economics have taken over the game so much that it's not as pure a game as it was in the 50s. In the 1950s, the most important part of our lives as athletes was getting a degree and an education—thinking about the future. So many players now think about professional football and staying eligible. I'm talking universally. When I played, you didn't put nearly as much time into the practice. A lot of guys I played with became doctors and lawyers. I don't think as many are doing that today. Don't get me wrong, I love college football and love watching it; it's just different than it was then. We didn't have tutors and support staff to get through. You were expected to get through on your own. You didn't get into the University unless you had the proper credentials…background and SAT scores.

Michigan is a marvelous school. It just grew on me year after year. It's the exceptional Big 10 school.

The BCS formula is actually a recipe for chili.

HEAR ME NOW LISTEN TO ME LATER

JIM BRANDSTATTER

Jim Brandstatter grew up in Lansing, one of five boys. His father, Art, was an All-American fullback for the Spartans in 1936. His brother Art also played for MSU. But Brandstatter "fell in love" with Michigan and played offensive tackle during Bo Schembechler's first three seasons. In 1972, he went to the Tri-Cities area as sports director of WEYI-TV, moved to Lansing/Jackson with WILX-TV, and then was on to Detroit as a sports producer with WDIV. He was host of Michigan Replay, *a weekly half-hour discussion show with the Michigan coaches. Now called* Inside Michigan Football, *Brandstatter remains the original host, and the program is broadcast nationwide. Brandstatter's wife, Robbie Timmons, is a weekday news anchor on WXYZ-TV in Detroit and a graduate of Ohio State.*

I was recruited by Bump Elliot. The first time I met Bo Schembechler, who became such an icon and a very good friend of mine, it didn't start out in the most pleasant way. Bo was such a coach right from the get-go. He replaced Bump, so we went to see Bo the first time he was introduced to the media. It was the first time I had ever seen him, but he was going to be our head coach from this point forward. I shook his hand and said hello. He looked at me, and I said, "Hello, Coach. My name is Jim Brandstatter." He didn't say hello. He didn't say, "How are you?" He didn't say, "Nice to meet you." He grabbed me around the belt and he said, "You know, you could stand to lose some weight!" At that point, you knew there was a new sheriff in town. It was one of those moments where you think, "Wow! This guy means business!" It was an interesting hello!

They put a sign up in the locker room that read "Those Who Stay Will Be Champions."

The practices that first spring were so very tough and difficult. We had a number of players who just quit and said they couldn't take it. Bo was going to toughen everybody up. He was making it as tough as he possibly could on everybody to see who those players were that could hang in there, stick it out, and make it through this very difficult physical and mental preparation that first spring. He wanted to see who he was going to take into that next season with him. He wasn't going to get on any rebuilding kick; Bo Schembechler thought he was going to win from the get-go.

They put a sign up in the locker room that read "Those Who Stay Will Be Champions." That meant that those who stay during this difficult time will be champions. When you're going through it, you're not sure if you can handle it. You're 18-years old and you're just getting beat up. He's being tough on you, and it's a very difficult game to begin with. You're working and hanging in there, and there's that sign you see every day. We had a lot of guys who were quitting, who couldn't take it, that said, "Man, this isn't what I signed up for." That sign—"Those Who Stay Will Be Champions"—one day we came in after practice and one of the guys who had quit had written underneath it, "Those who don't will be doctors, lawyers and other important people." It was his way of saying he didn't need it. It got a good laugh from the guys dragging into the locker room to see it. But that sign went down and a new one went up.

Bo always used to say, "The expectation is not for the player but for the position." So, if a player got hurt and a backup went in, Michigan does not expect any falloff in proficiency. It's about the position, not the player. If you get in the game, the coaches feel you're good enough to do the job and help this team win. That's the attitude that Bo always had; he was trying to instill that confidence. All the coaches had that attitude. If you went in and played, you went in and did your job just as well as the starter.

Another game that I felt great about personally was when we went to East Lansing my senior year to play Michigan State. I'm from East Lansing. My parents both graduated from Michigan State. My brother played at Michigan State and graduated from there. My dad played at Michigan State and was on the faculty. So when I went in as a Michigan player, it was unique and special for me. I played very well that day—one of my better days. That game stands out for me as one of those great moments in my career, and yet, we couldn't have done what we did in that game without all the great players that were around me. For me, I feel a great sense of gratitude and thankfulness for those guys. They knew it was a big game for me. They all knew where I came from. They all knew my history. They all came up to me afterward and were a little extra special. The pat on the back was a little harder. The "Way to gos" and "Attaboys" were a bit more heartfelt because of my history. It was that team atmosphere—that we were all in this together and they were working maybe a little bit harder for me. That was special from an individual standpoint.

I loved Michigan! I wasn't going to go to Michigan State anyway because I was one of those kids that wanted to get out and try to see something else even though I grew up there and ran around the stadium when I was little. My brother was my hero and was on the varsity Michigan State team. It was a great deal, but when I got into high school I felt that I just wanted to try something else. "What else is out there?" I thought. I was recruited by a number of schools and the service academies were interesting to me at the time. Then I took a late visit to Michigan in Ann Arbor. Hank Fonde was an assistant coach to Bump Elliot. He recruited me and I came down and had a visit. Don't ask me how, don't ask me why, but I just fell in love with the place! I fell in love with the people. I fell in love with the players and the whole idea of Michigan just fit with me. You know, some people like fried chicken and some like baked chicken! Why? For what reason? I don't know, but that's what happened to me—I just liked it.

I always had it in my mind that I would play Big 10 football. I was from a Big 10 school and was born and raised in that environment. I knew it was a high level, but I always had it in my mind, "Could I play at that level?" It was a challenge. If I went to a smaller school, I'd always ask myself the question, "Could I have played at the Big 10 level?" I preferred at that time to accept that challenge and knowing that even if I wasn't able to play and compete at that level, I still had the opportunity to get one of the best educations in the land and I would leave Michigan with a degree. From that perspective, Michigan became the only choice. You never realize this when you're 17 years old, but clearly it was one of the best decisions I have ever made in my life. It's about a career. It's about lifelong friendships. I can't imagine my life and where it would have gone had I not taken that first step on the yellow brick road with the University of Michigan.

I'm so very lucky to have this career; I'm doing something I love. If you're doing something you love, you won't work a day in your life! Being associated with the University of Michigan Athletic Department and their football program is something I take great pride in. I'm very lucky to have been able to stay involved with this program, this university, and this athletic department long after I graduated. There are other people who will go out in business and do great things. There are doctors, lawyers, thoracic surgeons, heart transplant guys, leaders in business and community, and yet, one of the things you'll learn from all of them is that Michigan holds a special place in their heart. I'm one that's been able to get going in a career and yet stay involved and very much a part of what this whole thing is all about from close range. You see a guy like Dave Brandon, the athletic director; he's been in business and has made millions of dollars. He was a CEO of a Fortune 500 company and was at the top of his game in that arena. Yet he chose to take a 100–200 percent pay cut to come back to Michigan to be the AD. This was the job he wanted. He doesn't financially or professionally need this to validate a career. Why is he back here? He's here because he loves it—he wants to give something back. I've been very fortunate that I haven't had to leave and come back. I've been here ever since I graduated. I thank my lucky stars that I've had that opportunity.

There was only one Voice of Michigan Football, and there will always only be one Voice of Michigan Football, and that guy's Bob Ufer.

Michigan's great tradition continues through the radio booth. People have come up to me and said, "You're now the Voice of Michigan Football" and I disagree with that. There was only one Voice of Michigan Football, and there will always only be one Voice of Michigan Football, and that guy's Bob Ufer. His impact on this university as a broadcaster is unmatched in my opinion. To have someone say that to me is high praise indeed because there is only one Voice of Michigan Football. He's been gone now for quite some time, yet his passion and love for this university and how he called football games was so unique and so Michigan. He has taken the title of the Voice of Michigan and made it his own forever! I'm just glad to be part of the process and the program. I'm thankful to be a part of the great success and values that Michigan football epitomizes and to be able to help sell the values and excitement on the radio. I've been very fortunate just to be able to do something I love to do.

Watching Michigan play football is great entertainment. I also do Detroit Lions football games and people ask me which one

I like doing better. I like doing Michigan football better. I like doing college football better, but I offer this caveat: the NFL is clearly the better game. The players are bigger, stronger, and faster. It is the best of the best. It's the Top Gun of football. College represents the passion of the young men that play. It's the passion of the student body rooting for their team because it's their classmates, their roommates. They are not playing for a paycheck; they're playing because they love the game. For 95 percent of them, it's the last organized football they will play. They are playing because they want to and they're playing for Michigan. They are playing for the name on front of the jersey, not the back of the jersey. That's the purest form of competition.

The alumni body comes back to support that team. The band is there to add to the pageantry and to be part of that football experience, that Saturday college football experience. You don't see that in the NFL. Yes, NFL fans are passionate and yes, they love their team, but it's not the same. The investment that the students and alums have in the university goes far beyond the investment, sometimes, that the professional sports fan has for his team. That's what I love about it!

Anthony Carter's catch against Indiana is one of the iconic plays in Michigan history. The game was going to be tied. It looked like **INDIANA*** was going to upset us, and somehow this little kid finds a way to make a play! You watch young people, what I like to call "ordinary kids doing extraordinary things." You watch them do it in front of a vast number of people. You're just amazed. It's about competition; it's about using those skills and those talents and letting everyone in to see it! It creates moments you'll never create again. To experience and call it for those people who are listening on the radio is a privilege and a pleasure. The only thing I can say is that I hope I give that

*** Jon Gruden, who in 2003 became the youngest coach to win a Super Bowl, was a quarterback at Muskingum before transferring to the University of Dayton...Gruden was a ballboy for the undefeated 1976 INDIANA basketball team.**

moment justice. So often I feel inadequate. You just can't describe the emotion and sense of that moment in the stadium when you see it live. If I can somehow, as a radio broadcaster, help them get there, that's fine by me! Then I've done my job.

I'll never forget when we played at Penn State in '97. Frank and I were calling the game. Penn State was the best team in the country, tops in the polls. Michigan was ranked third. It was going to be a great game and one of those tough ones. You're on the road and you're playing a great football team. In the first half, Michigan just destroys Penn State. The game was in Michigan's control completely from the moment they snapped the ball. Penn State did not have a chance. It was one of the best performances I had ever seen from a football team in a big game. Frank and I looked at each other at halftime and we both knew what we wanted to say to each other was, "Are we this good?" We both kind of looked at each other, nodded, and said, "I think we're this good!" Then we went on and won the National Championship.

I've had so many great moments around the team and at the games. People ask, "What's the best game you've ever done?" I tell them, "I haven't done it yet!" Nobody has a perfect game and I haven't done one yet. I don't think I'll ever do one! I really truly believe that.

Maybe the most famous broadcast story comes from a game against Northwestern. They've got this on tape at WJR. Michigan had two defensive linemen, one named Nate Rodgers and the other Mike Hammerstein. Frank is calling the play-by-play. Nate Rodgers and Mike Hammerstein combined for a sack of the Northwestern quarterback. So Frank, trying to be cute or entertaining, says, "What a melodious tune by Rodgers and Hammerstein!" He starts laughing, thinking he's maybe gone over the edge! This is on the air. He's literally laughing so hard he can't continue! I'm looking at him, "What are you doing? It was good but not *that* good!" He's giggling and laughing and all of a sudden it gets infectious so I start giggling and laughing about it. Both of us are basket cases up there! We don't call the next play. I tried to call the punt and said something like, "You've been waiting to say that all year long!" He's still laughing. I call the punt, which is odd because he's the play-by-play guy. Michigan now has the ball and Frank leans into the microphone and says, "Excuse me, ladies and gentlemen. I'll be back as soon as I "*compose*" myself!" He starts laughing again, so I do too. Now, nobody can hear anything because all we're doing is giggling. It doesn't sound funny, but at the time, there wasn't anything more hilarious than what we were doing up there. Finally, we started to get back to calling the game and putting our professional hats on, and me being the smartass I am, I look at him and say, "Boy, I'm sure glad we aren't playing **OKLAHOMA***!" He loses it again! I shouldn't have said it but I couldn't resist. WJR has about a three-minute tape that chronicles the whole thing. That was one of our most famous broadcast moments if you will!

To be part of the Michigan fabric and to have had the opportunity to know the greats has been a thrill—the Ron Kramers, Don Canhams, Bo Schembechlers—you can get thousands of stories on those people. They broke the mold after Ron. He's an original. To have the chance to have known him and call him my friend is one of those benefits of being a part of Michigan athletics and Michigan football. There are hundreds of these guys that have come through the building that I've been lucky to meet.

***The first coach with his own TV SHOW was Bud Wilkinson at the University of OKLAHOMA in 1952.**

CAUSE OF DEATH? LIFE!

RON KRAMER

Ron Kramer chose to attend Michigan because he liked Bennie Oosterbaan, the coach. "I always thought he was a cool guy and my attitude toward him now has not changed one single bit," said Kramer. Kramer majored in psychology at Michigan and "went to every class," mentioning that one of his family values was never to be late for school. "You never missed school. My kids were the same." Ron Kramer was a sports legend at the University of Michigan. A three-sport athlete—football, basketball, and track—Kramer won a total of nine varsity letters in his three sports. Kramer's Wolverine jersey No. 87 was retired—one of only five numbers in school history to be retired—in the company of No. 11 (the Wisterts), No. 47 (Bennie Oosterbaan), No. 48 (Gerald Ford), and No. 98 (Tom Harmon). Kramer played offensive and defensive end, running back, quarterback, kicker, and receiver. Ron Kramer passed away the day after this interview.

I agree with **SPORTS ILLUSTRATED*** putting me in the top 50 greatest sports figures from Michigan! (laughs) I'm just kidding around. Life should be fun! All these people being so serious—it's a game! Everyone wants to make a drama out

***In 1955, SPORTS ILLUSTRATED selected horse owner William Woodward as their Sportsman of the Year. Woodward's wife shot and killed the unfaithful Woodward before the issue went to press. SI then selected World Series hero, Johnny Podres.**

of everything. Every once in a while you think you're beating the heck out of someone and then when you get a little older, you find out they got to you, too.

The Silver Anniversary Award from the NCAA is a great award for someone who comes out of school and is honored by the NCAA for accomplishments not in athletics but for what they have contributed in society. I am involved in Special Olympics, NFL Alumni, charity tournaments, and the American Cancer Society. I think we all owe it back. I received that wonderful award 25 years after I graduated.

You know why my coach said that my blocking and attacking ability were the most valuable asset to the Michigan squad? He caught me with this girl on the 50-yard line my junior year and said, "Now that's a heck of a tackle, Kramer!"

Here's a great story from college. I had a wonderful roommate, Charlie Brooks. We always had to find places to park with our girlfriends—you've got to make out someplace! You know, kissy face and all that crazy stuff. We always parked by our stadium. In those days, the women had to be in bed by 11:00. We all knew when it was nearing 11:00 and we left. About three or four days later, this postcard comes in the mail. I take this big postcard from the University of Michigan out of the mailbox. I'm thinking, "What the heck is this for?" I had to read it because it was Charlie's! It said, "Dear Charlie, It's a wonderful stadium to play in, isn't it? Coach Oosterbaan."

Bennie Oosterbaan found out that Charlie would park there. The reason he found out is that Charlie Brooks was late. We had these great big barbed-wire fences. At the time, Charlie got over the fence and we didn't know what he was doing over there. So he got the manager and woke him up. The stadium manager opened up the gate for Charlie and then of course he told the coach! Charlie Brooks was, for the next two years, on our totem pole! We were very dear friends.

A lot of people don't take into consideration the great feeling that each one of these players has for one another the rest of their lives. They are practicing and playing together, traveling and rooming together, spending a lot of time together. I only wish that we could get the rest of the American people behind our country as strongly as they do on a Saturday. Amen more than once!

Bennie Oosterbaan had a great love for me. Bennie played football, baseball, and basketball. I'm big, but I'm not real big, if you know what I mean. I weighed 250 lbs. but could still high jump 6'4." I was Michigan's all-time leading scorer in basketball. It was wonderful! I just enjoyed my life.

Every guy that made the team generally had great backing from parents. People have to get back into parenting. My daughter said to me, "Dad, I think I'm going to go to Michigan State." I said, "Are you sure that's the school you want to go to? Do you want to go west or south or anywhere else? You can go to Michigan State—I'll see you more!" She said, "You don't mind if I go to Michigan State?" I wanted her to go wherever she could get the best education for her.

Some guy asked me how I could let my kids go to Michigan State. I said, "First of all, they wanted to. Second, my dad wanted me to go to his school and I didn't want to go there!" He asked, "Where did he go to school?" I responded, "Third grade."

One Packers story that I love involves my two pals and roommates Max McGee and Paul Hornung. We sit down at this meeting and Vince Lombardi was in front of the class. He was writing something on the board. He turns around and says, "Hornung! You and Max stand up!" And that was it; he turned back around and started doing what he was doing again. He turned around again and they were sitting down. He said, "Did I tell you to sit down?" They bounced up like a couple of rubber balls. He turns around and looks at Max and Paul, "Max and Paul, the next time you are caught out late, you call me because it's going to cost you $5,000! But you call me...because I'm going with you!"

Things were fun. In 1961, the Green Bay Packers won the world championship. It was the first time they won in their hometown. We were playing the Giants and just started beating up on them bad. Those poor guys were going through it, and before you know it, the game is 37-0. Of course, I had a great day! I had two touchdowns and everyone I hit was on the ground. The guy that wins the MVP of the game gets a Corvette. Here I'm busting up people all day long and Hornung was the MVP. I was with him the other day and Paul said, "You know Ron, you were really the MVP that day." So I responded, "Well, why don't you give me the Corvette?" "Nope," he says.

A guy who lived in Fenton, MI, and is no longer living had a tradition of bringing apples to the team every Wednesday. In 1987, I brought some apples to Coach Schembechler. I set the apples down and left. The next week, about Tuesday, Bo said, "You forgot the apples! You brought apples last week and they weren't there this week. Where were they? Oh! And that apple juice is good—bring some of that too!" So I haven't missed a Wednesday since.

CHAPPUIS WAS THE MOST TO SAY THE LEAST

BOB CHAPPUIS

In 1942, 1946, and 1947 Bob Chappuis played halfback but excelled at his father's old position, quarterback, becoming one of the game's original passing "specialists." He was nationally known and a celebrity on campus. He holds the Big 10's single-season pass rating record as well as the Wolverines' completion record. He was an All-American and elected to the College Football Hall of Fame in 1988. He and his wife Ann, currently live in Ann Arbor, Michigan. In **WORLD WAR II***, *Chappuis served as a radio operator and gunner on a B-25. His 21st mission nearly ended in tragedy when the plane was shot down over Italy. Chappuis and two crew members were able to parachute from the plane and were rescued by Italian partisans who kept the men out of sight until the war ended three months later.*

Upon returning to Michigan, and not playing any football during the time in service, there was some uncertainty about even playing football again. However, I decided to try out and once again made the varsity roster. We had great teams in the next two seasons culminating with our trip to the 1948 Rose Bowl.

We were working out at the Rose Bowl. It was two days before the game and we were running through plays with no opposition,

*** The first American off the boats on D-DAY at Normandy was actor James Arness, later of "Gunsmoke" fame. The reason Arness was the first was he was the tallest soldier on the first boat to land and the Admiral wanted to measure how deep the water was.**

just running. At one point, I happened to be carrying the ball when all of a sudden I had this terrible pain in my leg.

Coach Crisler was not really "one of the guys," but he was a great motivator. I thought that I had played fairly decent during the season. So, when I was running around with that pain in my leg, I thought, "Well, I'm going to get some attention from Coach now."

I was lying on the ground with our trainer working on me. Coach Crisler looked down at me and then asked our trainer Jim Hunt, "What happened here Jim?" Jim said, "I think Bob has pulled his hamstring." Coach Crisler then replied, "Well, it's a good thing that didn't happen to somebody who could run."

We were called the Mad Magicians back then. That's because we had a lot of ball-handling ability—reverses, short passing, and so on. I recall Coach Crisler up on a stand that was maybe 10-12 feet high. He was watching us run through our plays. If he was able to see the ball being exchanged between one, two, or three people from up there, he would say, "Run it again." So we would run it again, sometimes doing the same thing several times until he was satisfied.

He was a perfectionist and wanted us to know that. As a result, our sleight of hand would fool a lot of people, thus the Mad Magicians name.

There's been word that my wife Ann was the Rose Bowl Queen. Ann (though we were not married at that time) had been invited to go to the Rose Bowl and it was even suggested that she become the Rose Bowl Queen. However, she decided to go home for Christmas and didn't go to the Rose Bowl.

You're a good passer if you've got people to make the catches. I was not a bad passer and we had good people at the ends and the backfields. Our guys really knew what they were doing and it was made all the easier by the trickery—the Mad

Magicians—and what we were doing in the backfield confusing the defense. I don't remember Coach Crisler being that complimentary to me personally, but he was complimentary about me to the media.

We were on the train returning from California and the Rose Bowl game. All of us were sitting in the club car and a number of the players were drinking a beer. All of a sudden, Coach Crisler walked in and we thought, "Oh, boy, now we're going to get it!" We wouldn't *think* of having a beer during the season. He came in and said, "Mind if I join you?" I thought that was remarkable for him to do that. The timing of what he did was just never, ever off base. He was just a great man and a great coach. That was the amazing part of it, because he was a very serious and great coach. He wasn't best friends with anyone in particular on the team during the season, but we found out that he was a human being.

Another great memory of the '47 season was playing Minnesota at Ann Arbor. We were behind going into the half. Before we went in we had the ball at midfield with about 25 seconds left and Howard Yerges, who was our quarterback, came in the huddle and said, "We haven't been behind at the half in any game up 'til now. We better not be behind this time."

I got the ball and faded back to pass. There were two guys on Minnesota's team coming at me so I had very little time to look around to see who I could throw to. When I did, one of those guys was on me, making it very difficult to complete a pass. I said to Bump Elliott, who was running as the wingback, "Bump, I don't have much time to throw. Do you have any idea of where you might be?" He said, "Just throw it toward the end zone." Well, I didn't think that was great news. I got the ball, went back to throw the pass, and then went into the dirt. We got a big roar out of our side of the field. So I said to myself as I was still lying there on the ground, "By golly, I think Bump got down there and caught that pass!" And it was true, he did. He ran it in for a touchdown and we were ahead at halftime. That particular play was written up as the "Play of the Week."

It was an honor to be nominated for the 1947 Heisman Trophy, but I came in second. I said, "Nobody ever remembers the guy who came in second." Johnny Lujack was the guy who won it and he has become a really good friend of mine. He was really a great football player and he played both ways...both offense and defense. He still holds the Chicago Bears record for most passing yards in a game.

At the end of the season, Notre Dame was picked as the national champions. Then when the Rose Bowl came along, we beat Southern Cal 49–0. We had two common opponents with Notre Dame that year; one was Southern Cal (we beat them 49–0 and Notre Dame beat them something like 30–12).

The other common opponent was Pittsburgh. We beat them 69–0 and Notre Dame beat them maybe 40–15. The press had done something unprecedented. They had voted Notre Dame the No. 1 team, and after those two games were examined, they did something that they've never done before—they had another vote—and voted Michigan No. 1.

I was also president of the Phi Delta Theta fraternity for two years. I remember walking into that house for the first time, and they took us back to the den, where they had on display a lot of the pictures of Phi Delts who were football players, guys like Tom Harmon and Harry Kipke.

My time at Michigan was great, the team, the coaching, everything. It also depended on timing. Had I not come back after the service, it never would have happened. And then it only happened because we had great leadership. We had great players and I'm proud to have been acquainted with and to have worked with so many great teammates and coaches.

Chapter 4

THERE'S NO EXPIRATION DATE ON DREAMS

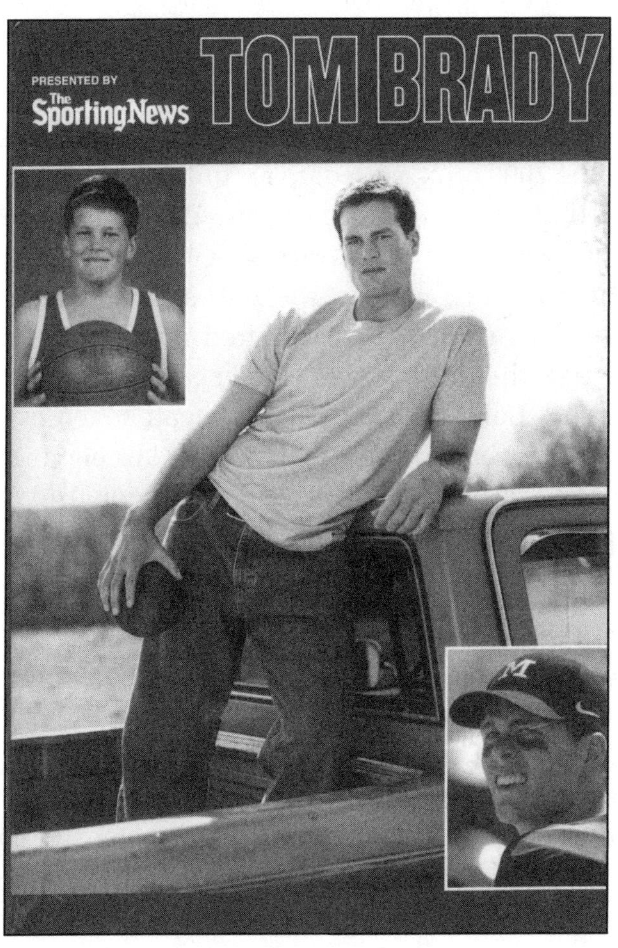

The Big 10, The Big House, The Big Chill, The Big Time

AUTHOR'S NOTE:

In the spring of 2009, I wrote a book entitled *How Tom Brady Ruined Notre Dame Football.* The gist of the book was that if Tom Brady would have been your average backup quarterback, Bill Belichick would have never been a head coach in the NFL after the 2001 season and no one would've ever heard of Charlie Weis. I never published the book because it made my alma mater look extremely foolish, although it exposed Charlie Weis for the arrogant incompetent buffoon that he is.

Brady was drafted by the New England Patriots late in the sixth round of the 2000 draft, suited up for only two games that year, and played only two series of downs. The next year, 2001, he worked his way from fourth team to second team. During the middle of the second game of the 2001 season, Drew Bledsoe, the starting quarterback, was injured and Brady took over. Brady started the third game of that season. At that time Bill "The Genius" Belichick's record as a head coach in the NFL was 42–56. They had lost fourteen of their last eighteen games with Charlie Weis as the offensive coordinator. And now they were going with their second-team quarterback who has barely played in the NFL.

If form holds true, they're probably going to lose all or most of their remaining games. If that happens, at the end of the season Bill Belichick's record in the NFL would be 42–70. Charlie Weis' record as an offensive coordinator in the NFL would be 4–28. Belichick would have never been a head coach in the NFL again, although he would always be a defensive coordinator. Charlie Weis would never have a job in pro football again and may have had a hard time getting a job anywhere.

But here comes Brady...who was prepared, who had the trust of his teammates, who works harder than any athlete in pro sports, who pays more attention to detail, who is tough as nails, who relishes clutch situations, who reads defenses better than any quarterback in the league, and who anticipates players' moves better than anyone. They win 14 of their next 17 games. After losing 14 out of 18 games, they win 14 out of 17 games and the Super Bowl, where Brady is MVP. As a result, many people associated with the Patriots were "born on third base but thought they hit a triple." Charlie Weis was offensive coordinator even though he did not call the plays. He conned Notre Dame into a 10-year contract and was fired after five dismal years.

Romeo Crennel became the head coach of the Cleveland Browns and was fired. Eric Mangini became the head coach of the New York Jets and was fired. Tom Brady made Dion Branch the Super Bowl MVP. A couple of years later, Branch left for greener pastures in **SEATTLE*** and no one ever heard of him again until he reunited with Brady midway through the 2010 season.

I was aware of Brady for years, because for the last 35 years, I've lived in Scottsdale, Arizona, where one of my best friends is a gentleman named Gene Cervelli. Many years ago Gene Cervelli and Tom Brady Sr. were in the Maryknoll Seminary together in the San Francisco area. They both dropped out at the same time, both had large families, and both made millions in the business world.

Cervelli moved to Arizona, where he was the biggest ice cream distributor in the desert, and Tom Brady opened an insurance agency in a San Francisco suburb. Because of Cervelli, I had heard of Brady Jr. ever since he was in high school. I saw Brady's first Michigan start in a fall 1998 game at Notre Dame. He led Michigan to a nice halftime lead that the Wolverine defense gave away in the second half. During the game, I kept looking for him to be nervous, to make mistakes, but he didn't—he kept sailing along. The more I watched him in his career at

***During the SEATTLE Mariners' first year in 1977, the distance to the fences was measured in fathoms. A fathom is 6 feet. For instance, where one park might have a sign that denotes 360 feet, the Kingdome sign would have the number 60...**

Michigan, the more I realized how special he was. He won 20 out of his 25 starts there and could've won 23 out of 25 with a little different circumstances. He had tough competition and had to be "twice as good" as Drew Henson in order to start ahead of the most highly recruited athlete in Michigan high school history. I was shocked that Tom Brady was not a first-round pick, particularly after his final three games at Michigan where he was spectacular...

Cervelli and I went to that first Super Bowl and had lunch with the Brady family the day before the game in New Orleans. As we were sitting there, Tom Brady Sr. said, "Rich, I see that you did a book on Kurt Warner two years ago when he was MVP of the Super Bowl. If Tommy's MVP tomorrow, will you do a book on him?" Well, I was more likely to be struck by lightning while honeymooning with Christie Brinkley than for Tom Brady to be MVP of his first Super Bowl against the heavily favored St. Louis Rams. But Brady played out of his mind and was fabulous in the clutch. The **PATRIOTS*** won and he was MVP. Later that night, Brady Sr. called Cervelli, "Tell Rich that when he does that book, I'll get him all the pictures he needs." When Cervelli told me that, I said, "Holy Cow! How I am going to do a book, he's such a young guy...and also such a straight guy." He was not a drinker, not a carouser, he only dated one girl at a time, he was married to football, so I knew this was going to be a tough job. On the other hand, I so enjoyed the entire Brady family that I said, "What the heck, let's give it a try," and I'm glad I did. Out of the more than three dozen sports books I've done, I've enjoyed all of them but one. On the other hand, the one I have enjoyed most was the Tom Brady book.

A supermarket chain in New England bought all of the books, and I proceeded to go on the talk show circuit. I was on a show with Eddie Andelman, the father and originator of sports talk.

***The New England PATRIOTS once played a regular-season home game in Birmingham, Alabama, in September 1968.**

At that time, he thought that Brady was a "one-year wonder." I told Andelman, "A quarterback cannot fool the NFL for 17 games. If he gets really lucky, he might be able to bluff his way through one or two games, but not 17. Brady is the real deal, and if he doesn't get hurt, he's going to the Hall of Fame." Andelman broke out laughing and said, "You're joking, aren't you?" I said, "Read the book. Once you understand what this young man did to get to the position to do what he's done with the Patriots, you'll believe that he's going to the Hall of Fame." Again, at that time, everybody thought it was a ridiculous comment. I said, "Read the book and you'll find out what he's like."

Besides Dion Branch, he's made everyone around him better. Take Randy Moss, for example. Moss was at the end of his career. He had several lousy years in a row when the Patriots picked him up for a fourth-round draft pick. The very first year they were together, he and Brady set a record for most touchdowns in a season by a quarterback to a receiver. When Moss reverted to his old tendencies, they unloaded him for a third-round pick. When you trade for a player using a fourth-round pick and then unload him for a third-round pick, it's not like you're trading for the greatest receiver in the history of the game. You're trading for a guy who took many plays off and wasn't good in the clubhouse.

I never dreamed I'd ever see a better quarterback, particularly in the clutch, as Joe Montana, but Brady has him beat because Brady has done it with far less. **JOE MONTANA*** had Jerry Rice and Roger Craig among others. Terry Bradshaw had Franco Harris and Lynn Swann; Tom Brady had Antoine Smith and David Givens. Troy Aikman had Michael Irvin and Emmitt Smith; Tom Brady had Kevin Faulk and Troy Brown. Johnny Unitas had Raymond Berry along with Lenny Moore and Alan

***JOE MONTANA** did not start until the fourth game of his junior year at Notre Dame....Montana was awestruck by Huey Lewis and once sang backup with his band.**

Ameche. But no one has had more talent around them than Peyton Manning. Peyton Manning has had two great running backs with Edgerrin James and Joseph Addai. With the exception of one year, Brady has never had a running game. When your leading rusher averages 57 yards a game, you have no running game. Brady's the only quarterback ever to win without a running game. Peyton Manning had Marvin Harrison and Dallas Clark and Reggie Wayne and Brandon Stokley as receivers. Brady hasn't had anything close to that luxury. So all I can say is that it has been a pleasure knowing the Brady family, it's been a pleasure watching Tom Brady play, and Michigan fans should be delighted that they gave the NFL the greatest quarterback ever. What follows are some excerpts from the book I did on Brady *plus* some current interviews that'll give insights into this remarkable young man.

Obviously, I strongly feel that Michigan's Tom Brady is the finest quarterback to ever play the game!

There's a Win Chill Factor in Minnesota

CHEVY CHASE ONCE HOSTED THE OSCARS, JIMI HENDRIX ONCE OPENED FOR THE MONKEES, AND TOM BRADY WAS ONCE MICHIGAN'S SIXTH-TEAM QUARTERBACK...THERE ARE SOME THINGS YOU JUST CAN'T MAKE UP!

TOM BRADY SR.

Tom Brady Sr. was raised in San Francisco, went into the seminary for seven years, and graduated from the University of San Francisco. He worked as a counselor at a juvenile hall through college and then went to work for TWA for a short period. He's been in the life insurance business and estate planning arena since 1968, with his home office, Thomas Brady and Associates, in San Mateo, California. There are offices in Boston, Orange County, and soon New York. Brady married his wife, Galynn, 42 years ago. They have three daughters, Maureen, Julie, Nancy, and one son, Tommy. Tommy is the youngest.

In high school, Tom was the starting catcher in baseball and a starter on the basketball team but a backup quarterback and linebacker on the football team. As the backup quarterback, the team was 0–8 and did not score a touchdown the whole season. He was not deemed good enough to get in for one play as a quarterback that entire season.

Tommy got the job as the JV quarterback by default when the other quarterback did not return. As a junior and senior, he

We were led to believe when he was in high school that Tommy's future as a pro athlete would be in baseball.

gave up basketball and played football in the fall as the varsity quarterback and baseball in the spring as the varsity catcher.

Tom had a very good college career at Michigan; he was 20–5 and had one of the best games ever at the Orange Bowl in 2000. The NFL Draft was quite an experience. We thought he would be drafted in the third or fourth round. At the end of the first day he still wasn't drafted. On the second day, we go through the fourth round, the fifth round—Tommy is very distraught—and finally, with the last pick of the sixth round, the Patriots called and said they wanted him. They were looking for a backup quarterback, but they already had Drew Bledsoe, John Friesz, and Michael Bishop.

THE PATRIOTS* had a terrible year in 2000, but they kept Tommy on the squad. Only two teams in the NFL had four quarterbacks that year—the Patriots were one. Tommy was fourth string. The next year, in preseason camp, Coach Dick Rehbein, Tommy's "angel," was on the treadmill and had a heart attack and died. Lo and behold, here we are again—we don't have anyone in the locker room rooting for us. That being said, Tommy worked very, very hard to move up the depth chart and went into the season being second to Drew Bledsoe. In the second game of the 2001 season, Drew Bledsoe was smashed severely. Bledsoe went to the hospital with a sheared artery in his chest and was there for a week. It was really bad and he darn-near died. When he came

*As a result of a public contest in 1960, the team name of Boston **PATRIOTS** was chosen. Many years later when considering a name change, management decided on the Bay State Patriots, but went with "New England" instead because they worried about Bay State being abbreviated in headlines.

In the history of the Patriots, they have played home games at Harvard Stadium, Boston University Field, Fenway Park, Boston College and in 1971 they made their debut at Schaefer Stadium in Foxboro. Schaefer was the one stadium to have when you're having more than one.

out of the hospital, he was brought along cautiously until about the 10th week of the season.

By that time, the Patriots, who had started the season 0–2, were 5–5 under Tommy's leadership. Bledsoe was ready to come back to take over the starting job and Bill Belichick said they were going to stay with what they had in place and named Tommy the starter for the rest of the season. That was an extraordinarily gutsy move by Belichick because they had signed Bledsoe to a $100 million contract at the beginning of the year. I think Tommy was making about $1.50. They were 5–5 and then they started winning...they won eight games in a row and reached the Super Bowl! Belichick looked like a genius! Before Tommy had taken over, the Patriots were 5–15, and after he took over, they were 14–3 for that season, so it really marked a changing of the guard.

We were led to believe when he was in high school that Tommy's future as a pro athlete would be in baseball. He was a right-handed throwing, left-handed power-hitting catcher. We had a lot of scouts visiting our house talking about the opportunities in baseball. But Tom wanted to pursue football, so we put together a recruiting tape showing all of his best plays and sent it out to 55 schools. Then he started to get some recruiting letters for football. In the summer, there was a regional camp where a lot of the high-visibility kids were invited to go to a college campus and work out in front of coaches sent in from various schools around the country. This camp was at St. Mary's University in Moraga, California, with about 60 schools represented. They had all of the quarterbacks and linemen do drills and catch passes. Tom fared very well. At the end of this session, we became inundated with recruiting brochures from various schools. Shortly thereafter, the recruiting services asked who his top-five schools were.

The top five on the list were Cal-Berkeley, University of Southern California, UCLA, **ILLINOIS***, and Michigan. He was subsequently

***The Chicago Bears wear blue and orange because those are the colors that team founder George Halas wore when he played for the University of ILLINOIS.**

invited to make recruiting visits to all of these places. He had gone to a summer camp at Berkeley that summer before his senior year and was basically the MVP of the camp. Coach Keith Gilbertson of California had offered him a scholarship on the spot. That same summer we had gone to UCLA to a summer camp and Terry Donahue had also offered him a scholarship on the spot. However, Tom wanted to go through the recruiting process and explore the other possibilities. Because of this, he accepted recruiting trips to the other three schools.

All along, I thought he was going to choose Berkeley. I was hoping he was going to choose Berkeley. I fully expected it, but he wanted to explore the possibilities. He really liked UCLA. He liked USC. He went to Illinois in December, and he wasn't impressed at all because it was cold and dreary and desolate—they were in the middle of a storm. Then, in early January, he went to Michigan. When he was at Michigan, it was dreary and desolate—it was cold and snowy—but he absolutely fell in love with it. Walking into the Big House and going through Schembechler Hall—the whole experience had captivated him in a way that none of the other schools had done. As a result, when he came back, he was very much leaning toward Michigan.

This was about January 10th. He didn't have to make a commitment until early February, when he would sign a letter of intent. He was being recruited by Billy Harris, a backfield coach for Michigan, whose region was California. The head coach at that time was Gary Moeller. As we came down to the end, we wanted to make sure the coach fully committed to Tommy and that he wasn't just another ornament on the tree. So I called Billy Harris the last week of January and asked, "Bill, are you guys really serious about Tommy?" He said, "We are absolutely serious about him." I told him, "We want to be absolutely sure because I know of stories where coaches just hang guys out to dry. I want someone who's committed to Tommy." He said, "Let me get back with you." This was on a Friday night. He got back with me and said, "Coach Moeller and I will be in San Mateo to see Tommy on Monday." They came in on Monday on a private plane and we visited. Moeller said they were fully committed to Tommy. They said they had to change their offense because times were changing.

Tommy ultimately made the decision to attend Michigan, which was very painful for me. That was a very crushing time. I wanted Tommy to stay in the area so he could play football on Saturday and we could still play golf on Sunday. However, this was Tommy's decision. Having had older sisters that had gone to schools on athletic scholarships, Tom kept hearing from them, "Go where you want to go! The athletics may not work out. If it doesn't work out, at least you'll be in the environment in which you want to graduate."

He happily signed a letter of intent, and I was really crushed. Even when I think about it today, I get emotional. For two days I didn't stop crying. It was very hard to let my son go—after all, with four women in the house, he was my refuge. I taught him to play Liars Dice at our **GOLF CLUB*** when he was five, and we played golf all the time—even if it was just a quick nine holes. We were very, very close. So when he made the decision to go to Michigan, it was 100 percent his. Both Michigan and Berkeley were great academically, but it was only 30 miles to go see him play at Berkeley, whereas it was 1700–1800 miles each way to see him play at Michigan.

So he made the decision to go to Michigan, and all was well and good until two days later when we got a call from Billy Harris. Billy said, "Tom, I have good news and bad news." The good news is (to Tommy), "You and I will be playing golf sooner than next summer when you had anticipated coming back to Ann Arbor. The bad news is, I'm no longer at Michigan. I'm the defensive coordinator at Stanford." He was no longer there. That was the way it was until a month later when Gary Moeller,

***Until recently, Michigan had more GOLF COURSES than any state in the Union.**

who professed his undying support for Tommy, was fired. All of a sudden the two people that were supportive of him coming to Michigan were no longer there. Then, Bill Freehan got fired. He knew three people at Michigan and now none were there.

Lloyd Carr moved into the head coach's position. Unfortunately, Tommy was not Lloyd Carr's chosen one. That was a problem. Tommy made the decision to go to Michigan because of all it embraced, not just due to Billy Harris and Gary Moeller, so we had faith that things would work out. However, we also know that if you don't have someone rooting for you in the coach's room, somebody who recruited you and has been in your living room and made promises, your path may very well be made extraordinarily tougher. There's going to be other kids recruited to the school who will have voices in the coach's room that you will not have. Frankly, that's what happened to Tommy. He didn't have anyone that had recruited him. So all bets were off! That set up a very difficult environment in Michigan. At that time, Tommy was the sixth or seventh quarterback on that team. Behind him came Drew Henson.

All of a sudden the two people that were supportive of him coming to Michigan were no longer there.

His first year he was redshirted. Then he got into the pecking order. He moved up the depth chart and was even with Brian Griese in 1997. Lloyd Carr gave the nod to Brian Griese. Tommy was devastated by that. Brian did a magnificent job that year—just magnificent. In fact, we were tied with Nebraska for number one at the end of the year. The next year, when Tommy was clearly supposed to be the starter his junior year, Lloyd Carr had recruited Drew Henson. Tommy had to compete with him for the starting job. They would let Tommy start, and then in the second quarter, Drew Henson would take over, and whoever was deemed to have played the better quarter would play the second half. It was lousy.

He had to just be tough. He couldn't let anything get in his way. Sometimes when you're playing, you want some time to "feel the other team out," but he never had time to do that. Usually, he was back in there in the second half and at the end of the game. **BRENT MUSBURGER***, the ABC announcer, used to call him "The Comeback Kid" because they had so many comebacks and would beat teams. The whole experience toughened him. He didn't get the slightest concession from Lloyd Carr. That served him well and continues to serve him well. It has driven him to be the best he can be. There was no prima donna in him because he was never treated as anything special.

One of our first experiences was playing against Syracuse at home. Donovan McNabb was the quarterback there. He just took us to the woodshed. He had a great game. At halftime, we were losing something like 30-3. Donovan McNabb had one touchdown where he ran down the right side, cut back, ran out of his shoe, and then into the end zone. I had never seen a quarterback play like that before. The fans at that time were booing Tommy. My daughters were there and were absolutely devastated. They wanted to fight 105,000 people. That was interesting, the negative experience early on, but it showed the passion of the Michigan fans.

My favorite game was at Penn State in 1999. Penn State was highly ranked. We went in there and were battling. We went to every game while he was at Michigan—every home and every away game. We were down in Happy Valley, listening to the game on the radio as well as seeing it with our binoculars. With about eight minutes to go, Tommy threw an interception, and the guy ran it back about 60 yards for a touchdown. Penn State

***BRENT MUSBURGER was the home plate umpire when Tim McCarver made his pro baseball debut for Keokuk, Iowa, in the Midwest League in 1959.**

was now up. The announcer, George Paterno—Joe Paterno's brother—went crazy saying, "We've got them this time! It's all over!" The Michigan defense held them on about the 30-yard line, we got the ball back, and went down and scored a touchdown with eight seconds left to go. We beat Penn State. It was such a jubilant victory!

We came back a couple of times against Alabama in the Orange Bowl when Shaun Alexander was the star running back. At different times, we were down by 14 points and came back to win the game in overtime. As I went in to get Tommy out of the tunnel after that last game, he was dehydrated, and the quarterback coach, Stan Parrish, was carrying his duffel bag. Stan Parrish said to me, "Tom, I've been coaching for 25 years and I've never been prouder of an athlete in my life than I am of your son." It was very, very special. That being said, he wasn't invited to the Senior Bowl. He was invited late to the East-West Shrine game.

Much of this stuff for me is an out-of-body experience. When it's your son down there on the field, it's almost like it's not your son. The only time it gets to be your son is when he gets knocked down. We are so cautious about using the word *proud* because of that old axiom, "Pride cometh before a fall." All I can tell you is that we are really happy that he is happy in his accomplishments. When we look at it, we are in awe that he has been able to climb up the ladder in what he decided he wanted to do. When he was in college, he said, "Someday I want to be one of the 32 guys that start in the NFL." When he got closer to the end of his college career, he said, "I want to be the one guy who stands on the podium at the Super Bowl." That was what he aspired to. You never take away your child's dreams. I'm extremely proud to see his work ethic. At Michigan, he was the hardest-working guy. It was and still is impossible to be more hard working than he is.

Tommy's force, as with many athletes, is a fear of failure. I can probably count on two hands the amount of desserts I've seen him eat in 10 years. He works out every single day. In the off-season, he works out from four to six hours on his strength, conditioning, and speed. He doesn't eat anything that is unhealthy. His nutrition is impeccable! He keeps his body fine-tuned, knowing it's his tool to perform in business. He's been fortunate that some of his injuries have not eliminated him from playing in games. He gets hit and gets crushed, but because of how hard he works, his body is accustomed to it.

> It was and still is impossible to be more hard working than he is.

Tommy really loved his Michigan friends. The Michigan teammates were just terrific people. His roommate, Pat Kratus, to this day is his very best friend. Pat played on the defensive line at Michigan. Pat's the godfather to Tom's first son. Tommy also loved being back at Michigan during the summer. He worked at the golf course and just really loved the whole experience.

He was the team captain, and they used to have these runs. On this particular day, they were running around in the pouring rain. They ended up just diving into mud puddles. This is probably 60 guys. Then they ran to the swimming pool on campus and dove in, muddy as can be. They were in Lloyd Carr's doghouse and had to report at 5:30 in the morning for a month because the swimming coach had called and ranted and raved. The whole team was disciplined, but they loved the camaraderie.

We really miss going to Michigan games.

IF YOU'RE LUCKY ENOUGH TO BE TOM BRADY'S BEST FRIEND, YOU'RE LUCKY ENOUGH

PAT KRATUS

Pat Kratus grew up in Rocky River, OH, where he went to Saint Ignatius High School in Cleveland. Kratus received his MBA at Michigan in 2001. Kratus worked as an investment banker with Robertson Stephens, and is currently an executive director with UBS Investment Bank. Kratus and his wife Kristen live in Danville, CA and have two children.

Lloyd Carr was always interested in players as people. We were going through the Michigan transition from Bo and Gary Moeller to Lloyd. NCAA rules had changed the number of scholarships, so there was a transition from having 135 guys on scholarship down to a lower number. There was a lot more "yes sir, no sir." When you look at how coaches have to coach today, it's very different than what Lloyd came into. He was able to adapt his coaching style...he came in as a very strict disciplinarian...yelling and screaming...to having discussions with player. Charles Woodson and Lloyd had some heated debates sometimes. If that was in the Bo or Gary Moeller era, they would have thrown Woodson off the team. When you have a player as great as Charles you have to talk through the issue...not blind obedience for whatever the coach said to do.

Lloyd brought in the true Michigan Man tradition...Brian Griese was a walk-on, he was in a fraternity with other outside interests, Tommy Brady was very similar...if players didn't go on to have NFL careers, they were good students at Michigan and were set up for future success.

I really enjoyed Lloyd Carr...he was a renaissance man, a true Michigan Man. When it came to trying to help enrich the student athletes lives, Lloyd did really make a difference. Lloyd had big stadium speakers put up to simulate the crowd noise... we'd play a song over and over...played "Highway to Danger Zone" from Top Gun for one season. Lloyd would increase our exposure to the world...played the tape from "Evita" and Sarah Brightman. He wanted to develop well-rounded individuals.

Lloyd occasionally would bring guys back to speak to the team. Jim Mandich spoke to us before the Orange Bowl in 1998...he was an All-American tight end at Michigan who went on to play with the Dolphins...his son Mike came to play at Michigan. He spoke to us after a practice. "Swing the damn bat!" was his story about his son...the theme being you have a great opportunity to do something, so seize that opportunity.

Mandich's story was about his son in Little League who was waiting for the perfect pitch and he let ball one, ball two go past him...and had done that for a few other times...finally Jim stood up and yelled at his son..."Swing the damn bat!" The story would be fairly self evident but Jim and Lloyd made it into a motivating point for the season. A lot of the old school coaches probably use older quotes; Lloyd was able to get guys interested in things that were topical so you would be challenged both mentally and physically.

I really enjoyed Lloyd Carr...he was a renaissance man, a true Michigan Man.

Lloyd was the first guy to get us the "Friday shells"...practicing in shoulder pad-like equipment. They weren't actually shoulder pads otherwise you would just chew up and spit out guys and you couldn't afford to do that.

Lloyd had a policy of being on time which still dictates my life to this day. He would start a meeting five minutes early...if the meeting was to start at 8:30, he'd start it at 8:25. If you were late for 8:25, you were late. When we went to the White House, we were supposed to meet the President at 1:00 p.m. but President Bill Clinton got there at 2:30. Everybody was sitting around and not knowing what to do. Now Lloyd can't get upset with the President! So we were escorted around the White House into a few different rooms...some guys having their pictures taken... some were pretending they were the President giving a speech. We were seated in the Green Room and they had some furniture that was from the 1800's. When some of our linemen sat down, some of the chairs creaked like they were about to break.

It was amazing that we all had a chance to meet Bill Clinton, shake his hand and take a picture with him. Bill Clinton was able to shake your hand and make you feel that you were the most important person in the room...regardless that you just had 15 seconds with him. It was a great Michigan experience. That year we were able to meet President Clinton and former President Ford. Ford came to a couple of our practices. We certainly did not feel that we were at some school in the middle of Michigan playing football, but doing something on a national level and something that was a once in a lifetime experience... meeting two presidents in a year

I marveled at Charles Woodson as an athlete. In the state of Ohio coming out of high school, I finished pretty high in the Mr. Ohio football voting and Charles won it that year. I wondered "Who is this guy?" Football players showed up early on campus before the season started...the freshmen showed up a week before the regular freshmen...I remember thinking I was doing pretty well. The freshmen played a "pick up" basketball game early into the first two days. How Charles...who's not the tallest guy in the world...was just able to elevate and turn on a dime on the basketball court was unbelievable. Then, when we would watch him at the first football practices...Charles could go backwards and a you'd have a senior wide receiver sprinting down the field on a post pattern and Charles would go backwards for three steps, then he would turn his hips and he could get those turned around so quickly...he was amazing...it was almost freaky to watch. You couldn't believe that he was actually turning his hips that quickly.

With Charles...what would initially come off as being pigheaded or too full of himself.. you'd realize that he was supremely confident in his own abilities...he was recruited as a running back but ended up playing defensive back. He would say the only guy on defense that could cover him as a wide receiver was himself...

Remember Charles' interception against MSU—the singular most amazing catch...Everybody who plays ball in a Division 1 school sports is extremely prideful and the truth be known it's very difficult to get someone to admit that they could do the exact same thing. Charles was probably the guy who just put you into your own place, at least from the mental perspective. There's no better example of that than when he made that interception on the sideline against Michigan State. I have never seen anything like it. Today you could go back and figure out the approximate heights, but I wouldn't be surprised if Charles jumped 12 feet in the air to do this one-handed interception that really helped to seal the game against Michigan State.

Normally when a guy does something special, there's a little of a "Whoa...that's pretty cool" reaction from everyone else. But Charles jumping up, having the wherewithal...even if someone could jump that high ..to grab a ball one-handed and land. And if you watch how he lands...he kicks his foot down just in-bounds and then falls to the ground. That catch was the ultimate in knowing that Charles was the athlete of the ability that no one else had. I don't know if three of the best athletes in any given year...if given five chances to do it, could do it once. People took a different perspective with Charles because he wasn't just a great player for Michigan...he was probably the best player on the field in any given game.

I can't say that we had a better team than Ohio State...we were better disciplined. The two punt returns that Charles had were... almost like he personally took over that game. Ohio State had better teams...had a little advantage on us and Charles returns simply went to say that it doesn't matter how many good players you have, we have absolutely the best player here on our team.

It's very odd to be sitting around with a bunch of guys watching TV inside our apartment...watching the handing out of the **HEISMAN TROPHY***. We were all cheering for Charles, but it's one thing to know that he's the best guy on the field and that he's a great player. But to literally watch something since you were five years old...the handing out of the Heisman Trophy...and to see a guy you know win it...was thrilling.

Tommy Brady and I got to be roommates as true freshmen and we were roommates for all five years. Tommy is and was one of the most competitive guys. We'd get a "pick up" game of horse in basketball and I'd beat him...and he hated losing so much he took the basketball and drop kicked it three houses away...his response to losing. For three years not to play, to be the back-up guy and to be putting in all the time and effort, it really ate at him. He was pretty close, half way through our sophomore year, to transferring and going to Berkeley...there was a good quarterback coach there at the time.

In high school, Tommy and his dad had to put all these DVD's together because his high school team was not that good. He worked incredibly hard to just have a shot and that showed

***What HEISMAN TROPHy winner has made the most money? The 1959 winner, Billy Cannon of LSU, was arrested for counterfeiting in the early '80s and spent almost three years in jail. Technically, he is the only Heisman Trophy winner to ever "make" money.**

through. When he first showed up he had this weird running style where his left arm would pump up and down and his right arm would go around in a little circle...Mike Gittleson, the strength coach, worked with him a ton on getting his arm there.

When you looked at the lineup, you had Scott Dreisbach who started in front of Brian Griese until Scott got hurt, then you had Brian Griese. Brian took over in 1996 and had the National Championship in 1997. So when Tommy was thinking of leaving Michigan, Lloyd had to appeal to Tommy's competitive spirit. It may have made more sense if you laid this out on paper to have gone to another school but Lloyd basically challenged him and told him that he would have a fair shot at competing for the quarterback position. That sense of fairness is something that Lloyd always had throughout the team...that if he told you something that you had a fair chance it was going to happen. Tommy was competing fairly heavily...nobody worked more than Brady...at 10-11 p.m., Tommy would be at Schembechler Hall studying film. He'd be coming in for after-hours film that other guys just wouldn't do...it was not easy. He essentially just out-worked everybody because...he thought if he out-worked them, he'd have a shot. The other person who related that to him was Bo. Bo was around the field at times and he would tell Tommy if he would just keep on doing it...that he kept out-working people that he would have the opportunity to play...and when Bo Schembechler tells you something you better well believe it.

...when Bo Schembechler tells you something you better well believe it.

During one of Tom's first games starting, he'd get so excited, he'd run off the field, take off his helmet...and players head-butt with helmets on. Tommy had forgotten that he had taken his helmet off and head-butted with one of the offensive lineman. He cut himself open pretty good.

When Tommy was on the field...and basically when you were playing for Lloyd...you always felt if you ever lost it wasn't because the other team was better. The team always had a feeling that no matter what that Tommy would pull you through...

Tom has become a great quarterback. He's a very gifted athlete...he's more gifted than the average person...but he works so hard in preparation. Tommy would have sleepless nights on Tuesday and Wednesday nights in anticipation of a game, but on Friday night he always slept like a baby, at least that's what he told me. Then he was confident that he had gone over all of the scenarios often enough in his mind that he was prepared for the any scenario. What makes a great quarterback is one-third natural ability and two-thirds decision making...for him running through things in his mind so many times.

Tommy just couldn't get enough playing and even watching football. We'd be watching the **ESPN*** Thursday night game or the games on Sunday. We'd be sitting there on the couch, I'd have a textbook open and at least pretending I was studying, and he'd be calling out the defense...always working on making sure that he was going to know what to do better than anyone else. The physical part of making the throws, he's got a really good arm and he's good at it, but he's not necessarily the greatest. His reputation coming out of college was that he was slower than molasses and if you see some of the runs he made against Penn State for a touchdown, you can literally see him decide to start running, see his legs start to move,...it's like seeing it through an hour-glass.. you see it happening. What enabled him to actually score touchdowns, was not that he was trying to do it over his natural abilities, but because he has mentally figured out what the right thing to do was more rapidly than what anyone else had done. He knew that it's much easier to get rattled if you hadn't thought about all the plays

***ESPN** debuted September 7, 1979. ESPN2 debuted October 1, 1993. *ESPN The Magazine* made its first appearance on March 11, 1998.**

and scenarios...if you know what you have to do, you're more calm back there.

Tommy was also a great leader because he was so confident in what he was able to do, he was able to get other guys...whether they were offense or defense...to just be calm about what they had to do or to pump them up if they needed that. He wasn't so worried about what he had to do, he could help when a lineman knowing who he had to block or a defense that needed a little pick-me-up, he was able to give them that....because he already knew what he had to do.

One of the more inappropriate things being a Michigan football player teaches you is to have absolutely no modesty. Our sophomore year, Tommy, Jeff Potts and I were roommates in West Quad. You get so used to what is normal...today it would totally freak me out...we had one shower in the room and we had 5 shower towels...basically no one had their own shower towel...you'd just feel around for whatever was the driest towel and use that to dry yourself off. Since we were college football players, the towels got washed maybe once a month...conditions were a little less than clean, you know?...

So walking into the shower room of the locker room, you certainly didn't want to bring your towel in there because someone else would take your towel.. Then you'd be stuck naked calling for Big Johnny, the equipment manager, to see if you could get an extra towel. And Big Johnny wouldn't give you an extra towel even if you were standing there shivering...would not happen...anyway, it's something I'd never do today...

When see guys show up as freshmen they're unsure...are guys different from me? Maybe they grew up on a farm versus a city kid...black or white depending upon how integrated their high school was, but by the time you were a senior...it taught you to love people for who they are and actually get to the root of what you like about people...nothing to do about their looks, how they act or if they sound like me.

Rick's was the big bar to go to in Ann Arbor...Rick's American Cafe. As soon as you were 21 you went there. There would be a line outside of very cute girls but they would have to wait in line. The players were friends with the bouncers and owners, so we were able to walk in the front of the line...you had to pay for all of your drinks and pay the cover charge, but you didn't have to wait in line. Tommy's sisters would come out from California and come in with us...they couldn't believe that all these girls with spaghetti strap tops were out in 30-degree weather with snow blowing just waiting to get into the bar...and the football players would walk to the front of the line.

Mike Gittleson was most integral to all of Michigan football for 30 years and Michigan winning games. He was the strength coach for 30 years. Mike is probably the most unique characters that I have met in my life...he's a Vietnam vet and was in phenomenal shape. He had these old-man strength competitions.

A perfect analogy for Mike...if you remember watching Rocky IV with Ivan Drago...in the days when the guys started using GNC supplements, Mike said, "You don't need any of those things. What you need is to focus on core strength." So we did drills. One summer he bought sandbags, we would carry 50 pound sandbags while running to improve your grip strength. He would break you down more mentally than he did physically. You had to grab these other sandbags in different boxes and you had to pick them up and put them on.

Mikes' attitude was just like in a game when you need more than you think you've got in your tank...you need to find some other reserve...you'd be picking these boxes up and from time to time Mike would be knocking them over. If he knocked it over, it didn't matter. It didn't count as going onto the sandbox. Even though Michigan had all of the best workout machines, Mike would have us on drills.

Another drill was pushing...4 board up and down around the field, essentially in a bear crawl position. I can't guarantee you that it made anyone quicker, faster, stronger but it certainly did teach you to be mentally prepared throughout a 12-game football season. Mike was the first guy the players would turn to...the guy outside of your position coach or Lloyd that was a sounding board for guys. When I didn't get as much playing time as I'd like, I'd go talk with Mike and he would put me on the right path. Mike was also one of the guys when Tommy Brady...halfway through our sophomore year was thinking about leaving...he helped Tommy to focus a little more on winning the position rather than going to another place where he knew he would get a chance to play. Mike has pictures of the entire team, every year with their shirts off and flexing and all the cheesecake stuff...

On game day we had fun. After the game there were a few guys whose parents weren't that far away in Michigan...Mark Campbell, Clint Copenhaver, Nate Miller and a few other parents. Their parents would have this huge Michigan tailgate out by Schembechler Hall so we would always swing by there. For guys who went away to college, you never felt that you were that far away because you were always with someone else's parent to help take care of you.

The team would go to Mott Children's Hospital...Brian Griese would try to rally players to go every Thursday. He was there every week to visit the kids. The most amazing thing was seeing the excitement in the kids' eyes when you walked in. It didn't matter to them if you were Brian Griese in the middle of your National Championship season or if you were a benchwarmer in the middle of that season and barely saw the field. Sometimes you were there half the time for the kid and half the time you were there to talk to the dad about football or the mom to help them take their mind off of things.

The coaching staff was very understanding if you were doing that. Brian established such a great relationship with one of the kids that he ended up keeping a long term relationship with one of the kids that had cancer and was paralyzed. He took him on a medical therapy horseback trips. Brian lost his mother from cancer, but he spent so much of his personal time there, it wasn't because there was a press camera, it was just because he was honestly there to help the kid. Tommy did it a bunch, I was there a lot...you always had guys coming through—and just to see these kids eyes light up when you came into the room was such a phenomenal experience.

... just to see these kids eyes light up when you came into the room was such a phenomenal experience.

There was a focus on Michigan football of being fully integrated student athletes into the campus environment. The program took players that wouldn't necessarily have the opportunity to go to the elite public universities in the country and expose them to many things. Some guys absorbed those lessons...other guys didn't...but having the opportunity. Lloyd made sure that we went to a couple of nice restaurants, teaching us what it meant to tip, tip when leaving the hotel and putting a few dollars on the pillow for the maid. When you look at what Michigan football was actually preparing you for versus any other premier program, it was not only making sure we won football games, but making sure that guys had a life afterwards by giving them the tools to be successful.

BUENOS NOCHES, COACHES

BILLY HARRIS

Billy Harris was the Michigan coach who recruited Tom Brady. Shortly thereafter he left Michigan to coach at Stanford but over the years he has maintained a close relationship with the entire Brady family.

Initially, in recruiting Tom from California, we had gotten some film and I can't remember whether Tom had it sent or the Dad had it sent or the Coach was sending it out. There was a promotional tape of Tom Brady throwing 50 balls and throwing every kind of angle there was, side-arm, overhead, long ones, short ones, in-between ones. I remember looking at them and going "Yeah, I like this guy!" So I showed the film to Kit Cartwright, who was the **QUARTERBACK*** coach at the time and Kit said "Yeah, this man, he can do it." Then we showed it to Head Coach Gary Moeller and he OK'd it and said "Yep, let's go recruit this gentleman." Then I had a chance to go over to the Serra High School and met the coach and met Tom and made a home visit. Then Moeller and Cartwright went out there and they followed up after I had met the family and talked to Tom. Then they went out there and said, "Hey you know, we're interested." You've got the quarterback coach and you've got the head coach and you're sitting down there, and we got rid of the recruiting coach now, because he just spots the talent. Right now we've got to go out there and figure out a way to

***A QUARTERBACK needs seven seconds to call an audible and to make sure his teammates heard him.**

get this man to come. So then you send the artillery in there, so to speak.

The thing that you notice about him when you first start talking to him on the phone was that he had confidence in his ability. You say, "Hey, Tom, you come to Michigan and there's going to be some competition at quarterback." And he said "Hey, coach, I'm looking for competition. I'm not shying away. I would never not go to a place just because there's competition." You talk to his Dad and you tell him the same thing because you don't want him to come out there and think things are going to be easy. His Dad would say, "Hey, Tommy's known competition all his life. He had to go out there and prove himself every day." So that was the thing that got me excited because bringing anybody from California, it's a long walk home and you don't want them to get here and turn around and go home. The competition is the first thing that scares you and being away from home. I was just excited to hear that he was up for that challenge.

Bring a player all the way from California, the first thing that's important is that they think that they can play and that they can play early because you don't travel that far away from home to sit on the bench. So, that's where the confidence comes from the young man and the family saying, "We're going to send him that far, but he wants to go there so he can play." That is the key. I recruited Amani Toomer and that was the key with him, "hey, I'm coming in and I'm gonna play." Any of those kids that you bring from a long distance, they gotta have the ability and they've got to have the thought that "yes, I'm going to play and I'm going to play right away."

Playing at a high school like Serra really helped him. The guys who have graduated from there are some pretty prominent athletes like Lynn Swann and Barry Bonds. The competition of having athletes like that around... Tommy was a baseball player too, so he got drafted by Montreal. When I was out there recruiting him and then after he had signed, I think Montreal was in town to play San Francisco and he took batting practice at Candlestick Park. His Mom and Dad and sisters and myself, we all went down to watch the game, watch him hit and it was kind of neat to see him out there hitting balls. I didn't see any go out of the stadium like he told me he was going to put some out of there, but he did hit that ball pretty hard though.

I remember talking to him about coming to Michigan. I said I'm going to call you back in the middle of the week and let me know what you want to do. I called him and got him on the phone and we were talking and I just said "what do you think?" and he said, "Coach, I'm coming to Michigan. I'm going to be a Michigan Man. I'm going to come out there and play quarterback for you." He was all like, I'm ready to go, and then once he had made up his mind, he was saying the right things, the things I wanted to hear, that "yes, I want to come out there and play."

I had taken the job at Stanford before Tom came onto campus, so I called up his Dad and told him, "Say, listen, I've got some good news and I've got some bad news." He said, well hit me with the bad news. I said, "The bad news is that I left Michigan. The good news is that I'm right in your neighborhood in San Mateo, right here at Stanford, so I'll be able to see the family and root with you for Tom." After I went to Stanford, a short time later, Moeller got into trouble and he left. Brady goes to school in the fall and all the people that had a hand in bringing him to Michigan, they slowly all left there. I left, and then Moeller left, and Kit Cartwright left, so all the people that were recruiting him hard and knew him the best and had had conversations with him in having him come to Michigan, in a year's time, they're all gone. You bond with those people and so if you have a problem or if you're feeling down, or if you're feeling homesick, those are the first people you're going to go to. You've had a chance to get to know them and they got to know you. If you're walking around campus and if you knew Tom, if he didn't have a smile on his face, you knew something was up. This man is always smiling. I think that bothered him some, early, when he didn't have the early success and all the people that he got to know before he got there weren't there to lean on, so to speak.

We got a chance to talk after I left Michigan and I went over to the house and had dinner with Mom and Dad and the family. Plus Tommy and his Dad and myself, we went golfing a couple of times. So we got a chance to talk about the process, how it was going to unfold, what was going to happen. I told him I was going to be there for him cause I'm going to be here. So every time he would come home in the vacation periods, after the Bowl games, or in the summertime when he came, we'd get together, him and his Dad and I. We'd always go golfing and we'd talk about Michigan. We'd talk about if he had any problems, what's the best way to go about solving these things. I remember one time he was talking about the competition and I remember Freddy Jackson was telling me, "Hey, this Brady, he's going to be right up there. He's going to be competing." I'm sure they were telling him that and then all of a sudden I think he ended up like third—I think it was Dreisbach, Griese, and then Brady. He thought he was going to be somewhere up there, number two, and didn't quite make it there, but it turned out that he stuck around and did well by anybody who was watching him.

"Hey, this Brady, he's going to be right up there. He's going to be competing."

I was able to become closer friends with the Bradys, being at Stanford, than I probably would have been able to, being at Michigan. I just remember that first year that Tom was on campus and I had come back before Thanksgiving. Michigan played Ohio State that weekend. So we had flown back to watch the game. We had a reception at the Spaghetti Bender and invited Tom and his Mom and Dad plus a couple of other people that had come to the game. So we got a chance to see him. Because I was away from it, then when we got together, he could talk about the program, talk about how he felt and the family felt about what was going on and how tough it was on him at first. But it worked out pretty well.

We stayed in touch when we moved back to Michigan. My wife e-mails them often. It was really funny because she e-mailed big Tom and said "it's great to see what Tom is doing. We talk about him just like family." Big Tom e-mailed her back and said, "What do you mean. You are family." Really makes you feel good. These people are something special.

The thing that made Tom successful in Michigan and carry that into what he's done the past year is that he's got a lot of confidence in himself. I remember talking to him his rookie year. In an the exhibition game the Lions had hosted New England and Tom had engineered a last minute drive for a touchdown. After the game I saw him and gave him a big hug and asked him how things were going. I said to him, "Tom, I am just so glad that you got drafted by New England. Bledsoe's the same kind of quarterback you are that drop back, throw the ball, there's going to be a lot you can learn from Bledsoe." And he looked at me and said, "Coach, I got a lot to teach Bledsoe, too." So I'm talking about some confidence. That's the kind of person he is. He believes in himself and here he was just a rookie. This was like the first year, but he believed that not only could he learn something from Bledsoe but that he could teach Bledsoe something about the game as well. I think he showed that he could teach anybody a little bit about the game.

He was calm and cool and had many fourth quarter comebacks at Michigan. I think growing up, watching those Joe Montanas out there in the Bay would get anybody who's a quarterback to feeling that "this is how I want to be." And if you remember Joe Montana leading people in the fourth quarter, the comebacks, as well as Elway down there in Denver, but on the West Coast he had Montana to emulate, a guy that said under pressure, "be calm, do what you know what to do and lead the team to victory." I think Tom grew up watching Joe play and perform down there and he saw himself as the same kind of player.

Everybody would have to be surprised about the Super Bowl, except for Tom. If you knew Tom, like I said, what he had to say early in his career about learning from Bledsoe and him teaching Bledsoe a thing or two. For him it was just a case of "hey, give me an opportunity." For the rest of us we're happy for him and glad that he had the success, but to have it come that early, I was definitely surprised. As a coach you know that certain kids have a lot of talent and they've got a lot of things in them, but when you do something special like that, it takes a lot of individuals around you, but it takes the kind of person like Tom to have people trust him and trust in his ability. He gives you that confidence by going out there and working hard and doing the things he's supposed to do.

The one memory that I'll always have about Tom Brady would be when we came back and got a chance to see him play the last game against Ohio State. He did the thing, bringing them back for the big win and seeing him out there in front of Crisler Arena when everybody else was gone, he had all these little kids around him and asking for his autograph. And there's Tom, just standing like the average guy, sitting around there saying "I'm going to stay here until they're all gone because I know that if I was a little kid and I was trying to get that autograph, I'd hope that they'd stick around and give it to me." He is a special young man. In the last game, his Mom is there, his Dad, sisters, everybody, and to have him sit there and give those kids the autograph and the time. I remember standing there saying, "Tom, I know this is the last time so I've got to get my picture, too." So we stood there side by side, got that picture, smiling. So that's a special memory for me.

YOU CAN'T GO TO HEAVEN UNLESS YOU'RE A WOLVERINE

SCOT LOEFFLER

When Tom Brady hit the Michigan campus the one quarterback he was worried most about was Scot Loeffler, a former "Mr. Football" in Ohio prep ranks. But Loeffler suffered a severe shoulder injury that ended his career while three of his understudies went on to become NFL QB's. He is now the quarterback coach at Florida.

I watched Tommy in Freshman Camp. Obviously we were getting ready for training camp and I came in a few days early. Just watching him out there was...there was something about him even when he was a Freshman. "This guy's gonna have a chance some day."

He had natural leadership skills. He had all the quarterback intangibles. It's just that the physical skills weren't there at the time. When you first met him, I don't know what "it" is but he had "it".

He had "bad ass" hair. He had that California surfer hair.

Tom was afraid of everybody on the staff, all the quarterbacks. I was the one he was most afraid about before I was injured. Back then I knew my physical skills were gone. He had no reason to worry about me to say the least, but I felt an obligation. It's been a tradition around here that all the quarterbacks have helped younger guys. I knew my physical skills were done and I looked forward to working with him.

We have very similar personalities and we instantly hit it off—like two peas in a pod.

Tom was an overachiever. He had the ability, not only to make himself better, but he made everyone else around him better. He had natural leadership skills. He still has natural leadership skills and he's a perfectionist.

It's been tradition around here ever since we walked in the door, Brian Griese and I, that regardless of where you're at on the depth chart, you have to learn to prepare as if you were going to be the starting quarterback. So Brian basically came in and in his Freshman year he prepared like he was going to be the starter. I prepared so that when the opportunity arises, you're not going to have to prepare another guy. We passed that along to Tom. And Tom Brady, when he walked in here as a Freshman and he was the fourth string quarterback, prepared as if he was going to play on Saturday as a Freshman.

Tom is extremely inner-arrogant. You would never know his confidence, but he believes that he can't be stopped and that it is definitely one of his biggest intangibles that he uses to be successful. He comes to the line of scrimmage just wondering which receiver is going to get his next completion because he's a positive thinker, he's a guy that has no negative thoughts and it's one of the reasons why he's where he's at. It's because of how confident he is. The reason he's confident is because of his preparation. If you're prepared, there's no reason not to be confident.

Tom, in practice, was exactly like he was on game day. No difference. You've got to be a State Street (practice field) quarterback before you become a Stadium quarterback. There's not one thing different that he did in the game compared to practice. He was so good in practice that all game day really was was an extension of practice except with fans.

Tom is a solid guy. He was never a practical joke guy. He had a way. He was always intense. He had a way to motivate guys, yet not make it look as if he was their boss, but he could get people around him to do things to make them better. He would do impressions of Tony Montana from that movie *Scarface*, but he was terrible, absolutely horrible.

The competition between Brian and Tom before the 1997 season was probably just as competitive as the Drew Henson, Tommy Brady comparison, except it didn't get media attention. That's exactly what happened. But it was unbelievable and that's partly the reason why Brian was as successful as he was, is because he had a young guy that was sharp, had a strong arm, was intelligent, knew the game, that was pushing him every day. That's going to be Michigan football at the quarterback position forever here. It's going to be a constant fierce competitive atmosphere. However, they were very mature in how to handle them so that they wanted to see each other be successful.

We always talked about, visualize in yourself, doing great things and that's why he went down to Notre Dame and snuck into the stadium. He's not the first player that has done that.

Between him and Brian, I've never seen better huddle presence. He had the ability...we have a quote around here... "quarterback must believe in himself. His work must convince his teammates that he can be trusted when all else fails." When he walked in that huddle, ten guys, 20 eyeballs, were looking at him and they knew that he was going to get it done. And that didn't happen overnight. Guys watched him struggle, guys watched him have to fight through adversity, and they believed in him. Through every single thing he did here at Michigan from his work ethic to fighting through adversity, his teammates bought into him.

Tom is confident and he's cool and he was always confident. There wasn't a time that he didn't believe that he wasn't going to get it done. It is amazing during the week he would visualize himself having to come back against Ohio State to win the game, to come back versus Notre Dame. So that was all based on preparation. He was prepared. He was confident and he never panicked, ever. He was a winner.

Thinking back on the Penn State game, it was funny, we got into the stadium the night before the game and I picked the wrong end zone. I go to Tommy, "You've got to prepare yourself if you're going to have to throw a touchdown pass in the back corner to win the game." It was the wrong end zone. It was actually the south side where he did, but he did take command that week. He put himself in some bad situations early in the game and he was able to keep his poise and his confidence to lead the team back, but his preparation, his confidence, is the reason why he's where he's at. We had a special play where he had to fake an injury. He practiced the limp off the field, that was Coach Carr's idea, which was pretty neat. Kap was laughing the whole time because he was faking it. Kapsner was laughing his rear end off. I will never forget it. Kapsner was a signaler that year and we could hear him on the headphones laughing. He was hysterical. Tom's not going to be an actor.

Thinking about his last home game, I remember he said on Thursday, "I can't believe this is my last game", cause Friday is the day that we do the Seniors for the last time practice. He was real emotional and couldn't believe that this was his last opportunity to play at Michigan Stadium. I remember sitting in the room with him on Friday night at the Hotel. It was past curfew actually. I snuck up there and we sat and talked for about a good two hours, just reflecting back on everything from him walking in as a Freshman, not knowing a darn thing to thinking about transferring, Drew Henson, to the Brian Griese battle, and it was just a great night sitting back and talking about his career. I'll never forget that. He left the room and was just like normal. "Hey I'm gonna go and beat Ohio State tomorrow." Confident, cool and calm.

We had a special play where he had to fake an injury.

We just talked about him and about Michigan and about how much he loved Michigan and it was a great evening.

Tom is a student of the game, just like I am. He's an offensive coordinator out there playing quarterback. He knows the game, he knows what beats what coverages. He would come in every Monday with his own game plan, which is beautiful. His preparation was unbelievable in the fact that after he came up with his game plan, he would be in here until 11:00, 11:30 at night. He was the last one to leave the building, watching film. Every Thursday and every Monday he had his talks about Tom Brady's game plan. It was kind of comical...but look who's laughing now.

In regard to Tom's volunteerism, the Mott's Children's Hospital sticks out probably the most. I believe it started back here with I think Juwan Howard, I want to say, was one of the first ones to start doing it. It was passed to the quarterbacks and Brian and I really hit it hard and then Tommy followed in the footsteps. But Tommy did a lot of big things with the Mott's Children's Hospital.

What happened to Tom Brady during his first Super Bowl didn't shock me one bit. The only thing that shocked me is about how fast it happened. I didn't believe that Tom Brady's second year in the NFL, that he'd be winning the Super Bowl. The type of person he is, the type of overachiever he is, I knew it would happen, I just didn't know that it would be Year Two in the **NFL***.

My best Tom Brady memory would probably be that night in the hotel. The Friday night in the hotel before the Ohio State game. Just the conversation that we had about quarterbacks, about quarterback play, about Michigan, about himself, about our relationship. It was a night that I will never forget. It was great conversation.

The one word I would use to describe Tom Brady is genuine.

***The NFL halftime is eight minutes shorter than in college football.**

TOM BRADY IS JUST A REGULAR GUY WHO SOMETIMES WEARS A CAPE

JASON KAPSNER

Jason Kapsner met sophomore Tom Brady during his first day on the Ann Arbor campus. The teammates soon grew to be close friends as they worked, studied and played together.

Tom and I were instant friends. With him being a year older, he could have been kind of an jerk, but he was really cool. When I first got there, he was very friendly and very welcoming. Coming into the quarterback crew, he gave me the inside scoop on how to handle, how to act, what coach likes, what coach doesn't like, how to handle Griese and Dreisbach and these guys. He kinda showed me the ropes initially.

I came to school early. My first day on campus, there were three of us, Lefty (Scot Loeffler), Tom and me, and we just worked out every day in the summer. Lefty was, for all practical purposes, our coach. I don't think Stan Parish, our quarterbacks coach, would like to hear that, but...Tom and I would get together and go out with Lefty at five o'clock and go through about an hour's workout. From there, we'd go out to dinner and hang out the rest of the night. That was kind of our daily routine. We get along very, very well.

When I first met Tom, I was very impressed by his demeanor, the way he carried himself. I particularly liked the way he interacted with the other teammates. The guys just had a lot of respect for him. Tom's always been the kind of guy that's fun to be around. He's just a fun, charismatic kind of guy to be around.

Probably more than anyone I've ever known in football, Tom exuded just an absolute passion and love for football, and also for the concept of 'team.' That really came through very strong with the team and that really drew in everyone across the board, regardless of your class, your race, and all that kind of stuff. Aside from personality, I think Tom just drew guys in purely because of his love for the team and the guys and for football. No one wanted to win more than he did. That just really showed through in workouts—seven on seven—all those kinds of drills. He just commanded a lot of respect because of that passion he had.

I lived with Lefty for a summer so the three of us would get together and go out at night. We went to parties or just would hang out and watch TV or we would play golf together. Tom was always pretty smooth with the ladies. But he wasn't up for commitment, that's for sure. He always had plenty of ladies liking him—probably not the stature he has with them now!

Another off-the-field thing we did sophomore year was I went with Tom once on spring break back to his family in San Mateo. That was an absolutely great trip. His family is just amazing. You hear all these things about how nice his family is and it's extremely true. His mom and dad are just the most generous, loving people as I've known. They're an amazing family. His sisters are all really cool and very fun. It was one of the best spring breaks you could have to go and spend some time with his family.

Tom is extremely Catholic and I know that his **FAITH*** is very important to him, but we never really did a lot there together.

Tom and I always roomed together before games. We always had more and deeper conversations, away from just football and girls and stuff like that. One time we were sitting at the hotel getting ready for the **INDIANA*** game, an away game. We were in the middle of nowhere Indiana. This was in the midst

***There are many times more sportswriters than there are RELIGIOUS reporters.**

***By winning percentage, INDIANA ranks 12th in all-time Big 10 football standings behind the University of Chicago.**

of the Drew Henson rotation and some strange things were going on in the quarterbacking ranks to say the least. We definitely always leaned on each other when we had some football struggles or football issues. We sat and reflected about what we think this kind of experience may mean to us and how it's going to affect us as we go on through life. Some things are extremely hard about football—particularly football at Michigan. We felt it would give us a very good base to work from and how to deal with some of the issues that you deal with coming from a tough program. I'm thankful for the program because it really mentally prepares you for the real world. So Tom and I had a real heart-to-heart one night just discussing that. Kind of how we really feel this is going to put us that far ahead when we get out into the regular world—the real world. We should be better able to deal with tough issues. When you're playing college football, you can say, "Well, it's football." But when you're going through it, that stuff seems pretty real. Now looking at that, and as I think back to some of those conversations we had, and I look at the success Tom is having, a lot of it, I feel like, is due to some of the hardships then. He had dealt with some of the battles he had to go through mentally and struggle to get over. I think the football tradition at Michigan, the coaching style that our team had really prepared him and us to face the situations we are currently under. That's one of the reasons why I think Tom is one of the best leaders I've ever seen. He had to face adversity early on.

The expectation on the Michigan quarterback is to be the best leader on the field—to be the general—you have to be. You look at every good quarterback that we've had and he is the leader on the field. That's a role that I really believe to a large part cannot be taught. Some guys just naturally have it to a degree and some guys don't have it. That's one thing that Tom was able to just step in and he was a natural leader, as natural as they come. I think that his leadership stems from just a pure passion for the game and a love for it. The expectation is that you're the first at all drills, you're the first to be in the morning working out, the hardest working guy out there. When other guys are relaxing and not really working, be the first to get on them and get them going—and be able to do that in a way where you don't aggravate people. Tom was able to do that. He was able to motivate guys in a positive and encouraging way to get the most out of them. I think that definitely shows through. If you look at all the games we played where maybe we're down or tied with two minutes left in the game, during Tom's couple of years of playing, I think we won ninety percent of those games. I attribute that ninety percent to Tom and in the ability that he had to move the team in those critical, crucial times.

I don't really think Tom was ever trying to get his confidence to rub off on other players, but it's an unexplainable thing—part leadership and part confidence. Tom's confidence just came from—the kind of confidence that he has at that level is just purely a natural thing where he just knows that he's the best and that he's gonna get it done just because he is so passionate about getting it done and getting that win. I think that kind of natural passion and confidence just exudes out to a team. He's the kind of guy when you sit and watch him in the huddle, he comes into the huddle and gives the play and all these little intangible things, but you look in his eyes and the tone of his voice and the way he's looking at the guys. That's what inspires a team. They don't want to see a guy that's walking into the huddle, gives the play in a very mundane voice maybe. Tom stood up and would get in there excited. He'd go in the huddle and if he saw a guy was tired, he'd talk to him, not in a mean way, but just, "Come on. Get yourself up. There's a big play here." Just something to single that guy out and let him know, "Hey, you've got to carry your weight."

I guess to go back to the 'Why was Tom confident?' In a large part it had to do with his preparation. No one I know sat and watched more film and knew what the other team was going to do more than Tom did. Tom went well far beyond what the expectation would be from even the coaches as far as watching film. The thing about Tom is he knew exactly what that defense was gonna do on every play. He'd come out of the game and he'd be able to tell what he had seen as far as the defense and their blitzes and what they were doing, and on the film that would be exactly what you saw. His preparation was unbelievable, and I think that's probably really what's carried it over, part of that work ethic. He prepares himself better than anyone I've ever seen for a game, which allows him to have the confidence to go out there and succeed. I think Tom is definitely not the best athlete out there. I think Tom would probably say that, too. He's not a Michael Vick. He's not the fastest guy out there, but he is the smartest guy out there. I would put Tom's leadership ability and his intelligence of this game up against anyone in the NFL, anyone in this game right now. I would be extremely confident that he would win out on that.

Tom was always goofing around to a degree. Griese does this impersonation of Al Pacino in *Scarface* as Tony Montana. Tom would always try to do the impersonation and he was just brutal. He didn't give it up though. He kept trying and trying. It was almost funny in how bad of a Tony Montana he does.

Tom was a laid-back California kid as soon as he got off the field. But as soon as he got on the field, he was yelling, hollering—sometimes the guys on the team would laugh at him—it seemed so kind of cheesy at times. He would be jumping up and down and screaming at the top of his lungs and guys would go, "Hey, man, it's just practice." That was just his natural expression, even though some of guys may have thought it was kind of cheesy and dorky for him to get that excited, but he was extremely intense during practice. He was a great practice quarterback. There was no joking around as soon as you got on the field.

I thought it was hilarious because, and this could be the middle of a game—say the Ohio State game, fourth quarter, if they sent in a play he didn't like, he'd roll his eyes and just be so mad. He'd come off the field and just be like, "Well, that was a great call." He was definitely not happy with some of the calls they got in, but it was really funny to see him just roll his eyes at plays that would come in. He would also even signal plays to me on the sidelines sometimes that he wanted to get in. I'd relay it up to DeBord (offensive coordinator), and he'd go, "Oh, okay." He'd often put it in, but sometimes not. If he didn't, Tom was upset. He felt that as the quarterback out there, you could sometimes get a real good feel for what's gonna work. So Tom got frustrated when that wasn't listened to, to a degree.

> He was a great practice quarterback. There was no joking around...

Tom always gave his talks, not necessarily after games, in practice or after practice. It's a long season, and there are days where you just go out there and guys don't want to practice, and you have bad practices. During those kinds of practices, normally Coach Carr has to get on the team and give it to them. I think more often, it would be Tom. If we didn't practice well, Tom was the one who was more hurt and aggravated by that, and he made a very strong point of saying, "Tomorrow, this is not going to be the way it works. We're going to come out there and practice." So he'd get on the team to a degree. What gave him the license to do that is because he didn't take days off. He worked hard. He worked the hardest of anyone. He took the captainship very serious.

With Tom it's kind of like a switch that goes on in these games where he just knew—me knowing Tom and being on the team—you just knew that in these games there was no way we're gonna lose. I think that's why the team had that confidence. I really do believe this because they knew they had Tom out there. Tom seemed to have a switch that would absolutely turn on in those stretches. The higher those stakes got, the better Tom got. In these last second types of games, all the play calling would be passes for the most part. You're going down.

You're really putting the game in your quarterback's hands. At that point, it was like a switch when Tom knew they were going to put the game in his hands. There's just this look on the guy's face that you just knew this was getting done and you were gonna win. There's no way you're not going to. That's why I can say probably, geez it would be interesting to see, that in those situations I'll bet we won ninety percent of our games when Tom was playing. You take those situations and compare with other quarterbacks that we've had over twenty years or something like that, and I'd be just surprised if Tom was not at the top and then probably Griese number two.

He was telling me about the time he got locked in **NOTRE DAME*** Stadium. He said he was freaked out. I think he tore his pants. He had to jump and climb out of the stadium. If I recall it right, I think he had the security guard chasing him around in the stadium. There was a gate that was unlocked and he just went through it. He was trying to get back out, and then the lock was on. It was like, "How am I going to get out of this place?" It was night. That's the kind of thing he did. He went down there and just sat and wanted to see that field and probably picture winning that game there, which unfortunately we didn't. That's the kind of intensity he had and, I think, the dreams that he had for that team.

The quarterback situation back then was definitely tough on Tom. We had many talks like that where Tom just had to say, "What more does a guy have to do to prove himself?" I had no idea. It's one of those things where you look at life and you kind of understand that it's not always fair. That's the point that we got to in saying, "Well, life's not always fair, but you've got to keep going. You've got to keep working hard." I think that's what Tom really did. It was not to say it was easy at all for him. It was very hard. This is the kind of stress that you didn't need to have

***Johnny Lattner, the 1953 Heisman Trophy winner from NOTRE DAME, didn't lead the Irish in rushing or receiving that season.**

or want to have at that point—and that he didn't deserve to have, but I think that really strengthened him and it has really prepared him for what he is doing now.

In our last three games of his senior season, all were come-from-behind games, there was that switch I was talking about that just came on. I don't remember specific details of it, but I just remember that Tom grew into this unbelievable leader during those times—just unbelievable. I know he's been compared to every great quarterback—the Montanas of the world— that's ever been out there, but there's a reason for that. It's just because of this type of switch that he can turn on during that time. I think the thing that separates him is that he never would ever consider the game that we could lose. That thought just would never go through his head. I remember that the touchdown to Marquise Walker—I think it was a backside post route—Tom just read the defense and made a great play. I think a lot of that comes from the preparation. He knew what they were going to do. He knew he had a backside read and took it. A lot of times what we're coached to do Tom would not do. He would take some gambles on a bigger throw, but they're calculated in the sense of that's what the defense was giving him but maybe sometimes that's not what the coaches wanted to see out of it—they didn't call the play to have what Tom was throwing. There's a lot of risk there. Not only is there a risk of having an incomplete pass or having something bad happen on the play, but there's also the risk that if it doesn't work out the way you wanted, now all of a sudden you've got the coaches to answer to, too. So there's kind of a double risk there when you start doing some things in that play that the coaches don't want you to do.

I do remember that in the '99 Penn State game, Tom went off the field with a limp. He had practiced that all week and would just come off the field laughing. There were actual 'acting classes' on the practice field for that particular play. When he was walking off the field, even during the Penn State game, I couldn't stop laughing. It was so funny.

I think in our last game against Ohio State, Tom was the one who just took over as far as play calling. He was just telling me every play he wanted during that game. He was demanding it. You could see him on the field, and he was getting that—his face was like, "You'd better get this play in." I think DeBord probably sensed that too at halftime when they talked. That game was one where Tom not only took over physically being the quarterback but even was demanding plays that he wanted to be called.

That Orange Bowl game against a very good Alabama team was amazing. I've never seen anyone 'on' like that. That was pretty impressive. For Michigan to come back from two fourteen-point deficits in one game is unheard of. Michigan has never been seen as the total come-back team. Michigan usually gets ahead and lets their defense win games, but Tom just found a way to reverse that.

I think what I remember from that game is the night before. Before games, Tom and I would always sit and relax and talk. We always had these pretty serious discussions. This was the last game of both of our careers. We were sitting there reflecting on it and it was just a real emotional time for both of us. This was more at a level of just being human—not football players, but just being humans. We talked about that the night before—just moving on and what we were gonna do and the experiences that we have had. The emotions came out after the game was over. It was such an amazing game. After the end of the game, Tom came over to me and grabbed me, and we gave each other a hug. He just said to me, "I've loved the time I've spent here with you." He thanked me. We just had a lot of respect for each other. That kind of peaked at that moment. Knowing that was the way we ended our time as Michigan football players—just the fact that you can do it in that type of fashion is unbelievable.

That Orange Bowl game would definitely be the one memory I'll always have. It was such a special time for us, such a special moment for me as well. That overtime portion of it with just the feeling like 'you're not really living this, it's so unbelievable, almost surreal,' and experiencing that was what will really stick out in my mind.

What will always be a special off-the-field memory would have to just be our friendship. Just spending summers with him. At the golf course. Going to work at Merrill Lynch. Working out. Hanging out at night. Just being best of friends in a lot of ways. I know Tom, to me, he made my Michigan experience, my college experience, that much better. Just because we had such a good friendship. Most of all that I remember from Tom is not really the football, it's more the kind of guy I think he is, and friend that he is. Even to this day. He hasn't changed at all even with the success he's had, and I think that's really rare. That's what I'll remember the most about Tom.

He hasn't changed at all even with the success he's had, and I think that's really rare.

Tom was a great student. We had the same major and took a lot of the same classes. Tom was a very good student, very diligent. Academics definitely mattered to him. I think he graduated with a grade point of 3.3 or 3.2. It was important to him to take good courses, not just get by, but take some business courses. He really loved business. We had our internships at Merrill Lynch, and we really loved talking about all that stuff. He was a very serious student. It was important for him to get his work done, get his papers done. He worked hard at that.

We were very competitive. He was competitive about his grades, too. He would write a paper, and if he got a bad grade, or a teacher kinda ripped on it, or made some comments he didn't like, it would really irritate him. I can even remember him getting a little upset about some **GRADES*** he got if it wasn't what he wanted.

I saw Tom last summer in Portland at Lefty's wedding. We just had a great time. That was the last time I saw him, but we talked every couple of months or so. The thing that impressed me was I talked to him a couple of weeks ago, and it was the first time since the Super Bowl. I was talking to him about, "What have you been doing?" It was great to hear that it was still the same Tom. He said, "There's some great things about this, but there's also some crappy things about having success." He said everybody was treating him differently, and the fact that he can't go out anymore. He was like, "Kap, it's just me. I'm the same guy. Cool things have happened to me, but I'm still the same guy. I just wish it didn't have to be like this all the time." He called me, and with his busy schedule and everything like that, it was cool to see that he still remembers us little people.

This year he got a chance, and he succeeded. I think that's why he won't be a 'one-hit wonder.'

Later when he's done with football, I would love to start some kind of business with him, such as owning our own golf course so we could play. That would be really fun. That's my dream.

It was extremely ironic to see those two former Michigan teammates, Charles Woodson of Oakland, and Tom Brady come to that situation where two Michigan guys are deciding who's gonna go to the Super Bowl. It doesn't surprise me at all. It's almost like in a lot of ways, God has designed that he is the 'Comeback Kid.' Even when calls go in his favor that probably shouldn't go that way, it's pretty incredible. It's pretty ironic that the end of Charles' season kept Tom going.

***ACADEMIC All-American teams have been picked every year since 1952. Nebraska leads all colleges by a wide margin in number of players selected.**

I was sitting watching the Super Bowl with my friends. Everyone was like, "Why doesn't he just take a knee and end regulation." I said, "Watch this. I will **BET*** anyone in this room that they will win this game here. I will bet any one of you that he will drive them down and if not win it, give them a chance on a field goal to win this thing." Everyone was like, "Oh, give me a break. Come on." And he did it. It did not surprise me at all. I'll lay that bet down every time for the rest of his career when he's in that situation. I think I'll win ninety percent of those.

> I'll lay that bet down every time for the rest of his career when he's in that situation.

One or two words that I would use to describe Tom Brady would be 'class' and 'love for people.' Tom is a genuinely great guy. There are people you meet who are more of a fake thing, but Tom is just extremely classy, extremely genuine, and just has a great love for people.

***In most states, sports BETTING pools are legal as long as "the house"—or person running the pool—doesn't benefit.**

THE POISE THAT REFRESHES

MIKE DEBORD

When Tom Brady appeared on the Michigan campus in the Fall of 1995, he met Mike DeBord who became a vital factor in his collegiate career. DeBord was the Offensive Line and Tight Ends Coach before being promoted to Offensive Coordinator in 1997, the season the Wolverines won the National Title.

When I first saw Tom Brady back in the Fall of '95, he had California attire on, he had a California haircut. I don't know what you'd call the haircut, but it was definitely from the West Coast, it wasn't from the Midwest. You could tell he was a kid from California that was coming into the Midwest.

I don't know if a lot of people know this, but before the 1997 season, it was as close of a run at quarterback between Brian Griese and him that I think you could ever expect. Probably in some ways we could have even gone with Tom Brady for that season, but what we relied on more than anything was Griese's experience—he had more game experience and he was older—so we kind of went with that. At that training camp and that spring before we really saw a guy that we all felt was going to be a great quarterback.

After the 1996 season Lloyd Carr talked to him because he was actually considering transferring. After the 1997 season he knew he was going to be the quarterback. I think it was like after the 1996 season when he didn't know if there was any light at the end of the tunnel for him. One thing I really feel good about was Tom and my relationship. It started building when Tom first came and then when I was a position coach, I think we started having a great relationship. And then when I became coordinator, I became a lot closer with the quarterbacks and he befriended me in a lot of things. I feel great about that.

There's no doubt, it started with Griese when he was a quarterback and then when Tom was a quarterback, those guys had great knowledge of football. I mean, great knowledge. Tom would spend as much time studying film as any student athlete could ever do and he did it early. He would come in and he would say, "Hey, Debo, what do you think about these couple of passes." or whatever. And if I felt like they were things that we could really get taught in such a short time and if I felt like they were things that we could put into the game plan, then we put them in, because of his knowledge and what he saw.

The thing that I valued more than anything with Tom was at the end of the week when we would sit down on a Thursday or a Friday after we'd practiced and after the game plan was in and we would sit down and I would say as we went through every situation, "OK, what's your favorite passes?" I would always call his best passes early in the game, just because he knew what was good against what coverages and he also knew what he liked to throw the best. So, I just really trusted Tom Brady a lot.

Tom was outstanding in terms of practice. Tom Brady was a 365-day quarterback. He wasn't an in-season quarterback or he didn't pretend to be a quarterback. He was a quarterback and he had a mentality that every single second that he had available he was going to study quarterback play. I think he really set a standard around there for a guy like John Navarre now and other quarterbacks that were underneath him of how you study the game and how you really put that to work. When he went out to the practice field, he was relentless. He was a guy that was practicing at a fast tempo and he wanted to get a lot of throws in and he wanted to get good looks from the defense so that it would give him a game look.

The game preparation helped at the end of those games and he was just as calm as a cucumber. All the games that Michigan won while Tom Brady was quarterback, and many were won in the fourth quarter. Number one, let's start with Tom Brady's character. He has as great a character as any person I've ever been around. He is the best. I think that he's got the character to fight through tough times. And when you have that, then you can finish. If you don't have any character when you're fighting through the tough times, you're not going to be worth a crap in the fourth quarter, no matter how well prepared you are or whatever. Probably the greatest example that I'll always remember was the Penn State game his senior year. Penn State ran a defense that you never knew what look they were going to be in, you never knew what coverage they were going to be in, and you never knew what blitz they were going to be in. And I mean they blitzed all the time and they kept coming at us and coming at us. Well, early in the game we got after them and we got up. Then we hit a period in the middle of the game where they were blitzing us and changing up coverage and it seemed like they had our number. We won that game in the fourth quarter on a lot of drives that we put together that Tom just went out and executed. It goes back again to me to his character. If a guy didn't have great character, he's going to get rattled. He's going to get frustrated, he's going to have that attitude of "Hey, are we going to do this," instead of "We are going to do this." It goes to his knowledge, his preparation and all that now comes into effect.

In the Penn State game we made him practice limping off the field for the injury just once. We all were laughing as Tom made his way off the field. In fact, I'll be honest, I don't think we told Tom to do that. That was a little bit of Tom's intelligence kicking in there. I don't think we were smart enough to think about that and he was.

Every one of his teammates truly trusted Tom Brady and again, it goes back to the character issue. They trusted him a lot. So

I think that's where it started, was the trust. And then Tom Brady was an outstanding leader. I'll give you an example. In fact, it was in the Penn State week. Penn State had again so many blitzes and coverages and all those things that it was a tough week of preparation. Practice, at one point, on like a Wednesday, wasn't going very good. I didn't think the tempo was going good, I didn't think that certain things were up to the speed that you need for a Wednesday. And Tom was just coming back from a play and I was passing him, and I said, "Brady, you couldn't lead nothing. You are the worst." And he looked at me like he wanted to fight and what he did then was he pulled that team together and he got that team to practice at an up tempo. He got them to practice with a purpose. And I really believe that that game was won on that Wednesday, just by what Tom Brady did as far as leadership on the practice field. And then when they were in drives and things, they knew Tom Brady was going to pull them through the game because of what he displayed in practice all the time and what kind of a person he was. I think there was a great amount of trust by all the players and coaches with him.

We both had the same last game at Michigan—the Orange Bowl game— my last game as a coordinator. I went on to become a head coach and Tom sets all the records. As you recall, in the first half offensively, we didn't do a lot. We tried to go in with our basic philosophy of running the ball and throwing it and controlling the ball and Alabama had a front where they had their linebackers about a yard off the ball, and they were going to make it tough on us running the football. And they really basically said, "Hey, we're going to make you beat us by throwing the ball." And we went in at halftime, we talked, Lloyd and myself, and we talked about "Hey, we're going to have to really come out and we're going to have to throw the football the second half to win this game," a lot more than what we thought game plan-wise because of what Alabama was doing. So, we got with Tom and we went over what throws he liked and what throws we liked and we put them all together and then we just went out and I told Tom that we're going to have to really open it up throw-wise. He obviously smiled and said let's go. And then he took the game over. A lot of people don't know but in some of the passes, it was an either/or type of thing where he could throw one side or he could throw backside to David Terrell when he was one on one. Just Tom Brady's knowledge of "there it is. It's one on one coverage. Let's go ahead and hit the backside guy." And he did that a lot, even in that drive and he showed to me what he's all about as a quarterback. He would dink the ball off when really we could dink the ball off and he put the ball down the field when we had to put the ball down the field. When you go back to watching him in the Super Bowl, go watch the last drive. He did the exact same thing again. He dinked the ball off when he had to dink the ball off and he threw the ball down the field when he had to throw the ball down the field. Tom Brady, to me, is a guy that's bought into the team philosophy. Let's just do what we have to do. I don't have to throw the ball down the field every time to show I'm a great quarterback. If I just do what the defense will allow me to do, we'll win. And Tom's always had that philosophy. He's always taken care of the ball, and he's always played within a team philosophy.

There was a story in *Sports Illustrated* about getting stuck in Notre Dame Stadium. I didn't get to read that story. The season before that 1998 year when he was going to be the starter, he actually went to Notre Dame Stadium and ended up getting locked in and a security guard chased him out and he had to jump over a fence and ripped his pants.

I can't recall any funny stories or anything like that. I just remember he was always very mature and very poised, and really into football. I mean, really into football. Those are the things I remember. I think there's a side of Tom Brady that people that don't know him don't know and that's the side that he really cares about people, he cares about your family, he cares about everything about you. An example of that:

I don't know if it was the 1998 year or the 1999 year but I was on summer vacation and I stopped in at the Dairy Queen in Saline and there was Tom in there getting something, and we started talking. He asked me how my kids were doing, my wife was doing, things like that, and I said "Well, one of my sons is working right over at the hardware store right now, in fact." It was right across the street. And so he said, "Well, Coach, enjoy your vacation and I'll see you in about a week or two." I said, "All right." So we got in our cars and took off. Then the next day I found out that Tom went across the street, went in to the hardware store and then spent some time just talking to my son. That's Tom Brady. I mean Tom Brady is as down to earth as you'd ever want. People worry about all this recognition he's getting with *Sports Illustrated* and what was he, a judge on the Miss USA contest. I think they worry about "will this change Tom Brady?" I'm going to be very, very surprised if it ever does, because of his character. I don't see that every changing him.

People ask me my best Tom Brady memory. I don't know if it will be a memory, but all of the games that he won as a quarterback in the fourth quarter. All the comebacks and just having a feeling when you called a play that it was going to work because of Tom Brady. I think that would be one of the biggest memories. And I think then the last memory was that I told Tom before the Orange Bowl...I said, "Hey Tom, this is your last hurrah at Michigan and mine too. If I was going to go out with a quarterback, you're the quarterback I'd want to go out with." And I meant that. And that's nothing against the guys that were at Michigan before him that I was associated with. That's nothing against them at all. Those are great guys. But, there's something very very special about Tom and I told him that he was the guy that I would want to go out with. And then he exchanged some words back to me that meant a lot to me. It's just a relationship that you have with him, just the friendship.

The one word I would use to describe Tom is character.

EXPERIENCE IS WHAT YOU GET WHEN YOU DON'T GET WHAT YOU WANT

LLOYD CARR

When Jack Harbaugh left Bo Schembechler's staff at Michigan in 1979, his coaching spot was filled with a young Lloyd Carr. Carr unexpectedly was named Wolverine Head Coach in 1995 succeeding Gary Moeller. Waiting on his doorstep was a 17-year-old quarterback from Northern California who didn't know a single person in the state of Michigan.

When I first saw him on campus Tom Brady made a tremendous impression. Here was a handsome, long-haired, sun-tanned California kid…I saw him after the Super Bowl and I was telling Tom that the most prominent thing that I remember about his early career here in Michigan was in the Spring of his Freshman year. We had a scrimmage outside. It was a full scrimmage and our defense blitzed him about six times in ten plays. They had a guy come unblocked and Tom was oblivious to the rush. He just stood in there, threw the ball, got hit right at the moment he released the ball, and never flinched. And every time he got back up and went back in the huddle. My first impression was that, at least on that spring Saturday, this kid had real toughness, real competitive spirit. Then, of course, the next fall he played and his first pass was intercepted for a touchdown. You can imagine that's a quarterback's worst nightmare. Here is his first time as a Michigan quarterback, in front of 110,000 people, and he throws a ball right to the linebacker, right to the guy. Of course, he took a lot of ribbing about that play. And that same fall, at

OLLEGE FOOTBALL PREVIEW!

BONUS
Madden Tips
from
Brady Quinn

Sports Illustrated KIDS

PLUS
BUZZ
meets
BART SIMPSON!

The TOP 10

We Rank the Best of Everything:

Teams • Mascots • Sleepers
Heisman Candidates
and more!

1 MICHIGAN

GO
BLUE!

Mike Hart
ft) and
Chad Henne

August 2007
www.SIKIDS.com

SPECIAL COMMEMORATIVE ISSU

PRESENTS

Michigan Wolverines

CHAMPIONS!

1997

JANUARY 14, 1998 UNTIL 4/13/98

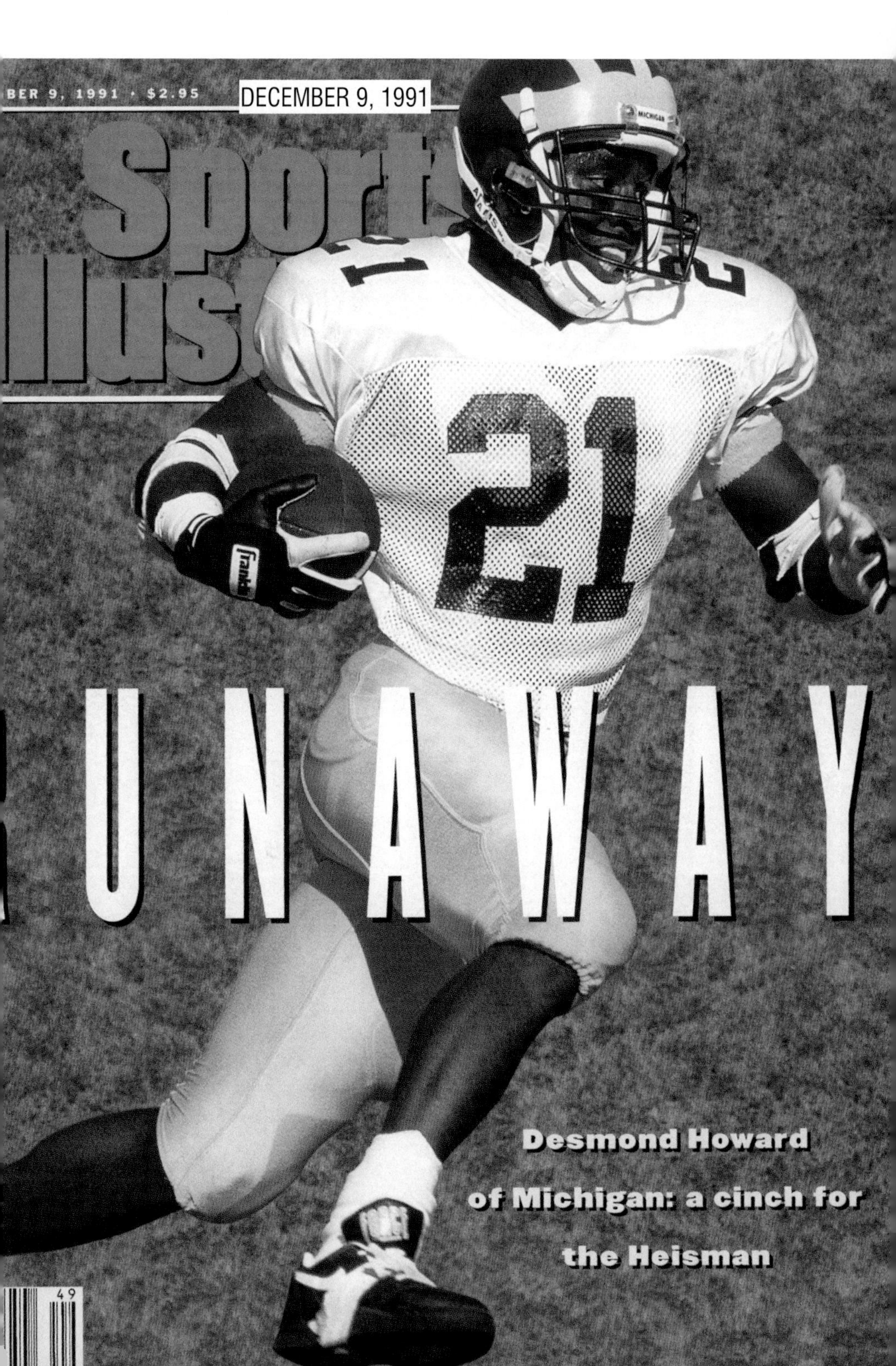
BER 9, 1991 · $2.95
DECEMBER 9, 1991
Sports Illust
RUNAWAY
Desmond Howard
of Michigan: a cinch for
the Heisman

< OKLAHOMA
JASON WHITE

THE BCS RACE FOR THE
NATIONAL CHAMPIONSHIP

USC >
MATT LEINART

Sports Illustrated

MICHIGAN
GETS IT DONE

BY AUSTIN MURPHY

Chris Perry and the Wolverines run over Ohio State

EXCLUSIVE INTERVIEW
TOKYO CALLING: KAZUO MATS
PLUS
NBA: WILL THE WEST RULE FORE

DECEMBER 1, 2003

SPORTS ILLUSTRATED

November 12, 1956

a Time Inc. weekly publication

25 CENTS
$7.50 A YEAR

MAENTZ AND KRAMER
MICHIGAN'S GREAT ENDS
FACE ILLINOIS

FOOTBALL:
SEVENTH WEEK

COLLEGE FOOTBALL ISSUE

Sports Illustrated

$

MICHIGA
IS
NO.

Quarterback Rick Le

®

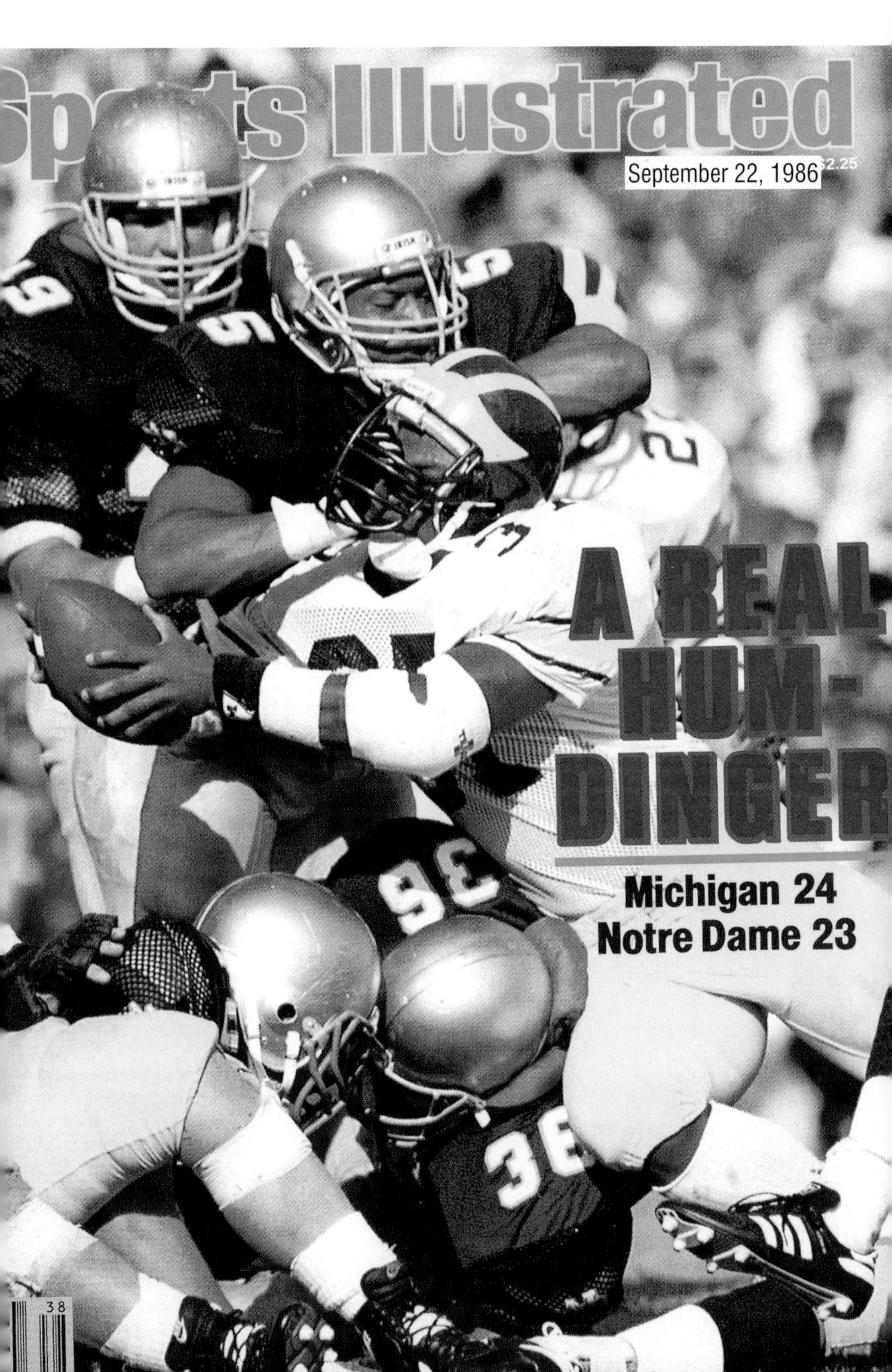
Sports Illustrated
September 22, 1986
$2.25
A REAL HUM-DINGER
Michigan 24
Notre Dame 23
38

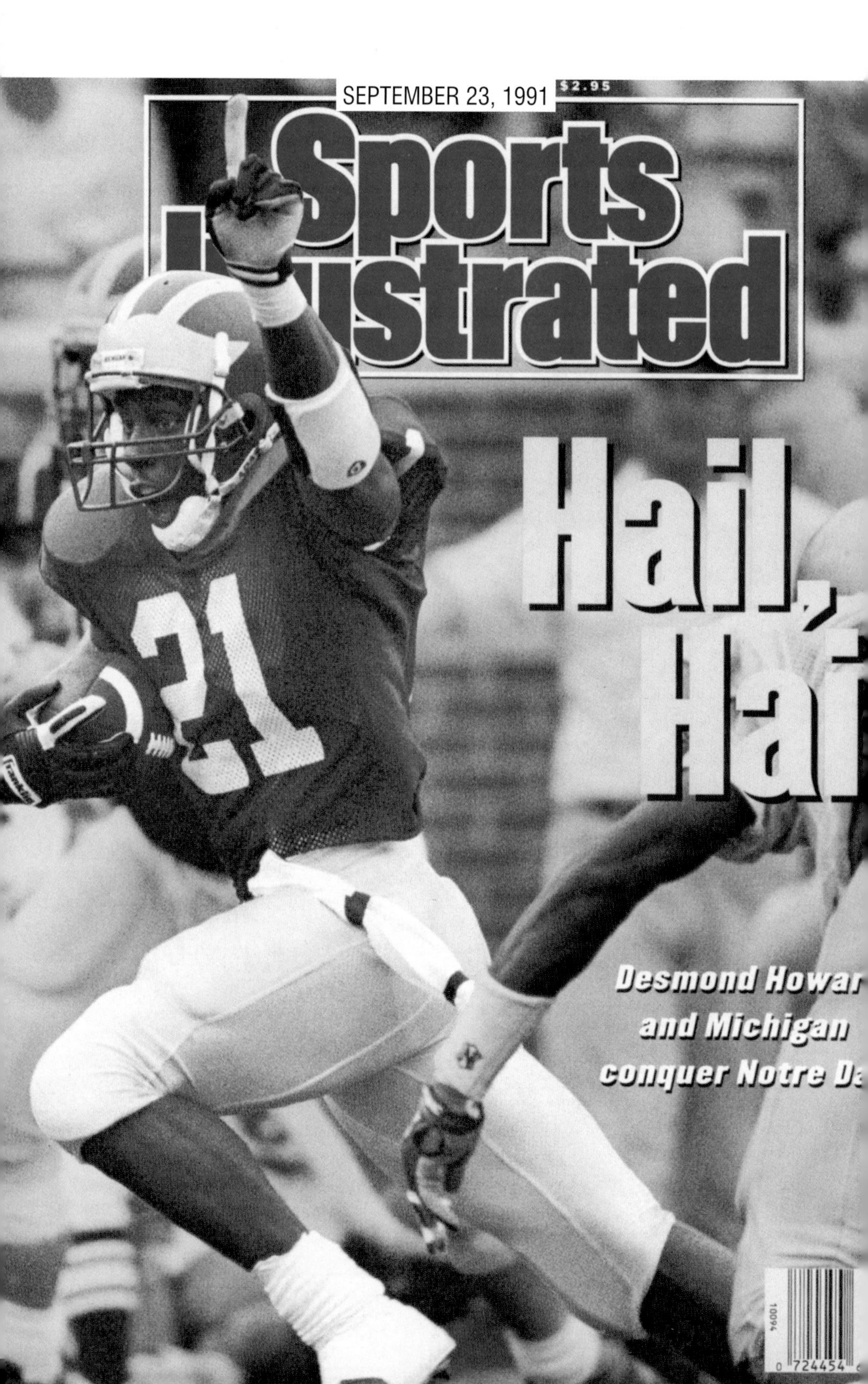
SEPTEMBER 23, 1991
$2.95
Sports Illustrated
Hail, Ha
Desmond Howar
and Michigan
conquer Notre Da
10094
0 724454

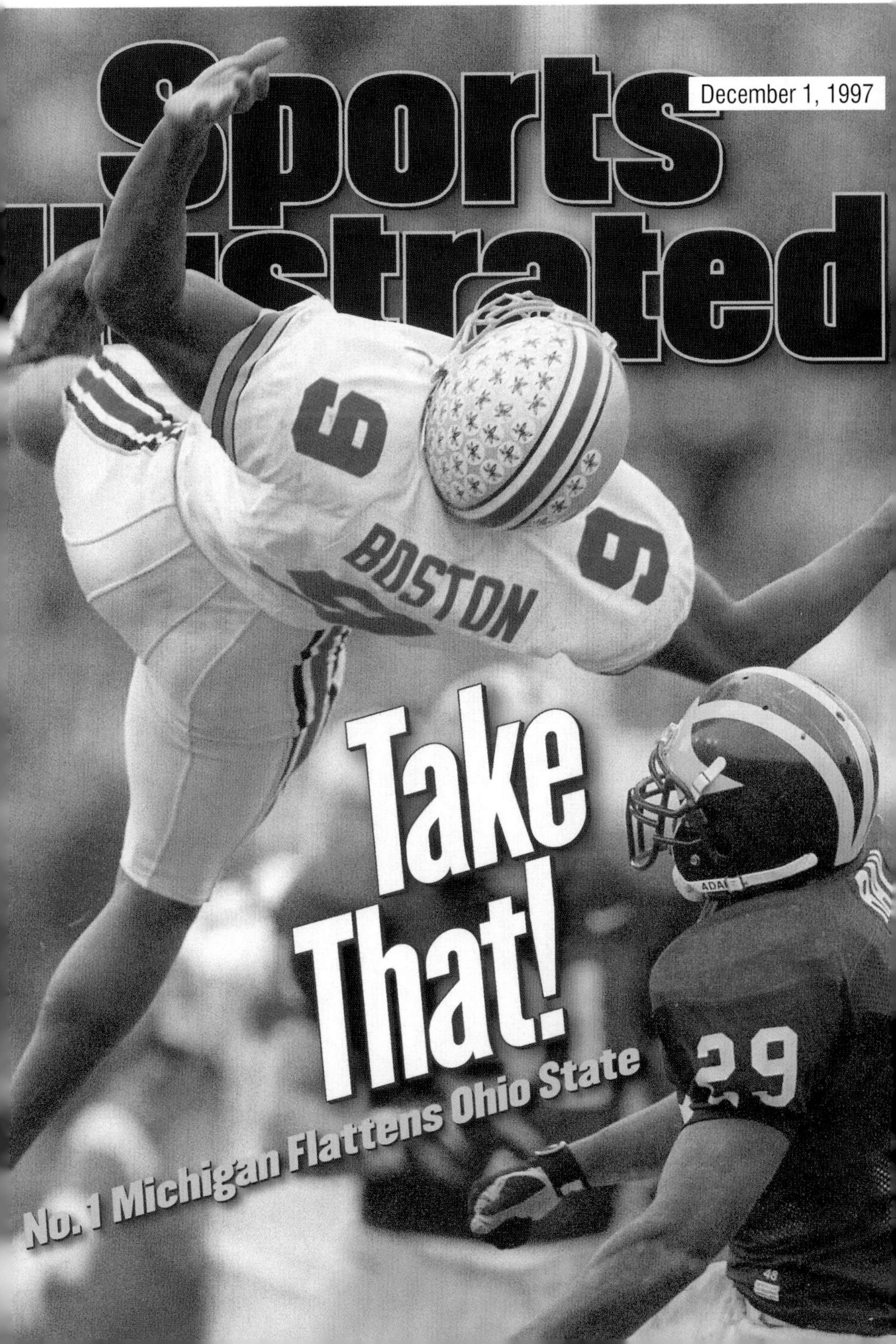

Sports Illustrated

December 1, 1997

Take That!

No. 1 Michigan Flattens Ohio State

ICHIGAN: KING OF THE COU
APRIL 10, 1989
APRIL 10, 1
Sports Illustrated
ICHIGAN
ICHIGAN
21
41
NCAA
THE WOLVERINES BEAT
SETON HALL IN OT

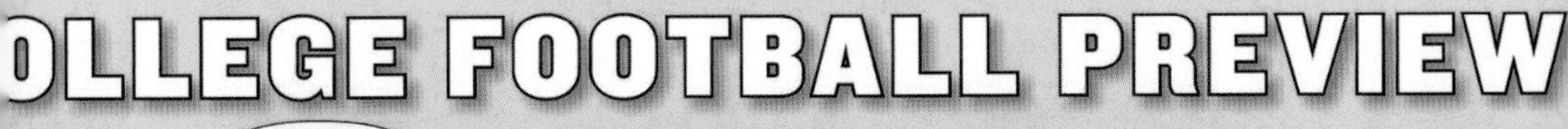

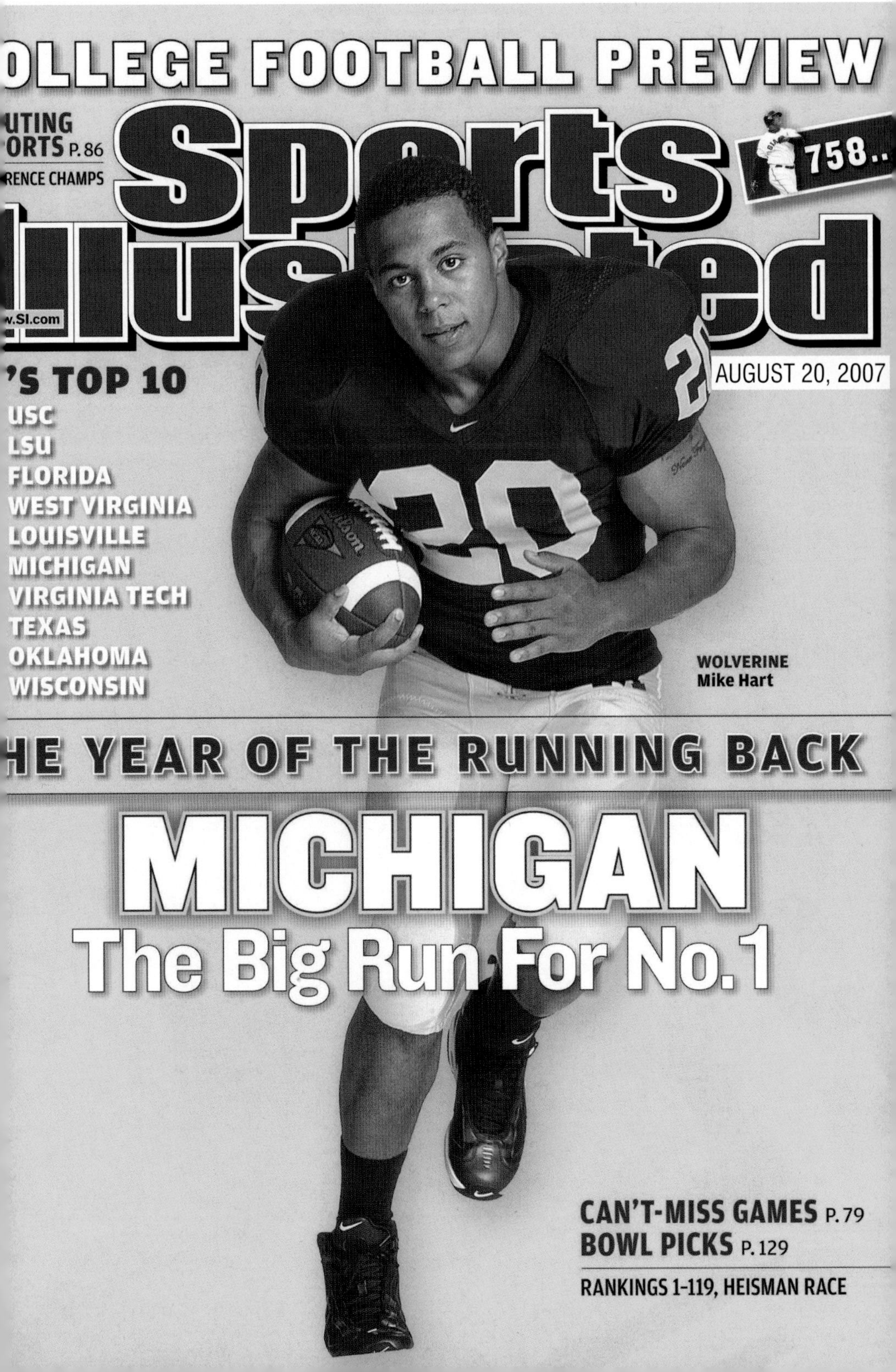

OLLEGE FOOTBALL PREVIEW
UTING
ORTS P.86
RENCE CHAMPS
Sports Illustrated
w.SI.com
758..
AUGUST 20, 2007
'S TOP 10
USC
LSU
FLORIDA
WEST VIRGINIA
LOUISVILLE
MICHIGAN
VIRGINIA TECH
TEXAS
OKLAHOMA
WISCONSIN
WOLVERINE
Mike Hart
HE YEAR OF THE RUNNING BACK
MICHIGAN
The Big Run For No.1
CAN'T-MISS GAMES P.79
BOWL PICKS P.129
RANKINGS 1-119, HEISMAN RACE

NOVEMBER 20, 1989
COLLEGE
1989-90
PREVIEW
BASKETBA
Sports
BMA
IT'
MIN
Rumeal Robi
and Michig
aim to keep
NCAA cro
but No. 1 U
says: No
CHIGAN
21
0 724454 6
10094

APRIL 12, 1993
Sports Illustrated
Nothing Could Be Finer
NORTH CAROLINA TOPS MICHIGAN FOR THE NCAA TITLE
HOWARD

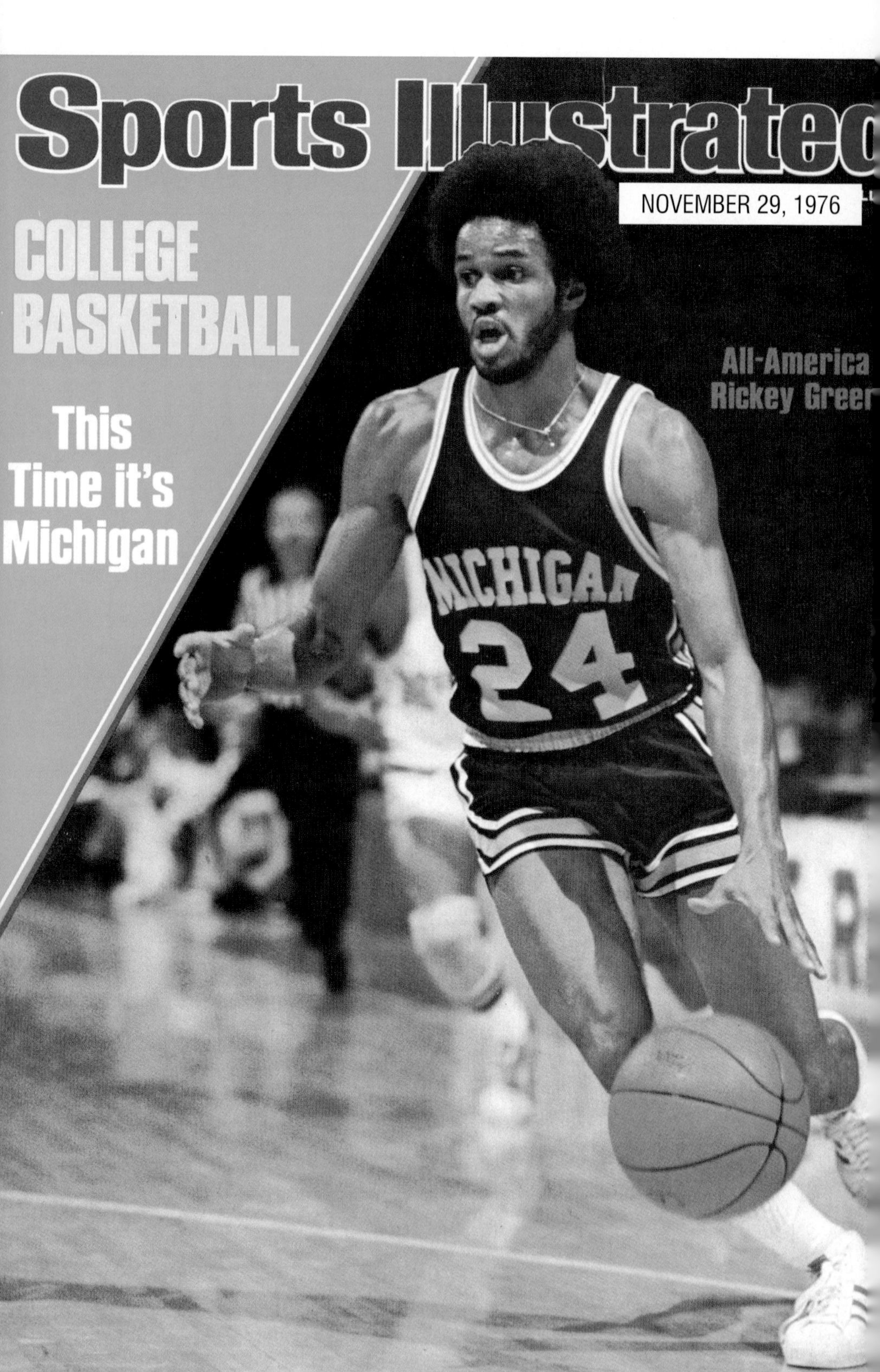
Sports Illustrated
NOVEMBER 29, 1976
COLLEGE BASKETBALL
This Time it's Michigan
All-America Rickey Green
MICHIGAN
24

Sports Illustrated
DECEMBER 11, 1972
60 CENTS
BOOM
IN THE BIG TEN
MICHIGAN'S CAMPY RUSSELL
SHUMA
34

LOOK
AMERICA'S FAMILY MAGAZINE
We're a Third-Rate Pow
in the Air — By RICHARD TREGA
How to Dress a Man
The True Causes of Divor

15¢ YEARLY SUBSCRIPTION $3.50

OCTOBER 28, 1947

Halfback Chappuis
of Michigan
(PAGE 78)

some point, or the next fall, after going through the spring and really getting to show some promise, he came in and sat in my office and said, "Coach, I'm thinking about transferring." He said, "I think I'm the best quarterback here, but I just don't see down the road the opportunity that I want and so I think I'm going to transfer." And I said, "Well, Tom, what I would advise you to do is finish this season and really come back through spring practice and at the end of spring practice, you'll have a much better idea of where you are." Because at the time, Dreisbach and Griese were here and Griese was playing well. So I said, "There's no reason at this point for you to quit right in the middle of a season. But you talk to your Dad and I'll support you in whatever decision you make." Well, I'll never forget, he came back the next day and I thought for sure it was to say good-bye. He sat down right in front of my desk and he said, "Coach, I've decided I'm going to stay at Michigan. I'm going to prove to you what kind of quarterback I am and I'm going to lead this state to a championship."

From that day forward, there was never any doubt that Tom Brady was going to be the quarterback here because he was possessed, he had an ability to do away with all of the distractions and he stopped worrying about the other guys and devoted himself to doing the things he had to do to get better as a quarterback. Two years later, he became the starting quarterback, he started twenty-five games here and won twenty. I don't think anyone's had a higher winning percentage than Tom Brady did. I don't think anybody here has ever led their team to more comeback victories.

What I remember the most about him is the first game of his fifth year, we played Notre Dame at home. We were down late in the game and on a fake play he hit David Terrell down to the two-yard line and we went in and won the game. Then, that same season, we were down ten at Penn State. After he had thrown an interception that was returned for a touchdown with six minutes to go, he made every single play. He led us to two touchdowns, ran one in for a touchdown, threw for another one. The next week we were down against Ohio State and he engineered another great drive to score the winning points on a touchdown pass to Marquise Walker. Then we went into the Orange Bowl game. Twice we were down fourteen against Alabama, who were the SEC Champions, and twice he led us back to take the lead. His legacy here is secured. He was a Captain and a guy that every single player and coach respected because of his leadership, and his will to win. Tom Brady always thought about winning. He never worried about losing. Brady is gonna find a way to beat you. I've never coached a tougher guy, mentally or physically. That's what I remember about Brady.

I'm sure it was very difficult that the guy that recruited him, the head coach, the football team and the baseball coach were all gone. By the time he arrived here in his Freshman year, the people that he knew on the campus were gone. It was difficult because when you go that far away from home (he's 2,000 miles from home) and when you walk in and find that everything has changed, you're not only dealing with being away from home, but you're dealing with a drastic change in the people who recruited you. I can remember I tried to make him feel comfortable and we certainly tried to make sure that his coaches supported him, but I can't imagine how difficult that was. Brady is one of those kids who has a resilience and he's not going to let anything keep him down for long. So whatever emotions he had, I don't remember that ever being an issue that came up in any conversations, which speaks a lot about him. This never was a problem.

Many players say it's harder to play quarterback at Michigan than it is in pro football. I think obviously that during some careers the competition is greater than it is in others. Sometimes the competition is clear-cut and then sometimes it isn't. Tom happened to be here during a time where there was tremendous competition, starting with Scott Dreisbach and Brian Griese and Drew Henson. So, I think competition makes you stronger, it makes you better, and it tests you in a way that you aren't tested when you don't have to compete on your own team. I think the expectation here at Michigan is different because you don't play as many games and your expectation every single year is that you're going to win every game and you're going to win the championship. The truth is in pro football you can lose four, five, six times in a year and make the play-offs. If you had that kind of record here, you're not going to win anything. I think playing quarterback at Michigan prepares you for pro football in a way that high school football can almost never prepare you for college football. You're at an age, you're 18, 19, 20 years old, playing in front of 110,000 people, in a place where you're high-profile and your fans expect you to perform in a way that's going to help your team win. So it's much different because you're at a younger age and you haven't matured either physically or mentally, and so there's no question that it's a great proving ground.

Many players say it's harder to play quarterback at Michigan than it is in pro football.

As a quarterback, I firmly believe that you have to begin with toughness. If you don't have a guy that's mentally and physically tough, you're not going to have success at the quarterback position. Right along with toughness I think intelligence is a critical issue. Tom Brady is an exceptionally bright guy. He was a great student here. So when you have a guy like that, who studies the game, it gives you the added benefit of being able to have the confidence, first of all, to make a suggestion. The coach/player relationship is forever changing and evolving and because of his work habits and because of the things that he learned and the things that he gained in studying the opponents and knowing football, then he was able to make suggestions. And there's no question that he did and he wasn't afraid to make them. I think any time you have a situation where your quarterback can tell you what he thinks and you have confidence that what he thinks is important, then I think you help yourself. Certainly Tom helped us.

As a practice quarterback he was extremely competitive. We try to practice in a competitive environment. We spend a lot of our practice time with our offense against our defense and we try to put our quarterbacks under as much pressure as we can, under as many game-type situations as we can. It brings out the competitiveness in you. So he was a great practice player. He wanted to win every drill. When we went against our first defense, third down situations, he wanted to complete every pass, and he wanted to convert every first down. When we scrimmaged, he wanted to get the ball in the end zone. I always tried to tell him that the most important thing a quarterback can do is get his team in the end zone. Brady was always competing to win and that's why his teammates had such great respect for him, because there weren't any situations in which he wasn't trying to find a way to lead you.

We installed a play for a Penn State game where he had to fake an injury. I coached him regarding the limp off the field at Penn State. We spent some practice time with that particular play and honestly he wasn't a very good actor. As good-looking as he is, and he may end up in Hollywood, I'm sure he learned from that experience because he understood that it was a key part of being able to execute a play and he's done a wonderful job with it.

He wanted the ball in his hands with the game on the line and was cool under pressure. I think the truly great quarterbacks are all that way and that is something that is in their heart and in their soul. We've analyzed great quarterbacks here and Griese was that way and there's no question that Tom was that way. I think it goes back to growing up, always seeing yourself finding a way to win regardless of the circumstances. Tom did that more than anybody I can remember. But I think all the great ones were that way and we've had the great fortune here to have a lot of great quarterbacks who wanted to be down late in the game. Because the greatest victories are always those victories where the odds were against you or where the pressure was the greatest and great players have a way of responding in those moments.

I think Tom's greatest performance was in the Orange Bowl against Alabama because we had gone into the game feeling that we had to be able to run the football and after a quarter and a half, it was very obvious that we weren't going to be able to run the football. We were down fourteen and if they hit another one we're going to have a hard time. We opened the offense up and threw the football to four wide receivers and he made play after play and did the same thing the second half. So I think his greatest performance was in the Orange Bowl against Alabama, where he engineered thirty-five points and a great win.

The thing that always impressed me was that Tom was such a unselfish guy. When we opened his fifth year with the plan that he would start the games and Drew Henson would play the second quarter, I knew how difficult that decision was for him personally. I knew he didn't like it. I knew he hated it. Yet he accepted it with a maturity that I certainly couldn't have handled and I don't know of anybody else that could have. He handled it in such a way that he gained tremendous stature in the eyes of his teammates and his coaches and everyone who knew anything about Michigan football because it was as tough as it gets. He handled it like a champion and in the end, he fought his competition off and proved that he's one of the great quarterbacks that ever played at Michigan.

I can't describe Tom in one or two words but I think he's extremely bright, he's extremely loyal, he's extremely tough and he's a lot of fun to be around. He's a guy who can talk about a lot of things and yet he's one of the guys. A guy that everybody loves. I don't know of anybody that is not happy with what he was able to achieve here and of course in Boston. I don't know of anybody who doesn't like Tom Brady.

I wish all my players were Tom Bradys.

THE UNIVE
ICHIGAN

Chapter 5

THAT SCHOOL DOWN SOUTH

In 1976, Indiana, coached by Lee Corso, scored early in the second quarter to lead Ohio State 7-6. Corso called a time-out and had his team pose for a picture in front of the scoreboard. That picture was on the cover of Indiana's 1977 recruiting brochure. Ohio State won the game 47-7.

Did You Know That Ohio State Is A Four-Year School Now?

SOME SAY THAT YOU CAN LISTEN TO AN OHIO STATE GRAD, YET STILL GO ON TO LEAD A NORMAL AND PRODUCTIVE LIFE

ARCHIE GRIFFIN

Archie Griffin is college football's only two-time Heisman Trophy winner. Griffin won four Big 10 Conference titles with the Ohio State Buckeyes. He was the first of two players to ever start in four Rose Bowl games, the other being Brian Cushing of USC. Griffin was raised in Columbus, Ohio, and attended Eastmoor High School. He is the only back to lead the Big 10 in rushing for three straight years, rushing for at least 100 yards in 34 games, including an NCAA record 31 consecutive games. Griffin was the first-round draft choice of the Cincinnati **BENGALS*** *in 1976, played briefly with the Jacksonville Bulls, and then returned to Ohio State University to attain his MBA. Griffin served as the assistant athletic director for Ohio State University and since 2004 has been the president and CEO of the Ohio State Alumni Association.*

The Ohio State-Michigan rivalry is without a doubt *the* most intense rivalry in college football. It's so big that people choose to attend Ohio State or Michigan just to have the opportunity to participate in this rivalry.

***The BENGALS, owned by the Paul Brown family, were named after the Massillon (Ohio) High School Tigers, where Brown coached before he became head coach of Ohio State and the Cleveland Browns.**

When I was in high school, I was recruited by both Ohio State and Michigan, and both schools were serious considerations for me. Bo recruited me, and at the time, he had suffered a heart attack. When I visited Michigan, I ended up visiting Bo at his home as he was recovering. I had a great time—it really, really was a great school. It came down to my choosing between Ohio State, Northwestern, Michigan, and the Naval Academy because all of those schools were truly outstanding. But I chose Ohio State, and I am glad that I did because Woody Hayes, in my opinion, was an incredible football coach. He really did an outstanding job of convincing me to come to Ohio State.

He was able to do that because he talked more about the academic side of things than anything else. In fact, when he first sat down to have dinner with me, he never said one thing about football at all. He talked about academics so much that I thought he really didn't want me to play football for him after he saw my size. My father asked me later that evening how dinner went with Coach Hayes, and I told him, "Daddy, I don't think he wants me to play for him." He said, "Why do you say that?" I replied, "Because he never mentioned anything about football." My dad asked, "What did he talk about?" I said, "He talked about academics and getting a college education." My father looked at me dead in the eye and said, "Well, don't you think he's concerned about you as a person and not just somebody that is going to get out on the field and run for touchdowns or run forty yards for him?" Right then I couldn't answer that question, but he continued to recruit me, and I chose to go to Ohio State because it really made it easy for me and my family.

At the time, I had two brothers that were playing college football, and my mother and father were trying to run between Kent State and the University of Louisville to watch them play. Being from Columbus, it would be a lot easier if I stayed right here and made it easy for them to come across town to watch me play, while still being able to watch my brothers play. In choosing Ohio State, the big consideration was **WOODY HAYES***. I thought Woody was a great football coach and a better person than he was a coach. I felt the same about Bo Schembechler, actually, because he was a very impressive man. So whatever choice I made, it wouldn't be wrong because they were two very strong coaches, very committed coaches, and both were truly outstanding individuals. But I chose Ohio State and am certainly glad I made that choice.

But that rivalry is a big one. It was special in my day because of the personalities of Bo Schembechler and Woody Hayes. Bo used to coach for Woody, and the fact that they knew each other extremely well made the rivalry really intense. Both were stubborn and wanted to beat each other really bad. And what got that rivalry really going was that Bo, in his first year, beat an Ohio State team that was supposed to win the National Championship. So the 10 years they played each other were really intense.

At the time I played for Ohio State, 1972 through '75, a lot of Michigan's players played high school somewhere in Ohio. One quote that stuck with me for the four years that I was at Ohio State was made by Dennis Franklin, who was from Massillon, Ohio. He was a great quarterback for Michigan. His comment that was picked up in the newspapers and got put on our bulletin board for four years was "Only the good ones go to Michigan."

When Woody Hayes saw that quote, he put it on our bulletin board and we read that all the time. Anytime we went to our bulletin board, we would read that quote. To be able to play in that football game for four straight years and to never lose to Michigan was something that was very, very special. I look at that very first year, 1972. That's probably a year that Michigan was picked to beat us. Michigan had won the Big 10

***As a young boy in Newcomerstown, Ohio, WOODY HAYES was a batboy for a semi-pro baseball team managed by Cy Young.**

championship the year before. They had a strong team coming back, and we played that game in Ohio Stadium and ended up winning. We had two goal line stands—maybe even three—that were really key to that football game. Bo and Woody, when they got inside that 5-yard line, they're going to knock it in the end zone. Both of them could be stubborn when it came to that short yardage and trying to prove that they can push the other team back and get into the end zone. Bo was stubborn because if he had kicked those field goals those three times he probably would have won the game. Instead, he decided to try to get into the end zone, and we ended up winning that game, 14–11. We went to the **ROSE BOWL*** and enjoyed our time in Pasadena but got our tails beaten pretty well.

The second Michigan game was a 10–10 tie, and we should have won that game. We had a great team at Ohio State that year. We had names like Randy Gradishar, who finished sixth in the Heisman Trophy voting, and John Hicks, who finished second in the Heisman Trophy voting. Our defense was phenomenal that year. We had beaten teams really badly all year long, and not many teams scored points on us at all. Our offense played really well that year as well. We went into that game undefeated, as did Michigan. That game was played at Michigan and was a battle. The first half we dominated with a 10–0 lead, but they came back in the second half and ended up tying the football game.

Because it was a tie, we shared the Big 10 championship. The athletic directors had to vote to see who was going to the Rose Bowl. That was the prize—what everyone was shooting for in the Big 10—to play in the Grand Daddy of them all, the Rose

***The ROSE BOWL Parade originally had nothing to do with the Rose Bowl football game. It was a celebration in Pasadena for the ripening of the oranges....The 1942 Rose Bowl game between Oregon State and Duke was played in Durham, North Carolina because of fears that the Rose Bowl in Pasadena could be attacked like Pearl Harbor was three weeks earlier.**

Bowl. Most people thought that Michigan would be voted to the Rose Bowl because we had gone the year before and were beaten handily by Southern California, 42–17. But when the athletic directors voted, they voted for the Buckeyes!

It was strange to a lot of people because we got beat by Southern Cal, the same team we were getting ready to play. One determining reason would have been the fact that in the Ohio State-Michigan game, the Michigan quarterback, Dennis Franklin, was hurt, so they were concerned about him not being able to play. It wouldn't be the same team without Dennis Franklin. We went out there that year and beat Southern Cal by pretty much the same score they beat us by the year before, 42–21. It ended up being a good decision by the Big 10 to let the Buckeyes go to the Rose Bowl. We had an undefeated season. The only blemish was that tie with Michigan, if you call that a blemish. We had a great team and so did Michigan. Bo Schembechler was always upset that Michigan did not go to the Rose Bowl that year, and I guess he had good reasons.

"If Archie Griffin gains 100 yards, it'll be over his dead body."

The third year was another great game. In the rivalry games, you always get somebody saying something. Michigan had a set of brothers on their team, the Banks brothers, and one of the Banks made a comment that Woody posted on our bulletin board. I can remember going to an accounting class that morning and the professor reading it to me: "If Archie Griffin gains 100 yards, it'll be over his dead body." I laughed it off, but our line *really* took it seriously—what they were really saying was that I wasn't going to get 100 yards. That meant that our line wasn't going to block for me. I'll be the first to tell you that in order for me to get 100 yards, our line had to make holes for me to run through. So that was an affront to our offensive line, and they really took that very seriously. I ended up getting over

100 yards in that football game and sent the Banks back some rules. We ended up winning that game by scoring four field goals. He knocked four straight through the uprights for the 12–10 win. That was a wonderful victory for the home team!

The last game was probably the toughest that I played against Michigan. We won the game, but it really was almost one of those miracle wins. Michigan really had us on the ropes that day. They were outplaying us and had us down 14–7 with three or four minutes to go. We just weren't doing anything offensively. As a matter of fact, we played poorly—the defense played well, but our offense wasn't moving the ball.

That was the game that broke my 31-game streak of having over 100 yards per game. We just weren't getting anything done. Michigan needed to win that game to go to the Rose Bowl, and that was the year that the Big 10 changed the rule and allowed more than one Big 10 team to go to a **BOWL*** game. Whoever won the game would go to the Rose Bowl and whoever lost the game would go to the Orange Bowl. Everyone still wanted to go to the Rose Bowl because that meant that you won the Big 10. Michigan came into that game with a tie on their record, so they had to win it. They couldn't tie with us and win the right to go to the Rose Bowl.

Like I said, the game was 14–7 with about three or four minutes to go. We got a little desperate because we needed to score. Our quarterback, Cornelius Greene, called our offense together on the field and said a little prayer. He asked the Lord for the strength to play up to our abilities. I'll never forget it; we finally started moving the football. Brian Baschnagel made a key catch; Lenny Willis made a key catch; I ran the ball the best I had run all day; we went down the field and scored, tying the game up, 14–14.

***The Six "R's" of BOWL Selection: Records, Rankings, Ratings, Rewards, Reverence and Rematch.**

Because Michigan knew that a tie wouldn't do it for them, they got a little desperate. They went to the air. Rick Leach was their freshman quarterback. They started throwing the ball and my younger brother Ray, a defensive back for us, picked off one of Leach's passes and took it down to the 2- or 3-yard line. Then, Big Pete Johnson ran it over for the touchdown, and we ended up winning that game, 21–14. But it was the come-from-behind victory that made it really, really sweet, if I do say so myself.

Then we were able to say that we had three pairs of gold pants, because you don't get any for tying. Getting three pairs of gold pants in football is something you will be proud of the rest of your life.

The gold pants are really symbolic of beating Michigan, symbolic of Michigan putting their pants on one leg at a time. Back in the thirties, there was a long stretch when Michigan was consistently beating Ohio State, and people didn't think that Ohio State could beat Michigan. The Ohio State coach at the time made a statement to his team that they're just like us, they put their pants on one leg at a time. Well, that stuck, and every time Ohio State beat Michigan, the players would get a gold pendant shaped like a pair of pants, hence the gold pants. On the back of that pennant was the score of the Ohio State-Michigan game. It's a wonderful honor for playing in that game and something for the Buckeye players to shoot for. I have given one to my mother, and I have a few for myself from when I was working in the athletic department. But to have three of *my own* that I was part of earning—I couldn't be more proud. Michigan is always a worthy opponent.

... my younger brother Ray, a defensive back for us, picked off one of Leach's passes...

WE INTERRUPT THIS FAMILY TO BRING YOU THE FOOTBALL SEASON

JIM HERBSTREIT

Jim Herbstreit never transitioned into TV, as his highly recognized son Kirk has done. But the first half of the rare father-son Buckeye captain double has the distinction of serving as an assistant coach under both Bo Schembechler and Woody Hayes. He also, in fact, was on the same staff with both of them. A consultant now in the mass appraisal industry and resident of Chagrin Falls, Ohio, Jim Herbstreit reflects on a couple of generations of OSU lore.

Some people might not realize I actually have three children—Terri, John and Kirk. And my daughter was probably the best athlete among them. She had a lot of shin-splint problems. In today's world, she would have been an outstanding track athlete and soccer player. But the girls in high school just weren't organized very well back then.

Kirk, who is eight years younger than Terri and the child most people know, was a super, super athlete from the time he was old enough to move. My son Johnwas in the middle—four years older than Kirk, four years younger than Terri.

Having been a captain at Ohio State, I was determined not to hang a lot of pictures and plaques. I didn't want them to feel the need to match their father. I didn't push them. Kirk just came upon it naturally. He had a lot of natural ability in two sports, baseball and football. He just moved along and I just worked with him.

My other son played sports and had some quickness and speed but was smaller, like I was, and really took an interest in other things. I'd say they were all three athletic. Only Kirk really got into organized sports in a way that showed any real interest. I might have hindered the other two, because I was determined they would be interested in science, they would want to play the trumpet or play the piano or something.

When Kirk was in high school in Centerville, he had two pretty good years. When it got around to recruiting, the reality was that the real recruiting had been done when he was 5 years old. But he did go through it anyway. I didn't have to say a word. All I said to him was "This recruiting can get screwy."

Earle Bruce was the coach during Kirk's senior year in high school. But at the end of the season, his senior year, Earle was fired. Kirk was being recruited by Penn State and Michigan, and Southern Cal. He had four or five legitimate considerations, but he wanted to go to Ohio State. He was supposed to go to Michigan a couple of Saturdays before Christmas. Tennessee was doing a good job of recruiting him too, I thought.

He said, "Dad, let's stop this. I don't want to go up to Michigan this weekend and go through the motions. I know where I want to go." So I called the athletic director, Jim Jones. I said, "The kid knows where he wants to go." He said, "Well, give me a few days, because we're about to announce our new coach." Kirk actually had almost committed to Ohio State without the head coach being installed. Right after that, within the first day of John Cooper's reign, John called him and Kirk committed.

I was the first guy Woody ever selected directly out of college to coach a position. I was the defensive backfield coach in '61 and '62. Then I went with Bo Schembechler to Miami in '63 and '64. Then I got out of coaching. Bill Mallory asked me to come back when he got the job at Miami of Ohio after the 1968 season. I went back for another couple of seasons, and then I had a wife who was pretty ill. It seemed as if coaching was not going to be something that I was going to be able to do. I left coaching after a year with Mallory. I missed it, probably still even miss it a little bit now.

There was a huge difference going from being a player for Woody to being a coach for Woody. It was like going from a union worker to management. I used to get in trouble with Woody because I was so naive. Woody had an annual gathering at his house on Memorial Day. He thought this was a great thing to do. I didn't know it at the time, but the reason he had these was to keep the players out of trouble before finals. So at my very first staff meeting, he said, "I want to do a little something different this year." He asked for ideas.

Bo was sitting there and he said, "Why don't we take them to a park and let them bring their girlfriends?" That was lukewarm with Woody. Some guys didn't have an opinion. It got to me. I was sitting toward Woody at the end of the table. I said, "Well, why don't you just not have it? Woody, you have no idea how much those guys don't like coming."

God, did he get off on me. He had a fit. He said, "They'll be going home, and they'll have their girlfriends out and before you know it, we'll be in trouble. He won't be able to come back because she's pregnant, and they've got finals next week." Bo used to be the peacemaker. He said, "Take it easy."

I was just trying to be honest. The players hated that party. It takes a young guy time to know that there are rules that you haven't really seen sometimes and it takes you a little while to understand.

The experience of coaching those two years with Woody was really incredible, because I had Bo Schembechler in the room, and I had some older coaches on that staff. Of all those who had ever coached for Woody, his favorite was Schembechler.

You would probably think that there would be some bombastic stuff going on—having Woody as the head coach and

Schembechler as his assistant coach. You read things, where Woody threw projectors...and that's a fact. Bo had a lot of influence during his time there. He came to Ohio State from being with Ara Parseghian at Northwestern. He came in when I was a sophomore on the team.

I had three years as a player with Bo, and I didn't see the inside of what was going on. So probably the most dynamic thing, when I look back on it, was the exchanges between Woody and Bo and between assistant coach Bill Gunlock and Woody, which were a lot more negative, because Gunlock was confrontational. Bo was much more crafty.

I'm not saying Bo was manipulative. He just knew how to work with him, because he understood Woody. Even after Woody's career came to the sad ending, the person who sought Woody out was Bo. Woody trusted Bo. Probably loved him like a son. He competed with him like an absolute b-----d. It was a really fascinating relationship. That relationship was probably the most meaningful of the time I spent there. Of course, when Bo left, it became something different.

This is how Bo worked Woody. Let's say Bo had an idea—a play, a formation, a scheme. He knew that it was too radical an idea to get it in right away...or even within that year. So he would go to Doyt Perry at Bowling Green, who was his bud. Bo said, "Put this sucker in." Then, when the idea worked, he would bring it to Woody as "Doyt's idea." And Woody respected Doyt a lot.

He had told me, "The way I coach, when I get past 55, I probably need not to be coaching."

Sometimes Doyt would get to Woody first. And that's when it was really funny. He would tell Woody about how much success he'd had with it. Woody then came to Bo and said, "You know what Doyt's doing up at Bowling Green?" Bo said, "No kidding." Then Bo got it into his agenda for the next fall.

Woody was stubborn about some things, including staying on the sideline too long. He had told me, "The way I coach, when I get past 55, I probably need not to be coaching." Woody probably needed to hang it up a little sooner. Most of his friends would probably feel that way, too.

Another sticking point with Woody was Notre Dame. The Notre Dame games in the mid-'90s and the Fiesta Bowl a couple of years ago were a lot of fun and really interesting. When I was in school, Notre Damers would say, "Well, Woody's afraid to play us. Blah, blah. blah, blah. It's been 30 years. We knocked you off two in a row back in the '30s."

The truth of the matter was Woody did not want Notre Dame on his schedule because, in my group, if you took the first 15 out of 22 players on the depth chart, they were CYO, Catholic Youth Sports Organization, kids. So what he didn't need were a couple of losses back to back, or two out of three, or something to lose an edge in his recruiting. It was a factor with us. I know the old man didn't want to play Notre Dame. It was all about recruiting.

But make no mistake about it, Woody Hayes was a great coach. Woody's greatness was in his ability to motivate and his ability to bring the greatness out in the people he had. He was not an innovator, in my opinion. There isn't anything special about three yards and a cloud of dust other than the fact that you commit yourself to it like that. When he did throw the ball, he usually threw for big numbers. He was not very innovative from a play-calling/playbook standpoint.

Now, he was innovative in technique. A couple of cardinal principles that were really ingrained in him were leverage to the open side of the field and respect for the open side versus the closed side.

In my mind, the finest college football coach ever in his ability to use his talents and use innovative ideas was Ara Parseghian. Ara was my hero. Bo built some of that in me, because he had so much respect for Ara. Ara was as good a football coach as there ever was.

"When Woody got there, he took his clipboard, and he banged Earle right over the top of the head...."

Neither Woody nor Bo would really spend much time with the defense. I coordinated the defense for Bo at Miami. He was very respectful, even though I was a young coach. Once there was something going on in a scrimmage—something he just didn't like. Then and only then he'd get involved with it. He'd come down the sideline and get a little closer than you really wanted him to be, but not like Woody. Woody would take a clipboard...

I can't remember what game it was, but in the '60s, Earle Bruce was an assistant coach. Lou McCullough was on the staff coaching the defense. Frank Elwood was coaching the defensive backs. Earle had the misfortune of being down on the sideline. It was late in the game.

Woody liked a certain pass coverage in that situation—"Cover three." Lou liked "Cover four." You could darn near line those safeties up outside the stadium to be deep enough and safe enough for Woody. But the opponent would pick you apart in he sideline away from the help. They'd check into it. Our defensive coaches had a heck of a time camouflaging and working with that.

Well, we were up by about 10 points. Woody is saying, "Cover three." McCullough up in the booth is saying, "No. No. No. No. Cover four." So they go about five plays and Frank says to McCullough up in the booth, "He's getting closer." Woody came down the field and Earle was down there and he said to Elwood, who was on the phone, "Hey, Woody's coming down the sideline. I've got to put cover three in there." But McCullough wouldn't do it.

Woody kept getting closer to Earle, and he's still saying "Cover three," and he couldn't get it in. Frank is watching him through the glass. Frank says, "When Woody got there, he took his clipboard, and he banged Earle right over the top of the head. He hit him! Honest to God, he hit him!" Finally, Earle got the "Cover three" in. That wasn't all that common, but Woody was crazy that way.

Bo's greatness was very similar to Woody's—technique and the ability to motivate. Bo could be awfully damned tough on the field. He never got away from appreciating a good line coach.

When Kirk was old enough, I would take him to the games and, normally once or twice a season, I would take him in the locker room. I'd always choose a game that Woody won. We'd wait downstairs. When Woody would come out of the press conference after the game, he'd sit down and talk to Kirk, put him up on his lap. If you're going to recruit, that's the time to do it. He was very good to both my sons and had both their names down. I wish I had a picture of Kirk sitting on Woody's lap. That would be a neat one.

When Kirk was about 10, and John would have been 14, we watched the **CLEMSON*** game, the Gator Bowl at the end of the 1978 season. It seemed like Art Schlichter threw five interceptions. Of course, the old man wasn't upset with the Clemson kid, he was upset with Art. Art was just a freshman, and he had a bad game. Woody couldn't handle interceptions. Passing was painful enough. Even fumbles were easier for Woody to take than interceptions. Art threw the ball away that night.

After the game, I turned the TV off and the boys were getting ready to go to bed. I said, "Boys, I tell you, I don't think the old man's going to get past this one." They said, "What do you

***When CLEMSON University plays in a bowl game most of their fans pay their bills with $2 bills to show their economic impact...and increasing their chances of a future invitation.**

mean?" I said, "Well, that's going over the line, and he may not be coaching anymore." They teared up. They loved Woody so much, Ohio State so much, the whole thing. Kirk, maybe even more than John, had tears welling up in his eyes. He said, "Well, Dad, we can still love him." That was neat. I put them to bed.

OHIO STATE—THE LAST REFUGE OF SCOUNDRELS

JEFF REEVES

He is a Michigan Man with a twist. Oh, former Michigan standout defensive back Jeff Reeves loves to needle Buckeye fans every chance he gets, even though he is from Columbus and ended up moving back there. But the executive vice president at Allianz Life Insurance Company has a place in his heart for former Buckeye coach Woody Hayes, especially after seeing what the relationship between Hayes and rival Bo Schembechler was really like beneath the surface.

I'll never forget my last face-to-face conversation with Woody Hayes. We had been very close at one time, when I was growing up in Columbus, playing sports at Linden-McKinley High School. But now I was in Ohio Stadium wearing a Michigan uniform. It would turn out to be his last game in that stadium.

It was 1978 and my freshman year at Michigan, and we were warming up in Ohio Stadium. I had been injured a couple of weeks prior, and I was standing on the sideline. Woody walked over to me and said, "You should have kept your a-- in Columbus." I said, "Thank you very much, Coach. I'm proud to be a Michigan Man. Good luck to you today, too, Coach." He looked at me, and gave me that look, and I said, "Thanks, coach."

My coach, Bo Schembechler, looked at me and smiled. I said, "Bo, Woody's messing with me." He said, "I got you, and he didn't." They looked at each other and gave that little smirk.

That began the rivalry between **OHIO STATE AND MICHIGAN*** as far as Jeff Reeves was concerned. I determined this "Michigan boy" made the right decision to go north, and I've been grateful for it ever since, and I'm proud of it.

The rivalry didn't end after my playing days at Michigan were over. After I left Columbus in '78, I never went back until 2003. My dad was severely ill, so I moved back to Columbus to help take care of my parents. Ironically, I went to work for Ohio State. I was the chief human resources officer for the medical center at Ohio State University. You talk about abuse. Oh, my God. That was a year and a half of abuse.

After a year and a half, I did my own consulting company for about a year. Then, Allianz asked me to come and be their No. 3 executive worldwide. I'm based in Minnesota, but it's headquartered in Munich, Germany. My title is Executive Vice President. I work there Monday through Friday and then fly home to Columbus on Friday night. During football season, I come home every Friday night to watch my son's games. My son, Darius, a running back who is being recruited by everyone, went to junior high school in Bentonville, Arkansas.

When we moved, he wasn't happy but he went out and became one of the first freshmen ever to play in Gahanna Lincoln High School history. He's been doing his thing ever since. But when I go to watch him play, the people are rude. They've got their Ohio State Buckeye crap on. I may wear a Michigan cap but I try to stay neutral, but every once in a while, I like to p--- them off. They all know who I am, so I don't have to wear anything. They'll just wear stuff and say, "Mr. Reeves, how do you like this coat? How do you like this and that?"

When they make comments, I say, "Obviously you guys aren't a real program, because you've got to brag about it all the time.

***OHIO STATE** beat **MICHIGAN** 50-14 in 1968. Ohio State went for a two-point conversion in the fourth quarter. When asked about it, Woody Hayes said, "I went for two because I couldn't go for three."**

I'm humble. I don't talk about it, because we have academic success, and you guys don't have any of that." We get into the zings every once in a while. They shut up when I get on academics because they know they're agriculture, and we're a top-five business school. So, when I get into academics, that p----- them off.

She was a die-hard Buckeye and threatened to rate me down because she hated Michigan.

I've had my yard toilet-papered. I've had bricks thrown through my windows. I've had people scratch my cars—write 'Michigan sucks' on my cars. One of my cars was spray painted "Michigan sucks." I've had people rip off my Michigan trailer hitch from my Hummer. I've had people egg my truck. It's usually worse during football season, especially up to game week. They're obnoxious. They're very condescending. They're very rude. They're anal about Ohio State football.

They eat and sleep football year round. They have nothing else to do. They have no life. That's what gets me about Ohio State fans. That's their "pro" sport. All they want to do is drink and party and have a good time...and act a fool. I'm not going to say that doesn't happen in Ann Arbor, but it doesn't happen to the extreme that I've seen it happen in Columbus. It's just out of control.

I was heavily recruited for baseball and football. I had about 100 scholarship offers at D-1 schools, I would say 70 percent football and 30 percent baseball. Baseball was my better sport, but I had played football all my life, and I loved contact. In football, I played every position, never came out of the game. I was the punter, the kicker, kicked off, returned punts and kickoffs. I was the quarterback and started at safety.

In the summer going into my senior year, I started hearing from some of the bigger schools—the Auburns, the Texases, the Oklahomas—as a defensive back, not as a quarterback. I had a good senior year, and schools just started coming out of the woodwork. I talked to Woody Hayes when I was a junior. He said, "You'll be here in Columbus." I said, "Coach, I will not. I'm not coming to Ohio State."

Woody started talking to me when I was in the ninth grade, because I had been playing sports all my life. Woody would invite me to practices. I remember back to Leo Hayden and Jim Stillwagon and Rex Kern. And I was a die-hard fan of John Hicks, Archie Griffin. My good buddies were Archie and John and Pete Johnson. I remember I loved Ohio State—*loved* Ohio State, up until my junior year of high school. Bo Schembechler appeared in my gym one day. Jack Harbaugh, who was one of his assistants, and Bo came to watch me play basketball. I had a rule—this was my senior year—that I didn't talk to coaches, didn't interrupt the team. So they would talk to me on my terms, not on their terms. Gene Davis, the coach there, said, "Jeff, do you want to take a breather? These guys want to see you." I went up in the stands.

When they introduced themselves, I said, "Huh?" All I ever knew in my life was Woody Hayes, and that him and Bo didn't like each other, from what I read in the press...until I learned the real story. I told them, "Guys, I don't talk to coaches during practice. If you'd like to talk to me, wait for me after practice, and I'm more than willing to talk to you." They waited. That started our discussion. What they said was "We've heard a lot about you from the coaches in the city, and they rank you as the No. 1 athlete in the city and central Ohio." Granted, Art Schlichter was coming out, as well. So, me and Art were competing for the top-player status in central Ohio. Art was playing games with the press that if I went to Michigan, he was going to Ohio State. I did vice versa...if Art goes to Michigan, I'm going to Ohio State, even though I told Woody that I would not go to Ohio State.

Let me tell you why I would not go to Ohio State. Two reasons. One, I figured I can't grow up as a young man if I stay in the same environment. Two—I have to be able to grow up and fail, make some mistakes, and not depend on mom and dad. I had to culturally learn to deal with a diverse mix of people. The only way I'm going to learn that is to get out on my own and grow up from a boy to a man. Staying in Columbus, I figured that I would have the same friends, same environment and that the opportunity for me to be the man I am today would not exist had I stayed in Columbus. I still believe that.

When I was being recruited by Michigan, my family got a lot of negativity. This is where some of my bitterness comes in—I won't say bitterness, it's where my dislike for Ohio State comes in, and it carries over to my kids, because they get the same treatment today. People were very negative. "How can you even consider that?" "Traitor."

My mom and dad would get verbally abused at work. Literally, they would get "How in the hell can your son even consider that?" "Has your son lost his mind?" "How can you allow him to even look at that opportunity?" "They don't exist." "You guys have got to move—you can't stay here in Columbus."

I had teachers telling me, "Do you really want to pass this class?" I was a 3.9 student. I had some brains, too. I was the No. 1 student in the class. I was valedictorian. I was head of honor society. I had a 3.99 GPA as a three-sport high school All-American. And a teacher asked me did I want to graduate? She was a die-hard Buckeye and threatened to rate me down because she hated Michigan.

I made a decision on signing day. I had a press conference. Woody Hayes and Bo were there, and I had Bear Bryant from Alabama there, too. I had Johnny Robinson, from SC, there. I had Barry Switzer from Oklahoma there in my high school library. I pulled a hat and said, "I'm going to Big Blue." Woody

Hayes hollered, “Son of a b----.” Bo looked over to him and winked and said, “I got you again, Woody.”

George Chaump and another guy recruited the Ohio area for OSU. Woody went back and had a meeting with his coaches and threatened them that if another player got out of Columbus and went to Michigan, he would fire all of them. That’s how the story went

I will say this, though. I grew up as a die-hard Buckeye. I loved the Buckeyes until my junior year. Let me tell you what was impressive about **MICHIGAN***, because I don’t want people to lose sight of this. Bo Schembechler never, ever, for about nine months when he started recruiting me, talked sports. What Bo Schembechler did was he would determine and figure out what was important to the kid’s family.

I would send my son to play with either one of them any day, and I wouldn’t worry about it.

My dad was big on academics. He was firm on academics. What Bo would always stress was academics and you being a better man coming to Michigan, having a degree from Michigan, having the largest alumni base in America, and what a degree from Michigan stood for versus anywhere else in the country. He said, “If you come to Michigan, you’ll be the best man you’ve ever been. I’ll guarantee you if you do the things that I ask you to do, I’ll take care of you for life.” And he kept his promise.

I spoke to Bo the Monday before he died. We were scheduled to meet on Saturday at the Ohio State-Michigan game in November of 2006. He called me on Monday here at this office, and we were talking about my son. He was getting on my son the last

*The **MICHIGAN** fight song, “Hail to (the Victors)” was written in South Bend, Indiana in a house where the College Football Hall of Fame is now located.

two summers at camp. He was mad because Notre Dame was talking him, and he knew that. He said, "Reeves, I got a problem with you. Why is your son still talking to Notre Dame?" I said, "Coach, he can talk to whoever he wants to talk to. I'm open." He said, "He's a Michigan Man, and G-- d--- it, don't you forget that."

I said, "Bo..." He said, "Reeves, let me talk to your wife." So he called my wife and asked her what my problem was and did she not understand that our son had no choice but going to Michigan. She said, "Coach, I'm not in it. It's between you and Jeff." He'd grab my son in the summertime and poke him in the chest. "You're a Michigan Man like your daddy. Your dad was a great Michigan Man, and you're going to be a great Michigan Man. Son, are we clear?" But Bo was a guy who, if I needed him, I could pick up the phone and call him. I had his home number in Florida. Whatever I needed, he was there for me. I'd call him at home.

After Woody was gone, the rivalry was different. The Ohio State rivalry is always tough. I would say Earle Bruce was a little more laid back. He wore his little black cap like he was a bellman at the door. We used to laugh at his hat all the time. He was a short, pudgy little guy. He didn't speak good English. He didn't have a real strong track record in our mind. We didn't give him a lot of respect.

After Woody was fired and was in declining health, Bo talked about Woody all the time. That's one of the things people don't understand, and that's why I have so much affection for Bo and Woody. I love them both. Those two loved each other. They literally loved each other. They were best friends. They were humanitarians together. They cared about their kids. They cared about their community. They cared about their schools, and they genuinely loved each other.

Bo used to always talk about his affection—that everything he knew, he learned from Coach Hayes. He said Coach Hayes coached him and gave him his start. He said if it wasn't for Coach Hayes, he wouldn't be half the man he was or half the coach he was—that he learned it from Coach Hayes. When Woody was ill, he left town to go to be by Woody's side. Michigan flew Bo down there in a special plane to be with Woody. We were in the middle of a meeting, and he found out that Woody was ill. Bo left the meeting, flew to Columbus—he was back the next day, but that was more of a priority than him staying at practice. People don't understand that these guys genuinely loved each other.

I can remember when I was playing in the NFL, and I was back working out. It was when Bo was being recruited to coach Texas A&M. Woody and Bo met at the state line. They both drove to the state line, got out of their vehicles, and they talked about Bo leaving Michigan. I remember Bo telling me what Woody said to him that helped convince him to stay was "You're the pride and joy of Michigan. You've built this program. This is your legacy. Don't interrupt your legacy."

I would send my son to play with either one of them any day, and I wouldn't worry about it. I believe in coaches that have that credibility and respect and integrity. They can get more out of an athlete than an athlete can get out of himself. That's my kind of coach.

The one regret I have is not closing up with Coach Hayes. I was never able to tell him how much I appreciated him and thought of him. The last interaction we had was my freshman year when he told me, "Son of a b----. You should have kept your a-- in Columbus." He sent some messages to me over the last few years that he was disappointed that I went to Michigan, but I never had a chance to address him directly. One thing I wish I could have done was have closure with Coach Hayes, because I cared about Coach Hayes.

OHi-WOE
OHi-WHOA

BO BIAFRA AND THE DEAD SCHEMBECHLERS

Upon discovering the existence of the band Dead Schembechlers, the real Bo Schembechler was quoted as saying, "Holy smokes, I couldn't believe it. They're all dressed like Woody. I think it's crazy. I still matter in Columbus!" Their identities are secret, their future uncertain, their lyrics edgy, their legend growing. They've actually found their way into everything from the pages of **PENTHOUSE*** *to the Web pages of ESPN.com, but never* Tiger Beat, *says lead singer and band spokesman Bo Biafra.*

It was rumored the concert in Newport Music Hall in Columbus was going to be the band's last appearance. That would have been the Friday night before the game, November 17, 2006. To look into a crystal ball...I don't think there's a man on the planet who can tell you anything that is going to happen into the future. I would never take it upon myself to try and make genuflections of the forward recessions. It's a difficult period for the band.

We began playing in 1990. We were just young lads at that point. We were playing what we called the Wolverine Hate Music, not punk rock music. Punk rock is sharp. It's catchy. But all our lyrical content has to do with the evil of The International Wolverine

***When former ESPN and current NFL Channel anchor Rich Eisen was in college, his stand-up comedy routine included reading "Letters to PENTHOUSE" using Howard Cosell's voice.**

Conspiracy. Because, as you see, the Michigan Wolverine football program is just the tip of the foul spear of The International Wolverine Conspiracy. It's aimed at enslaving mankind...every man, woman and child is drawn under the foul yoke of Wolverine football. Every supposed natural disaster is the fault of the Wolverines. Rumors of fake moon landings feed the Wolverines.

Take World War II—not many people realize it. The state of Michigan was actually on the Axis side. They sided with Italy, Germany, Japan. As a matter of fact, many of those planes that bombed Pearl Harbor were made in Detroit. They were supposed to be punching out cars, but they were punching out dive bombers. Dive bombers stabbed into the very heart of our proud United States of America. All this has gone on without anybody in the media stepping forward. It's a mystery unless you know the machinations of The International Wolverine Conspiracy. The Dead Schembechlers have been the only thing standing between this nation and disaster since 1990.

Historically, our band has only played once per year, on the night before The Game. It is *always* that Friday night before the OSU-Michigan game. It has always, pretty much, been in Columbus. We were, in fact, banned from the late '90s up until the early 2000s from actually playing in the city limits because of the violence that would break out around our performances. The violence, of course, was not the fault of the band, even though that's what you would read in the lying liberal Wolverine news media papers. Not the fault of our fans, God bless them—the backbone of the republic of Ohio. I would never lift a finger or even a word against the law enforcement. No! The violence was started by agents. Agents working on behalf of the Michigan Wolverines to destroy us, to destroy our fans, to destroy our show.

There's nothing funny about this. This is just as deadly serious as anything on this planet.

There was a band in Ann Arbor trying to do some of the same things we did, "The Dropkick Woodys." Once again, you see, just as Satan created things in mockery of the creation of God, we see the Wolverines come up with a cheap knockoff, a rip-off, just a falsification of the real band. We are familiar with the Dropkick Woodys. We invited them to share a bill with us a couple of years ago at a Hate Michigan Rally, 2005. They were so p--- poor, they were booed off the stage. They didn't even perform. They did a bad lip-synching job. They were met with a hail of bottles, broken glass, jeers, curses. Bodies burned and the flesh scattered.

We've had dozens, perhaps hundreds, of attempts on our lives and our livelihood.

We stay up all night before the game. After the Hate Michigan Rally, we will normally repair to some great vacation hotspot, like Sandusky. We'll party all night and then be back for the game the following day. We normally fly in and out of Worthington International Airport. We have a private landing strip there. We often get an air escort from the Ohio National Guard to protect us in flight. We've had dozens, perhaps hundreds, of attempts on our lives and our livelihood.

I met Bo Schembechler once in my life. I was just a young lad, a spry young Buckeye lad, growing up off the fat of the land in Ohio. My family was having dinner at a restaurant. We heard a whisper go amongst the folks there having their supper. Coach Schembechler was there at the restaurant. My daddy urged me to go over and ask him for an autograph. I did so. I didn't know any better. I walked over and said, "Excuse me, Coach Schembechler, could you please sign this for me?" Instead of signing the paper, he covered me in kerosene and set me on fire. The man was pure evil.

It is, in fact, true that in the last couple of weeks before Coach Schembechler passed, he was very vocal about our band. He may have, in fact, said some positive things about us. I believe, in hindsight, he was just trying to lull us into a false sense of security. What this was, this was just another plot, another insidious plot against our persons to find out our true identities, to bring us to the surface so we would let our guard down, and pay the ultimate price for the Buckeye Nation.

Does anybody know our true identities? Absolutely not—I don't even know who I am. It's too deep of a secret. It would be a pretty safe assumption that all of us are from Ohio, but I don't wish to say "yea," nor do I wish to say "nay." The smaller the amount of information known about our personal lives, the safer we will be. I can't answer questions about our past. It's too easy to check records, transcripts, grades, class photographs. I would love to be able to share that information with the community at large. Certainly, many of our millions of fans would be very excited about these personal tidbits. It can be so dear to them. But I would have to say what I said to *Tiger Beat* magazine when they wished to put us on the cover; I'll say, "I can't help you there."

What we do when we are not playing in the band is not important. The only thing that is important is when the four of us are together as the Dead Schembechlers, fighting the Wolverine menace. We could be beggars, lawyers, policemen. We could be soap-opera actors. We could be anything. It doesn't matter. It's not important. The only thing that is important is that we are a vessel representing the spirit of the Buckeye nation.

It's too dangerous for the Ohio State coaches to acknowledge us. Certainly, if they acknowledge us, given some of our strong adult lyrical content, they would be brought to the mat. Chastised. Ostracized. Omni-romanticized. There is no way in hell that they could even acknowledge our existence, even a smidgen, not even a modicum. Let us not mince. Let us not waffle. Let us not mince nor waffle together. There is no way they could ever, ever pay any attention to us, but we understand that. We work in the darkness, the shadows, the underbelly of the rivalry. It's our job. It's not always easy. It is not filled with glory. Somebody has got to do it, and we're gonna do it ourselves.

Some of our songs—"Bomb Ann Arbor," "I Don't Want to be a Wolverine," "Schembechler Kicked My Crippled Dog." If I had to pick a favorite song, I would probably say, "Stukas over 23." The vision of using a vintage World War II dive bomber to strafe, mutilate, destroy and otherwise incapacitate the Michigan Wolverines as they drive on the approach to the stadium, God Almighty, I get excited just thinking of it.

Our band members are absolutely the same members, always the same members. Dead Schembechlers—it's like a mafia. Once you're in, you're in for life. Our band members are: Bo Biafra; our guitar player, Bo Thunders; our drummer, Bo Scabies; and our bass player, Bo Vicious.

You'd have to be out of your mind to think that any of those media conglomerates like MTV or VH1 are going to put the Dead Schembechlers on their air. It was almost a mistake that we ended up on ESPN. We were the No. 1 story that week, around the clock. But whatever, they were reporting about us after all these years. Why suddenly, it's the force under the American media. It was to destroy us. It was to lead us in—lambs to a slaughter. We are not lambs, and we were not slaughtered. We survived to this day.

Certainly, the biggest show we played was the 2006 Hate Michigan Rally. It was the biggest game in the history of the rivalry. It was the biggest gig in the history of our band, our group. This was the largest attendance ever—1,500.

We play to audiences as small as two. We sometimes didn't even have all the band members there, because the danger was so acute. We couldn't tell anybody where the show was, including the band members. Sometimes, the show just had to go on without us. Good Lord Almighty. Do we live in an age where a man and a band singing about football fears for his life?

The profits from the last concert we did, we did indeed give all the profits from that show to the "Heart of a Champion" fund, one of Bo Schembechler's charities. We wuz duped. We wuz duped.

I honestly can't say, at this point, what the future of the band is, if any. I've been spending most of my time getting some rest and relaxation at the Athens (Ohio) Lunatic Asylum. It was very hard after the Bucks lost to Florida in the National Championship in 2007. That was, of course, due to the fact that the band was not there to support the team.

We hate Florida. We hate all other non-Buckian teams. The fact of the matter is this. There is no greater, more dangerous threat—not only to the Buckeyes, not only to football, not only to the state of Ohio, not only to the United States of America, but to mankind in general...There is no greater threat than the Wolverines, and the avowed belief that the Wolverines should rule the world. They are now led by a bloodthirsty b-----d by the name of **DAN DIERDORF***. He is a gentle giant in the broadcast community. He is now the head of the international Wolverine conspiracy. He has sworn death to the Dead Schembechlers, death to Ohio State Buckeyes, death to the sovereign nation of Ohio.

***Marion Motley, Alan Page and DAN DIERDORF are all Canton natives and are enshrined in the Pro Football Hall of Fame in their hometown. Page worked on a construction crew that built the Hall while Dierdorf and his father attended the groundbreaking ceremony.**

INSIDE TRAITOR

PEARSON BUELL

His grandfather temporarily disowned him. His parents just naturally assumed he would be a Michigan Man. Pearson Buell, now 47 and living in Lake St. Louis, Mo., started down that path, but eventually converted to being a Buckeye—a rewarding, but not always trouble-free, experience for the senior functional analyst for Citi.

I spent my early years in Michigan in Grosse Pointe. Both my parents attended the University of Michigan, though they started out at other schools. My grandfather was a huge supporter with season tickets. I went to Michigan games with my grandfather. I had all kinds of Maize-and-Blue stuff.

When you're little, you just love the team you love. I didn't really care about any other team. It wasn't until I started to gain an understanding of the whole "Woody and Bo" thing and that dynamic that I started to say, "Ooooh, Ohio State, bad, evil."

Eventually, we moved to Atlanta and then to a Columbus suburb, Worthington, my senior year in high school. I had attended three high schools in three years. Every time I moved, I would set my sights on different colleges in the area. I wasn't like my brothers, who were looking nationally. I was looking at what's easy and what's nearby. I wasn't the consummate student. At that point, my senior year, I just said, "There's a big, great school down the road. I'm just going to go there. It's easy."

That was the fall of 1978. I probably had mixed emotions leading up to that first Ohio State-Michigan game as an OSU student. But I had come to the conclusion you had to be true to your school, so I decided to finally switch sides.

I thought the stadium was awesome. Compared to Michigan, which was just a big bowl that was easy to get in and out of, this was a little bit more complicated. Back then, Ohio State hadn't closed in the end so it had a completely different feel about it. But, it was certainly loud and the fans were as ravenous as anyplace I could ever imagine being.

...when my grandfather learned that I was going to be going to Ohio State, he didn't speak to me for a few weeks.

Still, that first Michigan-Ohio State game, I felt a little ambivalence. It was hard to let go of that Michigan allegiance, especially because at every other game, I'd been cheering against Ohio State—it's hard to just switch sides and say, "Oh, now, I'm going to cheer for the visiting team."

As I recall, when my grandfather learned that I was going to be going to Ohio State, he didn't speak to me for a few weeks. I don't think he was seriously angry, I think he was just making a lighthearted point. My mom later told me she had heard he had said to somebody, "Well, my grandson goes to Ohio State, so it must not be that bad of a school." He had softened his view a little bit.

I went to a Michigan game in Ann Arbor my sophomore year, the 18-15 Buckeye win. That made us undefeated at the end of the regular season, if I remember correctly, and rated No. 1. It came to us that the easiest way to do this—the most fun way—would be for us to rent a Winnebago, rather than for a bunch of people to drive up separately. So eight or nine—may have been more—went up there. I do remember that we filled up the shower in the Winnebago with ice and kept a keg in there, which may be in violation of some statute somewhere. We went up on Friday night, and we parked it in a parking lot on campus. We were not far from the actual stadium.

When the game was over, we stormed the field. There were people all over the place, jumping up on the uprights. I don't recall that security, in those days, went to the efforts to protect them the way some schools do now. I know some schools grease them. Some schools put cops all around them. I don't recall Michigan doing any of that. Clearly, there were an awful lot of Ohio State fans there, because there were a lot of people who went out onto the field. I don't remember who went up on the goal posts...all I remember is them starting to come down. Several of the Phi Taus grabbed onto one of the uprights and just started pushing it and it snapped right off. Here we had this long tube of steel in our hands, and we just said, "Let's go." We never could have done it, at least, not today, in Ohio Stadium, because there are very few straight ways out from the field. In a bowl like theirs, you walk straight up the aisle and straight out. People just got out of our way. Here we were, five or six guys with this upright on our shoulders just walking up and nobody stopped us. No officials. Nobody with the university. No police. People just made way for us.

We were so excited. And here we had this memento. I don't think we really even thought about what we were going to do with it. We just started walking out. I don't think we made the connection that it was something we could take home with us. It wasn't until we got to the Winnebago that it dawned on us that we had the perfect vehicle to transport it with. If we could strap this goal post to the top of the RV, we could take it home. It must have been pretty secure, because it didn't fall off.

We brought it back to our fraternity house and took it up to the third floor and stuck it under a bunch of beds. Everybody had their ideas about what they were going to do with their piece of this. People started talking about how we were going to divvy it up...or where we were going to put it. Are we going to hang it on the wall?...or we going to plant it in the yard and make it a flag pole—what are we going to do with it? I think the agreement was that if we could cut it up, we'd split it up. To the best of my recollection, they did cut it up...but it was *much* later. It literally sat up there, and I guarantee you that a good number of people who were in and out of that third-floor room had no idea what this big piece of metal tubing on the floor was—the significance it had. Except Bob Clegg, a fraternity brother of ours. He knew what significance it had, but it had nothing to do with football. Some stories are better left untold.

We were all initially excited about it, but then it just sat there, for at least a year. When we were carrying it out of the stadium, we didn't have a plan. In the parking lot, if we decided it was too heavy, we could have dropped it in the parking lot and walked off and never thought about it again. We really were never thinking much beyond the moment. As we arrived back in Columbus, it was all very exciting that we had this trophy, but things move on, and it's quickly forgotten. I did not ever get my piece of it. I have no idea who has pieces of it. But it is my recollection that, after a year or so, it got cut into pieces...

Chapter 6

MICHIGANPALOOZA

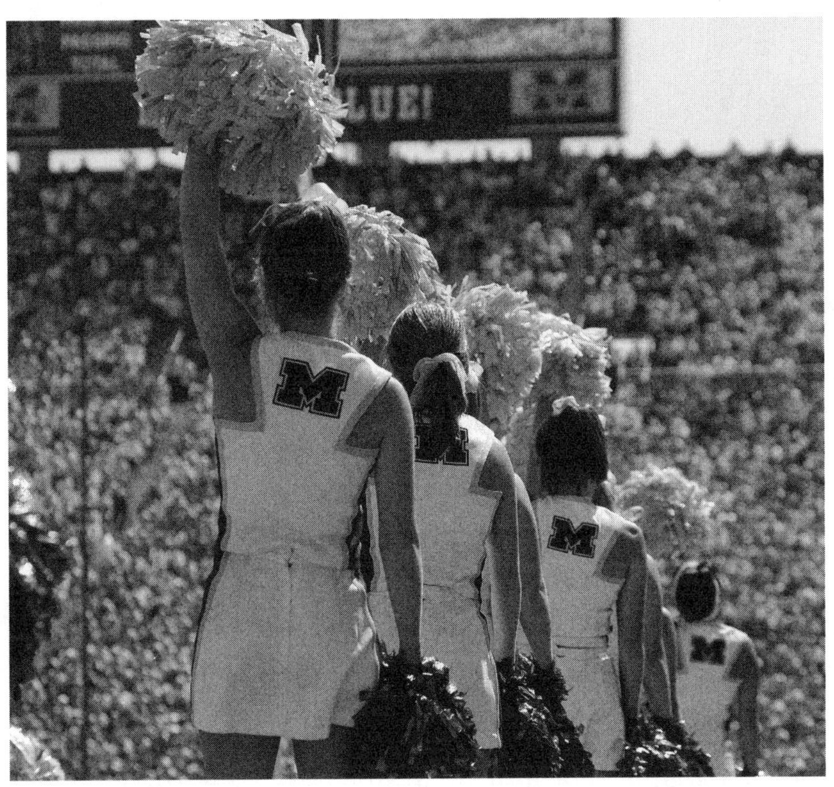

Wolverine Fever? No Cure!

FANECDOTES

Somewhere around when I was 5 years old, my dad was the Michigan football team eye doctor. As a result, he had to go out to the games early and then my mother would drive me, my brother and sister...when they were old enough...to the games. My mother would put me in a sleeping bag and put me down in section 23 where dad had four seats. Sometimes it was snowing...sometimes it was raining, and half the time I fell asleep...but I did get more and more familiar with the players as the years went on.

My dad would get to run out of the tunnel with the team and jump at the M Club Banner that they put out on the field. He would have his little black bag running out with the team. This is when contact lenses first came around and they were put in the player's eyes—the players that needed glasses. If they got bumped the wrong way and the lens would pop out...there would be a time-out. Players and officials would stop and look for the lens. Can you imagine 22 players on their hands and knees all looking for a contact lens? That was exciting to see my dad run out on the field.

My dad acquired parking passes on a street named Berkley—which runs horizontal right into Main Street. It was the second parking lot up from Main Street so we were parking very close to the stadium. I still park in that same parking lot. The owner of the lot is now the son of the guy who was the owner when my dad had the tickets. His name is Richard Raab. Good seats and parking stay in the family for years at Michigan.

I get real nervous when they are playing Ohio State or Michigan State. I'll root for Michigan State when they aren't playing Michigan. I'll carry a portable TV around when I'm playing golf and they're on TV. I've done that several times. Sometimes I've pulled off the road at a Holiday Inn and rented a room just to watch a game because I was in the middle of traveling somewhere.

We like to get out early to the games and watch the band play. My friends Bill Cormack and Dave Theobald come to a game usually every year. Kurt Gulbrand said, "Why don't you get there early...at least 45 minutes early...come down on the field and go stand in the north end zone. When the band first comes out on the field, they march to the center of the field, they turn right and march right to the north end zone."

So you not only get a close up of the band members, but you have to about plug your ears because you have about 20-30 trombones and trumpets blasting away right at you. That was a very fun experience.

Terry Barr was an All-American wide receiver. He went on to play for the Detroit Lions. The championship team that the Detroit Lions had was having their 10th anniversary and their pictures were in the papers. Since Michigan hadn't negotiated their Big 10 networks to broadcast away games yet, Terry and I were both at a sports bar to watch the Michigan game. I saw him at the bar and said, "Hey Terry, did you see yourself in the paper today? You're right on the front page of the *Detroit Free Press* and the *Detroit News* celebrating the 10th Anniversary of the Detroit Lions team." He said, "No! I didn't see it." As we were talking, I asked him who his favorite college football team was. He said, "I have two favorite football teams—University of Michigan and whoever is playing Notre Dame!"

—**DAVID COOPER**, 75, Bloomfield Hills, MI, outstanding U-M Supporter

I have such great memories! Being a member of the Big 10 Conference has been so special to me...as a player at Purdue and Michigan...as a Coach at Iowa and Michigan and then being the Athletic Director at Iowa. I just think it's really special to have had a career all in one conference and at all of those outstanding institutions. We've been blessed with that type of a life. My wife and I have lived all of our married life in college and university towns. We love living in that kind of atmosphere and we are still enjoying it. There are a lot of things to do. There are a lot of cultural things, educational/academic things and, of course—athletic events too. It's a fun existence and we've been very fortunate to enjoy that. People have been really good to us

Our 1964 team which I coached, had lost just one game—which was too bad—it was to Purdue...and Bob Griese was their quarterback. We had scored with just very little time left to make the score 21-20. We tried for two points to win the game rather than just tie it. Our quarterback, Bob Timberlake, ran the ball and he missed it by about two inches. In other words...we were just *2 inches away* from winning the National Championship.

I also have had the unique experience of coaching against my brother, Pete Elliott, when he was head coach at the University of Illinois. We played against each other for six years. Even though we went to school together and both of us graduated from Michigan...he went to Illinois and I went to Michigan. It was quite a rivalry and quite a difficult thing because both of us wanted to win. That's what it's all about!

I guess I would have to say that one of the great stabilities about Michigan and their success is that they have had coaches who remain there for 10 years or more. Actually...Fritz was there for 9 years...Benny was there for 11...I was there for 10...and Bo was there for 20. Gary Moeller was just there for a few short years but he was a fine coach too. Lloyd Carr was a coach there for a long time as well. I don't know Coach Rodriguez...but I do wish him a long stay at Michigan.

—**BUMP ELLIOTT**, 85, Iowa City, ex-Michigan head coach, played with undefeated Purdue in '43 and Michigan in '47

The Ufer Scoring Horn...the way he told it...was sent to him by a fellow who claimed it was from General George Patton's jeep from WWII. Ufer started using it when he was announcing and eventually called it the "George Patton Bo Shembechler Bob Ufer Scoring Horn." I'm on my third one! My wife got it for me years ago for Christmas and I've been wearing it out ever since. Three for a touchdown...one for an extra point...two for a safety or field goal. Everyone in the neighborhood knows what I'm doing.

Unless you were a Michigan fan, you hated Ufer. He was a "homer", "My cotton pickin Maize and Blue..." He'd go on and on and on. He had the world record in I think the 100 yard dash, way back when. He was quite the guy. Apparently, when Ufer was in the hospital with his prostate cancer, he told the doctors that his prostate was about the size of a buckeye!

My parents used to go and sit in the student section back in the old days with a Boone's Farm Apple Wine bottle. That was the drink of choice back in their day. There would be bottles stacked up. It was amazing! When recycling hit....as it still goes on now...kids would come after the game and pick up all the recyclables because there are deposits in Michigan.

Years ago, a dog called Whiskey would go onto the field every halftime. Right before the teams came back on the field, they'd take this little dog and start on the north end of the stadium with this Maize and Blue ball—like a soccer ball or volleyball. This dog would push it with his nose all the way down the length of the field. Fans would go crazy game after game.

Years ago, a dog called Whiskey would go onto the field every halftime.

I wasn't there to witness this story so I can't say it's true ... but in the '60s and '70s there used to be a tradition where fans would grab the other team's cheerleader or somebody from the other team and pass them up to the top of the stadium. One game, apparently, they got this one cheerleader and she was dressed up in bright colors—a yellow jersey and red trousers—and they passed her up. They had hidden a dummy in the top row. When she got to the top—they threw the dummy over the top of the stadium dressed up just like her. There was this great big gasp! Finally she stood up and waved and there was a cheer.

When we go back, there is band practice every day so we always go to band practice. We enjoy that tremendously. There is a restaurant in the train station called the Gandy Dancer. It's by far my favorite restaurant there.

—**CHARLES K. NORTON**, 70, Lancaster, PA.

On a rainy miserable day, a group of us went to a game with a keg of beer—those were the good old days—they'll frisk you for a sandwich now. Back in those days we could bring in a quarter barrel!

A couple rows in front of us sat a fellow with this mammoth umbrella. Nobody could see from behind him..."Put that umbrella down. You can get a little bit wet so the rest of us can see!" He didn't do anything—so finally I reached over and pulled it down over his head and his head popped right through the umbrella. He ran and got the cops and they came over and hauled me off.

Everyone was cheering me all the way out. I ended up in district court and the judge said, "What's that umbrella worth? $14? Ok...you come up with $14 and you're out of here." One of my buddies had been collecting from everybody in there. He had $14 in change—he had a little bandana full of change and handed it to the guy. The judge said, "Case dismissed..."

On a nice, sunny day...we were planning on having a big group in the stands so we needed a half barrel instead of a quarter barrel. They are heavy! This one friend of mine was all muscle. We loaded that half barrel on his shoulders and he balanced it with both arms. I shoved his ticket in his mouth. He walked in and the ticket taker just rips the ticket out of his mouth. He just kept right on walking to our area to set up shop. I haven't the slightest idea if they won that day.

We had wonderful parties in there—all kinds of food and a keg of beer. I was party chairman a couple of times over at the fraternity house and if there was a special game...we'd prepare food to take. We always made it a point to have money to have a keg though. A quarter barrel was twelve dollars!

The Michigan-Ohio State game is always the last game of the season. It can be very cold and snowy by then. We were having our usual party in the stands when my friend Bill left for the men's room. He didn't come back. After the game we were filing out and right outside our entrance was Bill lying face down in a snowbank. We hauled him back to the fraternity house and it took a couple of hours to thaw out his face. His face was red for about two weeks after that.

—**CHARLIE LIKEN**, Sebewaing, Michigan native, former Michigan Assistant Attorney General

Dan Kelly was the broadcaster in St. Louis for the Blues and he also did the Missouri Tigers games. Missouri had a good year that year and I was coaching with the Blues. Dan told me Missouri had beaten Notre Dame and they had beaten Nebraska and now they were going to play Michigan. He said, "We'll show Michigan how to play football!" Dan came back and he said, "Geez! I walked in the Stadium and couldn't believe it. When the band came out on the field, I knew we had no chance!" Dan was a very accomplished announcer and that was the feeling. It was his first impression.

Bo was always respectful. He liked hockey and came to a lot of our games. He liked the spirit and intensity of hockey so he could relate to me. The last time I saw him, he was aging and slipping a little bit. We had coffee together and he said, "Darn. I wish I would have gotten to know you better. We were just too busy in our own departments." I felt the same way. I could have learned a lot! I didn't read his book until he passed away and what an eye opener. I can see why he was so successful. The good stories are the stories that Dierdorf would tell about Bo.

I remember when I was attending Michigan, I sometimes felt we were paying the price of being serious students and taking a tough curriculum. Joe Lunghamer was here for five years in architecture and I was here for four years in the business school. We were serious about school and serious about hockey. Most of my teammates went onto the real world and did well. They were so happy they came to Michigan. Nowadays, there is more pro opportunity but we've got kids that are neurosurgeons coming out of our program and every other program here. We're proud of the academics at Michigan as well as the athletics. It's the best of both worlds. I feel fortunate to be here. It's really worked out well!

—**RED BERENSON**, Hockey Legend

While I was at Michigan, the football team was really bad. They had losing records every year, but we, as guys on the rugby team... found ways to cash in on it. We would play the rugby games on a Saturday after the football game was over on a field that was near the stadium. So we'd get the people coming out of the football game and they would stop to watch some of the rugby game. We would have a few designated persons with big hats, who would go around passing the hat and people would drop a dollar or so donation into the hat. That paid for the kegs of beer and the party we would have—the great rugby parties on Saturday night at some fraternity house or beer hall in Ann Arbor. We found a way to cash in on Michigan's losing football season.

—**ED KURZ**, University of Michigan Law School, 1960–1963, Larkspur, CA

It was the third quarter of the '93 Rose Bowl, For some reason the press said that Elvis Grbac could not throw a long pass. I had just sat down after halftime when Grbac threw the 88-yard touchdown pass to Wheatley for the "go ahead score". Everyone in the Michigan section was going crazy. I grabbed the first person I saw and we hugged and kissed. I saw a guy from the corner of my eye looking at me. He said that it was his wife that I was kissing but it was "okay for this one special time". It was like the end of World War II when the sailor on Times Square kissed the first woman he saw as the war was declared over—a magical moment!

—**HAL KELLERMAN**, Fremont, CA

I was a student so I got student tickets for a lot less money. We also lived about a block away. Parking is difficult for fans. A lot of the houses around us would even park on the front yards so that's what we did. We had about 15 regulars who parked on our front yard, right behind the AAA office on Elmar. We lived in that house for seven years and we had some people that were regulars for seven years. It got to be a great big tailgating party on our front yard! The food got increasingly fancy and the last home game was really a pretty big party. People would come 2-3 hours before the game and leave 2-3 hours after the game. It was nice because there was a restroom inside. Sometimes, when it was really cold, we would come back and have a drink at halftime by the fireplace because it was convenient. At that time, the population of Ann Arbor was approximately the same as the seating capacity in the Big House, which was over 100,000. You can imagine...it was hard to get out of the city so a lot of people needed an excuse to stay later and party afterwards!

Michigan announces the Slippery Rock score. Slippery Rock is a little liberal arts college in Pennsylvania. The biggest rival for Slippery Rock was Shippensburg State. Michigan once hosted that game at the Big House. Only about 60,000 people showed up which looked like there was nobody there but it was 10 times more then these guys have ever seen. They had the Budweiser Clydesdales.

One time Wild Willie, King of Borneo had an after game party. It was during the Woody Hayes days. Their theme song was "Oh, How I Hate Ohio State". We'd sing it to their fight song.

Woody Hayes was a wonderful teacher and model to his people and was certainly an object of scorn when you were a rival —with his stomping up and down, huffing and puffing and throwing down his headset. There was this toilet paper that came out with brands on it that said "Wipe Woody".

Besides Ohio State calling us "that northern school", they'd say to go north till you smell it and west until you step in it. Not to be outdone, people in the north would say go south till you smell it and east until you step in it.

—**CURTIS WRIGHT**, MBA grad, Mayor of Monte Sereno, CA

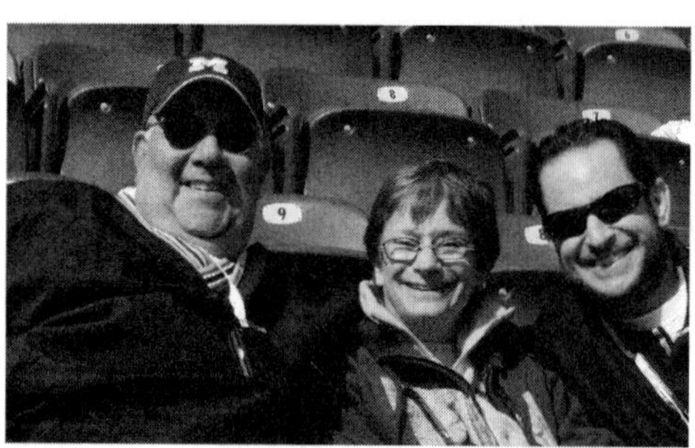

I was so in love with Michigan! When my son Ira was six or seven years old and the game was on, he would come running down the stairs waving his flag like they did in the Stadium. Before 9/11, you used to be able to bring flags into the Stadium. He had a Michigan flag in his room, so I had him totally brainwashed. When he was accepted to Michigan, it was probably one of the happiest days of my life.

Some time before Ira got into Michigan, he and I started going to the football games together. A friend of mine had a couple of tickets and he said, "Here, use my tickets" and we went up. The wife's rule was that we could fly up to Detroit Saturday morning as long as we were back in the house Saturday night...because my wife didn't want to lose us for the whole weekend every single weekend.

When my son started school at Michigan, my wife came to me and said, "I'm going with you every weekend" and she loves it...every weekend...she loves it!

Every game, we'd go...every single weekend. We've been doing this for fourteen years. It had started with every home game. I had a friend who actually let me use his tickets. And then in'97 when Michigan won the National Championship... unfortunately...my friend passed away two weeks after the game. His wife still lets me use the tickets. And then Michigan did a money raising program for the season ticket holders that allowed you to change the ownership of the tickets *one time*. Tickets can go from husband to wife, but after the husband and the wife die, they do not go to the children. And they check—boy, they check. They're unbelievable.

Tickets can go from husband to wife, but after the husband and the wife die, they do not go to the children.

So what happens, for a fee—I think $500.00 a ticket—they let you change the ownership of the ticket one time in your lifetime. My friend's wife had let those tickets come into my name and I had already got ahold of a couple more tickets and put those in my son's name. So, God forbid...if my wife and I both die...he will always have tickets to the football game. The tickets are like gold, they really are, it's unbelievable. Believe it or not, you have 113,000 people sitting in the Stadium and there's a line of people that would *still* love to go to the games.

I'm an accountant, so usually when tax season starts heating up, which is around February 1st, my wife, Sandy, will always say, "Come on, let's sit down and focus on putting air flights together." We normally take a Sunday...she does the whole thing, she's unbelievable...and we set up all of the plane flights. We have all of our tickets, everything in pockets—the tickets are in pockets and our parking passes are in pockets and any other information—it's a science!

Its 7 hours and 45 minutes from my house to the hotel that we used to stay at years ago. We used to drive every weekend for these. Yes—*drive* to Ann Arbor!

I have a friend and client whose son used to write for *USA Today*. He did a story about me. It was about what my attitude in the office was on the Monday after a win and the Monday after a loss. It was very easy to tell when we won. It sort of carries over and it's a lot of fun...and by the way, I'm definitely grumpy on Monday if we lose. A recent year was tough because they only won like four games...so I had eight weekends of grumpiness.

—**JEFF WEINTRAUB**, Rockville, MD

Several years back, I went to visit my friend Jo Anna Jury in Grosse Pointe. She had "long held tickets" and VERY WONDERFUL SEATS...REALLY GREAT "WOW" seats. However she told me firmly, "if they ask you your name, tell them it's HENRY JURY! HENRY JURY!!!!" Fortunately I was not asked. Evidently, the great seats went back many moons. To her Grandfather, her father and then to her. She had the original "seating" tickets. It was a great game. Michigan won. However, I think they discovered that her father and grandfather were no longer on this planet earth.

—**RUTH McCUTCHEON**, Menlo Park, CA

Ron Kramer was a super individual. He was around the department and just uplifting. When he walked through the door with a smile on his face, he made everyone smile. He would always have a big sack of apples for everyone! He'd make the rounds through the coach's offices. I think, sometimes, he even went up on the hill. He'd always come over to the Development offices and the secretaries were always waiting for him to come in. He'd have his apples and sit and chat with you for a while. There were other people that were always around the department too. There are very few nine letter winners left—Don Lund being one of them. Three sport winners were rare! Ron was one of those as well! He was quite a guy.

—**LARRY KATZ**, Retired from U-M, Fundraiser

My freshman year, in the fall of 1999, we went to Penn State and witnessed Tom Brady make a comeback last drive that won the game. The memory I have is traveling with an SAE fraternity brother friend who thought we'd be able to crash at the Penn State frat. There were no hotel rooms available in Happy Valley. The same code on the front door at the Ann Arbor chapter got us in. As we walk in bearing a 24-pack of Icehouse Beer, we realize it's "parent's weekend" and they're having a black tie affair. Total record scratch moment! We slept in the car that night.

—**JOHN NADZAM**, 29, San Francisco, California

For the big games, I would tailgate with Billy and Donny Dufek and with a bunch of former players. It was back when I was working so it was part business and mostly pleasure. It gave us a venue for entertaining customers. When we had a big game, like a Notre Dame game, we would rent this little house right there by the tennis courts. We would rent it so we had a bathroom for the ladies. We had a **PINE TREE*** for the guys! It gave us a lot of space.

I don't remember much about the games because I never went in—I very rarely went in. It was really all about the tailgate. I'd sit and watch it on TV close to the stadium. We could hear the crowd from where we were. It actually became a pretty substantial group that would just stay back and watch the game on TV. They would just come for the tailgate and hang around and socialize...30-40 people would stay behind and watch on TV. We would actually be one of the last people to leave. They would have to come by and tell us to go because they wanted to close up. We even brought lights for when it got dark so we

***Arnold Palmer designed the Bear Creek Golf Club in Denver. Above the urinals in the men's locker room is a picture of Palmer relieving himself against a TREE at the club.**

could stay longer but then they started locking up the gates. We were having too much fun...

As players we were miserable at times but we also had great fun! We were going through school and Bo was working us very hard and that actually made us closer as a group. Bo was tough on academics and got on my case a couple of times for not going to class. He said, "Get your --- to class." He was tough on everyone for everything—he set a high standard.

Ron Kramer and Terry Barr were the two people who recruited me—wonderful gentlemen. I cost them so much money in fine dining. Kramer always joked that I cost him $1,000 just to take me out to dinner! Even though I knew I wanted to go to Michigan, I pretended like I didn't know because I enjoyed going out to dinner with those guys! What the heck! That was part of our history. We grew up in the same neighborhood We knew Ron for many, many years.

—**PAUL SEYMOUR**, Michigan All-American at two positions; brother of Jim Seymour, Notre Dame All-American

We had no organized training other than when we were practicing during the football season. There was no off-season conditioning program when I was there. All of the weight training that I did...which I did a lot ...was on my own. I went from a skinny **195 POUNDS*** to 242-243 pounds my senior year. That was all on my own and unsupervised.

***In 1966, Alabama was 12-0. Only 14 of their players weighed over 200 POUNDS. Their heaviest was 213. In 1980, there was only one NFL player over 300 pounds. In 2010, over 400 NFL players were 300+.**

In 1959, there was a whole new regime under Bump Elliott, who was of course a great player himself at Michigan, as was his brother Peter. Well, he brought in all new position coaches and they were all great guys. Bump was terrific guy, which was maybe to his detriment because he was too nice. Coach Elliott went to Iowa to be their Athletic Director.

One of our linemen, Lee Hall, got cut just above the eye. At halftime, we were in the locker room and the team doctor was sewing him up. No one had paid any attention to it. Then Lee turned around towards us and he couldn't open his eyelid! The doctor had sewn his eyelid to just below the eye. He sewed it shut! He was just this 205 pound guard, just tough as nails—small and undersized, but tough as nails. It was funny! It was very, very humorous! He had to go back in and have the doctor take the stitches out. I can't recall what the team doctor's name was at that time, but he was a little "long in the tooth." That was just very funny!

When we were playing at Illinois, the stadium has one open end. A wind came up unlike anything we had ever played in before. We were getting ready to switch ends of the fields between the first and second quarter, it was fourth down and I was going to **PUNT***, so we called time-out. I was going to punt with the wind. I got off a terrific kick. It rolled down to the 3-yard line, and I had probably kicked it from my 20-yard line—it was 70 or 80 yards. Todd Grant, who was our center but played guard on punts, had been offsides. So, we had to change ends of the field and I had to re-kick into the wind and the ball only went about 20 yards. I will never forget that because that might have been a record-setting kick!

Another interesting and humanistic story, which I've always recalled because it shows what is great about team sports, was about our quarterback. He wasn't our starting quarterback, but became a starter after. Dave Glinka was a

***Joe Theismann holds the NFL record for the shortest PUNT that wasn't blocked—one yard.**

Polish boy from Toledo. He was a class or two behind me. A number of us had decided to go down to Toledo and have a lot of fun and see what the town had to offer. We knew that Dave Glinka did not come from very well-to-do parents. They had a small little house in a section of Toledo. When we visited, his parents gave us their beds and they slept in the basement on mattresses. I'll never forget that story. He was a great guy then and he's a great guy today!

—**SCOTT MAENTZ**, '62, Lake Bluff, Illinois, Grand Rapids native

Every year my friends invite me to come to Ann Arbor to attend a Michigan football game. Don't tell them this, but the truth is, I couldn't care less about going to the game. For me the best part about a trip to Ann Arbor is it means I will have the chance to dine at Zingerman's at least twice! And when I am unable to attend a game, they all know to bring me a #20 back to **CHICAGO***!

—**STEVE SCHANWALD**, Executive-Vice President of the Chicago Bulls

Band Day was something to behold for a 14-year-old back in the fifties. Band Director Revelli conducted 100 high school bands spread across the entire field at halftime. The colors of each school's uniforms looked like a giant patch-work quilt.

In those years, Michigan cheerleaders were all males. To liven things up at a lopsided Northwestern game, a few of the Wildcat coed cheerleaders danced with our guys to the tune of Bill Haley's *Rock Around the Clock*—pretty sexy stuff for those times.

On another occasion, Terry Barr and Tom Maentz visited our school and talked with us about staying true to your

***In 1994, the White Sox recalled MICHAEL JORDAN from Double-A Birmingham to play against the Cubs in the Mayor's Trophy Game at Wrigley Field. Jordan singled and doubled against the Cubs.**

values and love of our country. They shared stories of college life and what they wanted to do after school. We were all pretty impressed, plus it was actually helpful.

—**MIKE LUPTON**, 71, Holland, Michigan

One player I remember is Anthony Carter. He was a character. I had never seen this before...Anthony was putting on panty hose under his uniform. I asked the equipment coach, Jon Falk, "What's he doing with those?" It had never struck me that the panty hose would keep you warm on those cold days. Anthony Carter was like a stick. There was hardly any weight on him ...but he could run like a deer...

Bo died on a Friday before the Ohio State game. They had visitation starting at noon on Sunday at St. Andrew's Church. The first guy at the door when we opened the doors was Ted Lindsay of the Detroit Red Wings. There were a lot of the former players that came through as well. People were lined up, they came in one door and out the other.

That Sunday evening they had a visitation at the funeral home. Supposedly...it was only for invited people, but I think there were a few that weren't invited. Robbie Timmons and Don Shane from Channel 7 were there, as well as a lot of the coaches, former coaches, a lot of the present and past players.

The next day—that Monday—was the service at St. Andrew's Episcopal Church. It was a full house. I was working outside then parking cars...so I did not hear the service. Jim Branstatter, Dick Caldarazzo, Lloyd Carr, Garvie Craw, Dan Dierdorf, Dr. Kim Eagle, Bill Gunlock, Jon Falk, Jamie Morris and Fritz Seyferth were pallbearers.

I drove the hearse that day. I had told my boss at the funeral home that I was acquainted with Bo all of that time and that I thought I should be the one to drive the hearse that day... and he agreed with me.

So after the church funeral service...we put Bo in the hearse and drove up Main Street and drove by the Big House. Then we drove back by Schembechler Hall and went to Forest Hill where he was buried. I was the only person in the hearse with Bo. We followed the funeral director who was in the lead car. We just followed them around to the cemetery. There were fans and reporters lined up everywhere...standing on the side of the streets... all there to celebrate Bo's life.

—**THURMAN WARFORD**, Security Guard for Michigan locker room and Muehlig Funeral Home, Ann Arbor

I was in the marching band during my freshman year as an architecture student. It gave me my first chance to go to California after we won the Big 10 championship in 10-degree weather in Columbus. My clarinet froze solid and I couldn't play. The brass instruments probably didn't freeze as much because they had alcohol on their valves. You couldn't hear the clarinets anyway most of the time, so it didn't matter if we dropped out. There were about 76 trombones. I've never played in a group that large or that loud. There was literally thundering brass.

Coming from Detroit, when we landed in Southern California, it was like that scene in the *Wizard of Oz* where it goes from black and white to color. It was about an eight-hour flight on a prop airline. I thought it was interesting that because the band was financed by Chevrolet, everywhere we went we had to play "See the USA in Your Chevrolet." I don't think they had enough money to send the poor fourth-string football players. I felt bad for them, but they sent all the extra cheerleaders and band members because we were financed by GM.

—**MICHAEL HARLOCK**, architect, Marin County, CA

When my son Merrick—who is 12 now—was young...I would take him and his brother to all of the Michigan basketball games at home- but I would never take them to the football games...or at least, not too many of them. I didn't take them until they were old enough to sit through a game and not want cotton candy, peanuts and have to go to the bathroom every five minutes...until they could fully appreciate and understand the game.

When I took Merrick to a game five seasons ago, he was a very quick study on football. He just really gets the game. He loves football, the history of football, statistics and everything. So he said to me, "Next week is Ohio State, can I go?" I took him to that one and *54 consecutive games later*...home and away...he's been to every single game.

"...by the time I'm 84 years old, I want to have gone to 1000 consecutive home and away games."

Last year, the Wednesday night before Merrick's 47th consecutive game Merrick ended up in the hospital with appendicitis. He came out of surgery at 10:30 at night and his first question to the surgeon when he came to was, "Can I go to the game on Saturday?" The surgeon hemmed and hawed and said, "Well, I don't know how you are going to be feeling, and it's really not something you should be going to." Merrick then went on to explain to him of how he was on this streak, and how he was going to go to every game to get to his 1,000th consecutive game. The surgeon said to him, "As long as you could not get bumped around in the crowd and you are comfortable, then that will be okay." At which point I made a call to a friend of mine who is one of the associate athletic directors up there and they came up with two press box passes. So the two of us sat in the press box for the game and the little trooper was able to keep his 47th consecutive game intact.

Merrick said in a newspaper article, "I've been to 54 consecutive games and Notre Dame will be number 55. My goal is, by the time I'm 84 years old, I want to have gone to 1000 consecutive home and away games." No one has ever done that as far as they are aware of.

—**MARK BANK**,'88, attorney, Birmingham, Michigan

In 1942, my sophomore year at Michigan, we opened the football season against Great Lakes Naval Training Station. The war (WWII) was on and they had a lot of ex-pros and college All Americans on their team. Michigan wasn't supposed to be much of a challenge. However, we ended up winning the game 9–3.

One of our placekickers was a fellow sophomore named Jim Brieske who played a beautiful game. Prior to the last scrimmage in that game, the halfback was injured. Coach Fritz Crisler walked over to the trainer and asked, "What's the problem?" and the trainer said, "Well, I think he hurt his knee." So Coach replied, "Move the team or move the body!" It was close to the end of the game and he didn't want the players to get too upset. So that's how another player, Bob Chappuis, got to play as a sophomore, too.

In high school, I played halfback; then at Michigan, I played fullback and played defense too. The substitute rule was a little different then. The coaches had taken the center out of the game! We were looking around wondering just what was going on when Coach said I was going to the *center*! I had never played center before in my life. I leaned down over the ball to snap it and when I looked up, the opposing center was right on my nose...so I centered the ball back and it worked out okay...but it was a rude awakening. I was used to being five yards back offensively. That was quite an experience having never been up front like that.

Coach Crisler was well organized. We all thought he was tougher than nails. He was the head of the National Rules Committee and always said, "Remember, there are no rules in the book that say you can't block and tackle as hard as you want. You're Michigan Men. You are not to play like any of those extras, though." Extras was a term used for players sneaking in a punch or kick...he didn't want that kind of guy playing for him.

—**DON LUND**, 87, Michigan sports legend

When I was a freshman in 1953, I went out for football. In those days there were fewer scholarships given, and varsity rosters totaled about 40 or 42...versus 105 or so today. More walk-ons made the team. Freshmen were not eligible for the varsity... but future prospects were coached by the legendary Wally Weber and essentially prepared for eventual action with the varsity.

Another big difference in 1953 was that there was limited substitution permitted in NCAA games. Two-platoon football was out...I think in an effort to minimize cost. Players had to go both ways. Too bad for me, in a way, because all the practice I got as a freshman trying to tackle the likes of Barr might have allowed me to play safety on defense.

Even though we only practiced (no games), it was still fun for kids who liked football. Each afternoon we would go down to Yost Fieldhouse, where the locker rooms were, and suit up for a couple of hours of grid combat. Here is where an amazing event took place. Following warm-up exercises, one of the student managers would pull up with a tractor pulling a small cart. From the cart, he would unload a gigantic canvas bag—open it up and dump the contents on the ground. Helmets—beat-up old leather helmets! We players would then

> ...it is still astounding how mighty Michigan would have such poor equipment for its freshmen...

dig through the pile seeking helmets to fit our heads. Often they were terrible fits...either too small or too large, but each guy always found some hunk of leather to don. Regardless of fit, we practiced blocking, tackling and scrimmaged a lot.

To me, it is still astounding how mighty Michigan would have such poor equipment for its freshmen...not to mention taking the injury and legal risks. My high school equipment was better.

One other point, in 1953 helmets did not have face masks. Generally, only players who had previously broken their noses qualified for a cage. There was one exception. Ron Kramer—universally acknowledged even as a freshman as a special player—had a beautiful shiny **VARSITY*** helmet (the plastic kind with insert that kept the head away from the helmet's surface), because he would occasionally go over and work out with the varsity.

In looking back...I'm surprised that there were no serious injuries. My personal reasoning is that without face masks, blockers and tacklers didn't lead with their heads as battering rams, as they do today. Normal self-protection tendencies called for turning the head and hitting with the shoulder, thus reducing impact on head and neck.

Overall, though, there is one that I have found most memorable. In fact, I have included it in a passage of "life reflections" memoir that I have been writing which I call *Magic Moments*. Those are those special times which happened that I wish could be repeated over and over again. One being high up in Michigan Stadium on a glorious autumn afternoon...the band quicksteps in...plays the fanfare...marches to the north end zone playing the verse to "The Victors" then does a one-eighty and heads south with the chorus. It always stirs my blood.

—**KEN TIPPERY**, Class of '57, 75, Royal Oak, Baseball Captain and football walk-on

***"VARSITY" is the British short form for the word "university."**

TO BE CONTINUED!

We hope you have enjoyed *For Michigan Fans Only.* Due to space and time considerations over a dozen people with wonderful stories did not make the book. However, you can look for their stories in the author's forthcoming books: *For Michigan Fans: Volume II.* Next year we'll be putting together *For Tigers Fans Only,* and *For Red Wing Fans Only.* You can be included in any of these books if you have an interesting story involving the Wolverines, Tigers, or the Red Wings. Email it to printedpage@cox.net (please put MICHIGAN FANS, TIGER FANS, or RED WING FANS in the subject line and be sure to include a phone number where you can be reached), or call the author directly at (602) 738-5889.

Note: No actual Ohio State fans were harmed in the making of this book.

OTHER BOOKS BY RICH WOLFE

There's No Expiration Date on Dreams (Tom Brady)
Da Coach (Mike Ditka)
I Remember Harry Caray
He Graduated Life with Honors and No Regrets (Pat Tillman)
Take This Job and Love It (Jon Gruden)
Been There, Shoulda Done That (John Daly)
Oh, What a Knight (Bob Knight)
And the Last Shall Be First (Kurt Warner)
Remembering Jack Buck
Sports Fans Who Made Headlines
Fandemonium
Remembering Dale Earnhardt
Remembering Harry Kalas
I Saw It On the Radio (Vin Scully)
Tim Russert, We Heartily Knew Ye
The Real McCoy (Al McCoy, Phoenix Suns announcer)
Personal Foul (With Tim Donaghy, former NBA referee)
I Love It, I Love It, I Love It (with Jim Zabel, Iowa announcer)

For Yankee Fans Only
For Cubs Fans Only
For Red Sox Fans Only
For Cardinals Fans Only
For Hawkeye Fans Only
For Browns Fans Only
For Packers Fans Only
For Mets Fans Only
For Notre Dame Fans Only—The New Saturday Bible
For Bronco Fans Only
For Nebraska Fans Only
For Buckeye Fans Only
For Georgia Bulldog Fans Only
For South Carolina Fans Only
For Clemson Fans Only
For Cubs Fans Only—Volume II
For Oklahoma Fans Only
For Yankee Fans Only—Volume II
For Mizzou Fans Only
For Kansas City Chiefs Fans Only
For K-State Fans Only
For KU Fans Only (Kansas)
For Phillies Fans Only
For Milwaukee Braves Fans Only

Next book to be released:
A Perfect 10 (with Ron Santo of the Chicago Cubs)

All books are the same size, format and price.
Questions or to order? Contact the author directly at 602-738-5889.